Allegories of the Purge

ALLEGORIES OF
THE PURGE

*How Literature Responded to the
Postwar Trials of Writers and
Intellectuals in France*

Philip Watts

Stanford University Press   Stanford, California

Stanford University Press
Stanford, California
© 1998 by the Board of Trustees of the
Leland Stanford Junior University
Printed in the United States of America
CIP data appear at the end of the book

Preface

This book in its present form would not have been possible without the support, and insights, of colleagues, institutions, friends and family.

I am particularly grateful to the National Endowment for the Humanities for supporting this project with a summer stipend, which allowed me to complete the final version of several chapters. The University of Pittsburgh faculty development grant generously permitted me to pursue research in Paris.

Alice Kaplan has been a great inspiration from the time I began graduate studies to the present. I am grateful for her rigorous reading of my manuscript and her constant encouragement. Ora Avni encouraged me to present parts of this book as talks, and her comments on my manuscript were always extremely helpful. I have also benefited from the input and constant support of Antoine Compagnon. My thanks too to Suzanne Guerlac, who encouraged me to send the manuscript to Stanford University Press.

Yves Citton, Mathilde Doubinsky, Elizabeth Houlding, Cheryl Morgan, Aparna Nayak, Pani Norindr, Rosie Reiss, Dan Russell, and Mark Sanford provided me with intellectual support while I was working on this project. Rich Watts read the entire manuscript twice, and his suggestions about style and sources were always helpful. Special thanks also to Keith Sears for his advice on legal matters.

My colleagues and students at the University of Pittsburgh have always been extremely supportive and encouraged me to develop many of the ideas in this book. Monika Losagio provided me with valuable assistance and advice over the last few years. My thanks also to André Braga for his expertise in computers.

I am extremely grateful to Dennis Looney for his assistance and critical acumen. John Feneron and Mitch Tuchman were invaluable in bringing the manuscript to its final form.

My greatest thanks go to Sophie Queuniet. Her intelligence and generosity helped me bring vague ideas into book form.

One final note. My parents showed me unfailing support over the years. My mother tirelessly answered my questions and my father read several chapters of the manuscript: his comments and his arguments helped give the manuscript the form that it has today. This book is dedicated to his memory.

P.W.

Contents

Allegories of the Purge

Introduction

How many times have we been reminded that the purge isn't over? If we can be certain of anything about the *épuration,* it is that the trials of fascists and collaborators, the judgments, verdicts, and debates that took place in postwar France, are still with us, like an endlessly repeated epilogue to the drama of the Occupation. The trial and conviction in 1987 of Klaus Barbie, captured and returned to France from Bolivia; the trial, acquittal, and subsequent conviction for crimes against humanity of Paul Touvier, captured and returned to Paris from a monastery; the summary execution by a lone gunman of René Bousquet, who, fifty years after the end of the war, answered the door in his bathrobe and found himself face to face with a self-declared avenger; the dissemination in its many and perverse forms of Holocaust revisionism; the revelations about François Mitterrand's Pétainist past; the rediscovery of Heidegger's ties to Nazism; the scandal about Paul de Man's youthful enthusiasm for fascism—these are only a few examples illustrating that the purge today remains what French historian Henry Rousso has called an "unfinished project." Even in the immediate postwar years the purge of French collaborators was not a tidy affair. Not only were the trials a contentious and divisive moment in modern French history, but also, as Rousso points out, the Resistance authorities themselves often had to choose between an imperfect justice and an unrestrained revenge, between the continuity of the state apparatus and a complete renewal of the bureaucratic elite, between restoration and revolution (Rousso, "L'Epuration"). Today's conflicts and controversies about the purge have at their source not only the events that took place during the German Occupation of France, but the very imperfection, the ambiguity that surrounded the postwar attempts to judge those responsible for the horrors of the war.

The purge was intended solely as a transitional phase, from the Occupation to a renovated democratic society. It is one of the ironies of history that this transitional phase has lasted so long, but the reason can perhaps be found in the fact that the ambitions of the Liberation authorities were numerous and, according to Rousso, "sometimes contradictory" (Rousso, "L'Epuration," 104). The purge authorities had several goals in mind: to maintain security from a fascist counteroffensive in France; to release the animosity built up over four years of Occupation; to legitimize the provisional government and the different political parties that had come to power after the Liberation; and to rebuild the identity of the French nation (104–5). In order to achieve these goals, the purge authorities, many of them members of the Resistance, set up several tribunals and distinguished between capital offenses, such as treason, and lesser crimes, such as "national indignity," a rubric reserved for men and women who, by supporting Vichy and the Nazis, had failed in their duty as French citizens. The High Court was thus created in November 1944 to judge the most active collaborators, notably Marshal Philippe Pétain, head of the French state, and his ministers. The judgment of Pétain began in July 1945 and, in Peter Novick's words, was less a trial than "an elaborate ceremonial aimed at symbolically condemning a policy" (Novick, *The Resistance,* 173). Pétain was found guilty of treason—a crime that carried the death sentence—but the jury recommended that given his advanced age, the sentence be commuted to life in prison. As for Pierre Laval, he too was sentenced to death for treason after a trial that lasted only four days. In October 1945, on the eve of his execution, he attempted suicide by swallowing cyanide but was resuscitated just in time to be dragged before the firing squad and executed at dawn.

The government's attempt to bring about a successful purge was hampered by another series of events. While the provisional government set up legal channels for purging France of its collaborators, certain French men and women took justice into their own hands. In the months immediately preceding and following the Liberation, legality gave way to an often unrestrained popular justice, and courts of law were replaced by street corner tribunals. What Rousso has called an "extra-juridical" purge was responsible for the public beatings of suspected collaborators and for the *tonte*, the shearing of women suspected of having collaborated or of having had sexual relations with the Nazis. Opponents of the purge also liked to claim that this extra-juridical purge resulted in 100,000 deaths: the reality is closer to 8,000 or 9,000, a sizable number but one that could have been much higher considering that France was in a state approaching civil war (Rousso, "L'Epuration," 81–85). Whatever the exact number, what came to be known as the "unauthorized purge" (*l'épuration sauvage*) further eroded public confidence in the process and added to the French public's ambivalence toward the purge.[1]

The prosecution of writers and intellectuals who were suspected of having supported Vichy and the Nazi occupiers stands out amid the postwar trials. Never before in French history had the state put a caste of writers on trial for treason. The policy of the Liberation authorities to "strike at the head" of the collaboration meant that they were targeting both political and intellectual leaders. Because the writers were visible public figures, however, because they had left traces of their collaboration in writing, their trials often took place before those of the politicians, industrialists, bureaucrats, and soldiers who had declared their allegiance to Marshal Philippe Pétain after the armistice of June 1940. Writers and intellectuals carried an important symbolic weight in France, and public opinion focused on these trials

---

[1]The unauthorized purge is still a "hot" topic today as evidenced by a recent study claiming to reveal the untold truth about this "taboo subject" in contemporary French history. See Bourdel, *L'Epuration*.

at least as much as on those of political and economic collaborators. The most notorious of these intellectuals, Robert Brasillach, who as editor of the collaborationist weekly *Je suis partout* had become for many the very symbol of intellectual collaboration, was tried for treason, convicted, and executed in February 1945, fully two months before Pétain had been brought back to Paris from his exile in the German town of Sigmaringen. The swiftness of this and other judgments has led many present-day commentators to see in the trials of collaborationist intellectuals a symbol of the fundamental injustice of the purge. Novick points to what he calls the "crudely partisan use" made of the purge and the blacklists of writers by the Communist intellectuals in postwar France (Novick, *The Resistance,* 127). For Tony Judt, the hard-line position of certain intellectuals during the purge was motivated by "feelings of guilt" about their inactivity during the war and their search for "compensatory activities." This resulted, according to Judt, in a "notoriously unfair" purge.[2] Seen from today's perspective, the purge of intellectuals appears excessively violent, arbitrary, highly politicized, and on the whole, ineffective.

If contemporary historians agree that the purge was at best a botched and incomplete effort, it is perhaps due to the impossibility of attaining anything that resembled a consensus about the trials in the postwar years. Reactions to the trials were swift, diverse, and often violently antagonistic. As much as any event in recent French history, the purge became a *guerre franco-française,* a moment of conflict between different ideological positions, no less for writers, journalists, and intellectuals than for the political class. The hostility released at the Liberation had been building since the first days of the war, and one of de Gaulle's first preoccupations upon arriving in London was to declare the illegitimacy and illegality of the Vichy regime, thus paving the way for the juridical proceedings at the Liberation (121). In the world of letters things were no different: the very first issue of the clandestine Resistance publication *Les Lettres françaises,* released in

---

[2]Judt, *Past Imperfect,* 56, 59. For concurring opinions about the unfair treatment levied upon writers and intellectuals see also, Lottman, *The Purge,* 240–54; Assouline, *L'Epuration.*

September 1942, declared that its mission was not only to liberate France but also to "punish the traitors," and throughout the Occupation the Resistance writers accumulated evidence against intellectuals suspected of treason, collaboration, or complacency toward the Nazis. It is not a stretch to claim that the purge of collaborators began in spirit if not in deed as soon as Pétain signed the armistice at Rethondes. When the trials of writers began in earnest in October 1944 with the indictment of Georges Suarez, editor in chief of the pro-German daily *Aujourd'hui* and author of articles denouncing Jews, Communists, and members of the Resistance, writers from all sides began to comment directly or indirectly on these events that were once again splitting France in two. Whether they were imprisoned, blacklisted, or solicited to judge their peers, whether they had resisted, collaborated, or formed part of the wait-and-see (*attentiste*) majority, writers positioned themselves in relation to the trials and contributed to a process that took place as much in the forums of public opinion as in the courts. No moment in recent literary history better illustrates how writers and intellectuals defined themselves through what Bourdieu has called their "position taking" (*"prises de position"*), that is, their relation of "domination or subordination, of complementarity or antagonism" to the essays, novels, plays, poems, and speeches of other writers.[3] To understand a writer's position at the time of the purge, it is therefore necessary first to examine the multiple positions and choices that made themselves available when France began putting its writers on trial.

The position taking during the purge was occasionally met by equivocation, however. The itinerary of Albert Camus, a soul torn by indecision, illustrates the difficulty certain writers and intellectuals had when they were faced with judging their peers. At war's end Ca-

---

[3]Bourdieu, *The Rules,* 231–34. In a dissertation recently completed under Bourdieu's direction, Gisele Sapiro examines several literary institutions in France, including the National Writers' Committee (CNE), the body that was in part responsible for the purge of fascist and collaborationist writers. For Sapiro, during the purge "all individual 'choices'" are a product of the encounter between the writer's inclination and the "power struggles" between different positions available in the literary field. Sapiro, "Complicités," 7.

mus was a strong supporter of the purge, arguing for its swift implementation and deeming the whole enterprise "necessary" (*Combat,* 18 Oct. 1944). In his famous debate with François Mauriac, played out in the pages of his Resistance weekly, *Combat,* and in the conservative daily *Le Figaro,* he chose what he called "justice" over Mauriac's "charity," and throughout the last months of 1944 he reiterated the imperative that France must purge and purge well. In October Camus wrote of his country's need to excise the collaborators as if their presence were a health risk to the nation: "France is carrying, like a foreign entity [*"un corps étranger"*], a minority of men . . . [whose] existence poses a problem for justice." Justice could only be rendered through an ablation of these "foreign" bodies. But already, in the same article, Camus expressed reservations about the purge and about the justice he was advocating: "We have decided to assume human justice with its terrible imperfections" (*Combat,* 25 Oct. 1944). Within a few months doubt and indecision about the purge had begun to make their way into his declarations. In early January 1945 Camus wrote that "a country that fails at its purge, fails at its renovation" as if he were already sensing that France had missed an opportunity to create a radically new society (*Combat,* 5 Jan. 1945). In the last days of the same month he signed the petition in favor of Brasillach, written and circulated by Mauriac, though he insisted it was not in support of the man but in opposition to the death penalty. By August 1945 Camus had become entirely disillusioned by the purge: "the word 'purge' is painful," he wrote in another editorial for *Combat,* "the thing has become odious" (*Combat,* 30 Aug. 1945). From "necessary" the purge had become "odious." Camus's attitude echoed that of some French men and women who came to see the purge as little more than a political platform for special interests: the communists attempting to seize power through the tribunals; the collaborators and fascist sympathizers refusing to acknowledge the crimes of the war. As Novick writes, "The purge ended . . . with a universal sense of frustration" (158). Camus's articles in *Combat* presented an X ray of this frustration, of this incapacity to close what many hoped would be the final chapter of the war.

THERE REMAINS IN FRANCE today a rich and largely unexplored archive of texts surrounding the postwar purge, in which we can find the positions, arguments, and choices the French literary community faced in the postwar years. Though many of the juridical dossiers are still closed by law and accessible only through special dispensation, and Brasillach's is reported missing from the National Archives, numerous transcripts from the trials of writers have been published in book form. Indeed, it seems that transcripts of the purge trials became a relatively successful genre in the publishing industry of the postwar years. Jacques Isorni, Brasillach's attorney, published the transcript of his client's trial along with a sentimental account of his execution; the Albin Michel publishing house ran a series in the postwar years on the "great contemporary trials," which included the trial for treason of Jean Luchaire, editor in chief of the Nazi-sponsored publication *Les Nouveaux Temps* (Garçon, ed., *Les Procès*); for 70 francs in 1945 one could procure the transcript of Charles Maurras's trial, edited and commented by Géo London, one of France's best-known court reporters at the time. Along with documents of this sort, often released only weeks after the trial had ended, a number of defendants published defense briefs, called "*mémoires*" in French, which are still circulating today in a number of forms, from prestigious Gallimard editions to reprints that one can only find at the stall of a *bouquiniste* near the Pont St. Michel.[4]

The purge, however, was not limited to legal proceedings, and the debates generated by the trials quickly spilled out of the confines of the courtroom. In addition to the juridical dossiers, transcripts, and defense briefs the debates found their way into the entire literary production of the postwar years, from essays, criticism, and correspondence to novels, plays, and poems. High and low literature, public and private writings were equally affected and revealed the same anxieties in the face of this sometimes bewildering event. In the three

[4]One of the booksellers along the Seine specializes in *Action française* publications, and a sizable number of the books she carries are defense briefs and pamphlets printed in reaction to the purge trials. It was in this stall that I found a short text written at the end of the war by the editor of *Action française*, Maurice Pujo.

or four years it took me to prepare this study, the more I looked for material concerning the purge, the more I found, and I came to realize that the accusations, judgments, and verdicts of the purge inflected the entire intellectual production of the postwar years and left their trace on every genre and almost every writer of the time.

This book is about four writers—Sartre, Blanchot, Eluard, and Céline—whose works confront and respond to the purge of intellectuals in postwar France. It is an investigation of how their writing argues for or against the different positions outlined during the purge and how it reflects or distorts the competing theories about literature to emerge from the trials. These writers were themselves involved in the trials to varying degrees. Jean-Paul Sartre began producing his theory of committed literature and of the writer's responsibility within months of the first purge trials, though he rarely commented directly upon the trials themselves. Maurice Blanchot, always veiled in his references to historical events but always at the same time close to history, presents an argument for the autonomy of literature that is both a response to Sartre and a critique of what Blanchot called, perhaps with an eye to the purge, the "trial of art." Paul Eluard, one of the leading Communist poets and a member of several purge commissions, published in the clandestine Resistance press and devoted a number of his poems to condemning collaborators. As for Louis-Ferdinand Céline, he was blacklisted by the National Writers' Committee and accused of treason by the provisional government, though eventually condemned of a lesser charge. None of these writers dominated the debates that emerged from the purge the way Camus and Mauriac had. What distinguishes them is that their work constitutes a sustained and complex reflection on the status of literature in the face of political trials. While dependent upon the purge archives, their texts and their understanding of the role of the writer go beyond the debates taking place in the courtrooms or on the front pages of the dailies. Their writings exhibit a depth that, for reasons of political or juridical expediency, prosecutors, defendants, and journalists could only hint at during the trials. They all introduce complexities into their publications, or rather they develop the complexities that came with trying a group of French writers for treason. The four writers usually knew where they stood: Eluard repeatedly called for the execution of collaborators; with equal intensity Céline reviled the purge. Still their works often reveal an ambiguity, an equivocation that, perhaps more than anything else, mirrors the divisions of French society at the time. Proponents of the purge depicted the trials as a way of ridding France of its bad element: "Death to the traitors" was an oft-repeated slogan of the Communist partisans.[5] But the simplicity that might have seemed possible in August 1944 ended up in frustration. The texts of these writers, sometimes in spite of the authors' declared intentions, are often a reflection of the vacillation, the irresolution, and the ambiguities of the purge. Rather than simply issue judgments, though at times they do do that, these writers force the reader to confront the issues of ideological and aesthetic judgment implicit in the act of reading a literary work.

In their reactions to the purge, in their position-taking, the writers in this study also mobilized a number of discourses or registers, ranging from the historical to the sexual, from the economic to the medical and from the literary to the corporeal. To understand their take on the trails of collaborators and fascists, it can be useful to read their texts as allegories of the purge. One must be careful, however. In using the term *allegory,* one risks falling into a rhetorical imprecision that defines allegory as some sort of supertrope that would account for all types of metaphoric substitution. The danger of allegory is that it allows us to say whatever we want about a text.[6] Furthermore, Eluard, Céline, and Sartre on occasion all speak directly about the purge without having recourse to the type of indirection that characterizes this figure of speech. Nonetheless, the texts in this study do retain certain characteristics of the allegory. At one point or another they all

[5]See, for example, the headlines of *L'Humanité* in August and September 1944.

[6]In a recent study of Montaigne's essays Antoine Compagnon points to the vicissitudes of allegorical readings. Allegory allows the reader to "interpret works from the past in spite of their historical contexts and the author's intentions ... one says what one has to say and then attributes it to the text." Compagnon, *Chat,* 7, 11.

speak about the purge through a series of metaphoric substitutions maintained through an extended narrative—whether this narrative is a critical essay, a novel, or a collection of poems. The texts thus sustain both a literal and a figurative reading over time. The texts also all give the reader a key for reading them allegorically. They all remind the reader that there is a code to interpreting a second meaning, and this code is to be found in the purge archives. My contention is that the works by Sartre and Blanchot, Eluard and Céline all rely on the debates and arguments around the purge trials for their full significance. While pointing to a second, allegorical meaning, the works all retain their first, or literal, meaning, and indeed one of the characteristics of the allegory is that the reader is free to decide whether to choose a literal or a figurative reading. We can therefore read Sartre's essay "What Is Literature?" as a historical study of the evolving role of the European writer from the Middle Ages to the present. Yet at the same time "What Is Literature?" also gives us enough keys to read it as a commentary about the trials that are haunting France at the time that Sartre is writing. Likewise, Céline's obsession with the state of his intestines is both an exercise in scatological humor and a rewriting of the postwar purge in terms of the author's decrepit body. The force of the purge was such that it saturated all of the author's metaphoric registers.

One of the constitutive factors of allegory is that it appears in moments of historical turmoil: this is certainly the case in Resistance literature, and one need only think of Sartre's *The Flies* or even Vercors's *The Silence of the Sea* for examples of allegories of resistance. As I show, the literature of the purge also turns to allegory to communicate. But the relation of allegory to history is paradoxical. On the one hand, it arises in times of violent conflict and can serve specific political ends, such as thwarting censorship and disseminating a specific political message. On the other hand, in its avoidance of specific references, in its constant displacement of meaning, allegory is the very antithesis of history. Furthermore, if allegory has a didactic function, it can also lose that function through its constant references to itself as allegory. This is precisely the paradox Joel Fineman points to: allegory is both, in his words, "the most didactic and abstractly moralmongering of poetic figures" and "a clamor of signifiers signifying nothing but themselves" (Fineman, "The Structure," 34). For allegory to work, it must constantly designate itself as allegory: it remains a figure of self-reflexivity. Fineman's insights about allegory anticipate Fredric Jameson's claim that allegory "begins by acknowledging the impossibility of interpretation" (Jameson, *Postmodernism*, 168). It is possible to see allegory as a preferred figure of rhetoric in the postwar years precisely because it is a trope of indeterminacy. Allegory allows writers not only to speak about World War II and its aftermath but also to speak indirectly about the difficulty, if not the impossibility, of putting in place a system of moral and legal precepts about the roles and responsibilities of literature. Allegory speaks to us of the crisis of the purge.

These, then, are some of the paradoxes of literature produced during the purge. At a time when, for many writers, linguistic theory was determined by the Resistance credo "to speak is to act," several writers were turning to allegory, a figure of speech that consistently retreats from action. At a time when writers were called upon to take positions, they had recourse to a trope characterized by indeterminacy. Even for writers who were accused of collaboration and who, in some cases, were writing and speaking to save their lives, allegory often became their privileged figure of speech. In reading these writers who, at first, seem so close to historical events, we also realize that their negotiation with the purge archive, that is, with the transcripts, petitions, pleas, essays, and fiction generated by the purge, also depends upon a constant distancing of their texts from what at first seemed to be the object of their representation. The purge infuses all the registers of the authors' language, but it also seems to have created a distance between these writers and the historical circumstances they are judging and commenting on. In this sense an essay on Baudelaire or a paragraph about classical aesthetics can become an infinitely richer commentary on the purge trials than an editorial calling for the execution of Georges Suarez.

THE PURGE WAS, OF COURSE, about judging writers. I was reminded of this by one of those quasi coincidences familiar to anyone who frequents the archives. In the book containing the published transcript of the trial of Jean Luchaire, the editor of the collaborationist daily *Les Nouveaux Temps*, I came across a peculiar advertisement for an institute calling itself the ABC School of Writing (*L'Ecole ABC de Rédaction*). Endorsed by two venerable members of the French Academy, Claude Farrère and Marcel Prévost, the ABC School of Writing promised its students a "mastery of style" and a 50 percent increase in the graduate's personal worth. All this might have been nothing more than promotional hyperbole had the ad not also declared, almost as a warning to its future customers: "You are judged by what you write [*On vous juge sur vos écrits*]"—this in a volume that recounted in minute detail the judgment and condemnation of a writer. The advertisers knew their market, for they were at once reiterating a cliché—"you are judged by what you write"—and offering the school's future graduates a chance to control their fate through a "mastery of style." Not only did the advertisers link writing to judgment, they hinged judgment to a writer's style. If they worked well, if they *wrote* well, the advertisers seemed to say, the school's students would avoid the fate Jean Luchaire had met.

For the first time since the Revolution of 1789, and in an even more systematic way than during the Terror, France judged a class of writers as enemies of the state. As we read the trial transcripts as well as the essays, novels, and poems written in response to the purge, we are constantly solicited to judge, and this judgment has returned in full force today in what Henry Rousso has called the "phase of obsession" with the Occupation in the postwar years (Rousso, *The Vichy Syndrome,* 132). During the purge, and even between the pages of books about the purge, literature was put on trial. It's as if literary criticism had rediscovered its etymological root during the purge: *kritēs,* the critic is also the judge. Our relation to literature today seems once again to have become a relation of judgment: our understanding of literary artifacts almost invariably passes through a series of condemnations or exonerations as if the hermeneutic process were necessarily and irrevocably tied to a moral stance. Like the readers at the time of the purge, we judge writers by what they wrote. And yet our claims to certainty—and to understanding—when we issue judgments are perhaps less definite than they might at first appear. The purge archive in general and the four writers of this study suggest that the judgment of literature, like the purge itself, remains a difficult and ambiguous project.

CHAPTER I

Literature on Trial

Purging a society of its traitors is a messy business. There is little doubt that the French Resistance planned some sort of legal proceedings against Vichy from the earliest days of the collaboration. As Peter Novick writes, de Gaulle "had taken Vichy's juridical nullity for granted from the beginning" (Novick, *The Resistance,* 142), and the debates about the legality of putting the collaborators on trial began as early as 1941. The first official trial was that of Pierre Pucheu, Vichy's minister of the interior, who was condemned for treason in March 1944, that is, several months before the Liberation of France. Though this trial was held in Algiers and not in Paris, it was generally considered a successful prologue for the trials that would soon take place in metropolitan France. In the intellectual field, while the first trial of a writer took place in October 1944, from the earliest days of the collaboration Resistance newspapers had been preparing the purge. In its very first issues the clandestine Resistance publication *Les Lettres françaises* claimed that the intellectuals of the Resistance were dedicated to saving the honor of French letters and to punishing those they considered "traitors."[1] From 1942 on, the

[1]See the call to arms in the September 1942 issue of *Les Lettres françaises.*

writers at *Les Lettres françaises* as well as other Resistance periodicals were dedicated to identifying and denouncing the men and women whom they suspected of having collaborated with the Germans, and each new issue carried the names of fascist and collaborationist writers along with detailed descriptions of their acts of treason. If identifying collaborationist intellectuals was a relatively easy task, punishing them posed several grave problems.

During the summer of 1944 the Liberation authorities under de Gaulle's guidance created several tribunals whose role was to judge suspected collaborators, politicians, businessmen, and writers alike.[2] In June the courts, known as the *cours de justice,* were constituted in order to judge "in the name of the French people"; they were composed of one magistrate and four jurors, usually selected from a pool of members of the Resistance, which led critics of the purge to question the impartiality of these courts. The courts judged cases of treason and had the power to sentence guilty parties to life imprisonment, forced labor, or death. A second tribunal used to judge collaborators was the *chambres civiques* (civic chambers) created in August 1944. These tribunals judged what came to be known as "national indignity," a category that defined acts of collaboration less onerous than treason. Two other tribunals also functioned at this time: the military tribunal, which judged certain cases of treason and of war crimes, and the *Haute Cour* (High Court) created in November in order to judge the members of Pétain's government and high-ranking officials of the Vichy regime. As for the writers and intellectuals suspected of fascist sympathies or collaborationist activity, they were forced to appear mainly before the first two tribunals, but this did not guarantee leniency of any sort.

Approximately fifteen writers, journalists, and intellectuals were charged with treason of the same order as Pétain, Laval, and the ministers of Vichy France. Article 75 of the French Penal Code had been greatly expanded in 1939, shortly before the outbreak of the war. This article stipulated that treason was punishable by death and defined

[2]For a detailed description of the tribunals along with a statistical analysis of the purge, see Rousso "L'Epuration," 87–94.

treason as the act of bearing arms against France and delivering French troops or French military installations to a foreign power. For the writers on trial the applicable clause of Article 75 was the one that defined collusion, or intelligence, with the enemy.

> [Will be guilty of treason and punished by death ...] Any French citizen who enters into collusion with a foreign power in the attempt to engage the enemy to undertake hostilities against France.

For the purge courts collusion covered an array of treacherous activities, from delivering military secrets to the enemy to writing in favor of Nazi Germany. What distinguished the trials of collaborationist intellectuals from those of politicians and businessmen, however, was the debate these trials engendered over the status of language. Were the essays and articles that intellectuals had produced during the Occupation acts, or were they opinions? What was the place of pro-Nazi and Vichyite writers in the chain of responsibility that ran from Laval to the butcher who sold meat on the black market? These questions over the interpretation of Article 75 would continue to be asked well beyond the end of the war. For the prosecutors of the purge as well as for members of the Resistance the answer was clear: "intelligence with the enemy" included all forms of intellectual activity and equated a treasonous word with the performance of treason. To talk, to write was to act.

One of the major stumbling blocks for the purge was the possibility that Article 75 and the accusation of treason could be seen in 1944 as a retroactive law. Opponents of the purge were quick to argue that Pétain had been called to power by the Assemblée nationale of the Third Republic and that Vichy had been the legal and legitimate government of France, not only in the eyes of the collaborators but in the minds of the majority of the population.[3] The purge authorities, most notably the Comité français de la Libération nationale, the CFLN, used several arguments to counter these charges and justify the accusations of treason. First, they claimed that while foreign gov-

---

[3] For a detailed description of the questions of legality during the purge see Novick, *The Resistance*, 140–56. See also Laborie, *L'Opinion*.

ernments had recognized the Vichy regime, the Provisional Government of France had declared it illegal from its inception. According to the Resistance committees, "Vichy was not the legal government" but simply "the *de facto* authority" (ibid.). The CFLN's refusal to accept Vichy's legitimacy was one of the major arguments used in the prosecution of writers and intellectuals. If the purge authorities could show that Vichy was not a legal representative of the French people, then they could more easily counter claims that certain writers were doing their patriotic duty in supporting the collaboration. Furthermore, they maintained that even after the armistice of June 1940 Nazi Germany had remained the enemy, a distinction that allowed them to brand the collaborators as agents of a force hostile to France.

France's Provisional Government used a second argument when it claimed that Vichy had betrayed what France's minister of justice at the time called the "French soul" (Rousso, "L'Epuration," 86). In 1946 Pierre-Henri Teitgen defined the nation the collaborators had betrayed:

> France is, first and foremost, a tradition, a culture, a vocation ... France's soul is built on the belief of the primacy of man ... This French tradition ... is based on the faith, that moves us all, in the fundamental qualities of men of all colors, of all races, of all nations and of all beliefs, of all territories and of all horizons ... Accepting the politics of collaboration led certain men to forget these values.[4]

As Henry Rousso concludes after quoting this passage, the purge offered the opportunity "to reaffirm the values of the Republic and to rediscover the conception of a nation steeped in the tradition of 1789" (86). Along with the image of a democratic and tolerant France, certain proponents of the purge often either implicitly or explicitly accused the collaborators of betraying other French "values," such as virility, frugality, and the responsibility of the intellectual. If the purge authorities could not prove beyond the shadow of a doubt that Vichy was an illegitimate regime, they could nonetheless claim that the collaborators had betrayed a certain idea of France. And what was true

---

[4]Teitgen, *Les Cours,* 16. Quoted in Rousso, "L'Epuration," 86 (my translation).

for politicians, administrators, and businessmen was all the more true for writers who had left a lengthy paper trail behind them.

While the accusation of treason was reserved for the most active and notorious collaborators, the purge authorities put on the books a second law to prosecute men and women, including writers and intellectuals, who had committed lesser crimes of collaboration. This law, put into effect in August 1944, defined and punished what the courts called "national indignity" (*indignité nationale*). National indignity, as defined by Article 83 of the Penal Code, was not a crime in point of fact, but a state into which a collaborator had placed himself during the Occupation by committing certain acts (87). Acts of national indignity included having been a member of Pétain's cabinet (though, of course, high-ranking officials were accused of treason), having held an executive position in Vichy's propaganda services or in the Commissariat for Jewish Affairs, having been a member of collaborationist organizations (such as the Franco-German Cercle Européen), or having published or given lectures in favor of the enemy and of totalitarian doctrines (Novick, *The Resistance,* 147–48). The penalty for national indignity was a jail sentence that varied in length depending upon the severity of the crime, and national degradation, the loss of one's privileges as a French citizen, including everything from the right to vote to the right to belong to the legal, teaching, or journalistic professions (149). Again a problem arises concerning retroactivity, since the article was promulgated in the summer of 1944, that is, after the acts of national indignity had been committed. Adding to this juridical difficulty was the fact that the distinction between this state and the crime of treason was never crystal clear. Often the difference between being accused of national indignity and facing the death penalty was a matter of months, a defendant tried in the fall of 1944 running a much greater risk of facing a stiff sentence than someone tried of similar crimes in the spring of 1945. And in what constituted a case of rather bad timing, the collaborationist writers ended up going to trial well before the politicians of the Vichy regime.

Perhaps because the legal punishment seemed, at times, to rest on a shaky foundation, writers who had belonged to or supported the Resistance imposed a series of professional, or what they called moral, sanctions on the collaborationist writers. After Hitler's June 1941 invasion of the Soviet Union and the French Communist party's commitment to the Resistance, one of its first projects was to create a network of committees organized along professional lines. One of the most active and longest lasting was the Comité national des écrivains (National Writers' Committee), the CNE, which by the end of the war included many of the leading Resistance intellectuals. Aragon and Elsa Triolet were members from its inception, as was Jean Paulhan, who would violently break with the committee over its politics during the purge. Paul Eluard was a member, as was the critic Claude Morgan. The CNE never trusted Sartre enough to include him in its ranks. Working with the Resistance publication *Les Lettres françaises*, which carried its earliest declarations, the CNE denounced collaborationist writers throughout the war and began publishing blacklists of these tainted intellectuals as soon as the purge tribunals were in place.[5] The moral sanctions imposed by the CNE never threatened the life of the blacklisted writer, but they targeted a greater number of intellectuals than the courts could and were intended to reach further into the future, extending their judgments even beyond an author's death: "The moral sanctions taken by the CNE are not limited in time . . . there are writers whom even death cannot save."[6] The sanctions brought by this internal purge were, if not harsher than the court's verdicts, certainly more wide-reaching. They were intended not only to identify collaborationist writers but effectively to ban them from the postwar literary scene. In September 1944 *Les Lettres françaises* published its first blacklist with the following admonition:

> The members of the CNE unanimously refuse to contribute to the newspapers, reviews, anthologies, collections, etc. that publish a text

[5]The CNE was first known as the Front national des écrivains and published its first manifestos under that name. The committee renamed itself, however, perhaps to seem less closely attached to the Communist Resistance group the Front national.

[6]"Les sanctions morales prises par le CNE . . . ne sont pas limitées comme le sont les sanctions juridiques à temps. Et il y a des écrivains que la mort même n'en peut sauver, ceux qui ne peuvent avoir payé qu'aux yeux de la justice, mais non point de la conscience humaine." *Les Lettres françaises,* 22 Nov. 1946.

signed by one of the authors whose attitude or writings during the Occupation brought moral or material aid to the oppressor.[7]

In the October 11, 1944, issue of *Les Lettres françaises*, the CNE published a longer list of some 60 collaborationist writers with whom the members of the CNE "refused all contact," as if collaboration had become a virus and political purity a question of medical hygiene (*Les Lettres françaises*, 11 Oct. 1944). Some of the writers on this list would be put on trial—Robert Brasillach, Charles Maurras, Lucien Rebatet, Céline (who was tried *in absentia*)—others would not—Jean Giono, Marcel Jouhandeau, Henry de Montherlant, Paul Morand. In either case these moral sanctions, this professional purge was a boycott; indeed, perhaps it was nothing more than an attempt to control the literary marketplace. Not only did the members of the CNE refuse to publish with the tainted writers, but they also attempted to close public forums to any writer accused of collaboration. The result of this action, in the words of Jean Paulhan, who broke with the CNE over the blacklists, meant that "the entire press" was closed to these writers, at least in the immediate postwar years (Paulhan, *De la paille,* 57). For his own reasons Paulhan was probably overstating his case. Montherlant writes that the sanctions forbidding him to publish for one year, from October 1, 1944, to October 1, 1945, were a "pure formality." He goes on to add, not without his characteristic insolence, that "in no period of my life have so many of my books been published than during the three years that followed the Liberation" (Montherlant, *L'Equinoxe,* 273). Nonetheless, at a time when collaborationist writers were accused of having sold themselves to the enemy and of having profited from the Occupation, the sanctions imposed on the purged writers seemed to be as much about controlling income as they were about excluding the writers from the republic of letters.

[7]"Les membres du Comité national des écrivains se sont engagés à l'unanimité à refuser toute collaboration aux journaux, revues, recueils collectifs, collections, etc. qui publieraient un texte signé par un écrivain dont l'attitude ou les écrits pendant l'occupation ont apporté une aide morale ou matérielle à l'oppresseur." *Les Lettres françaises,* 9 Sept. 1944.

Along with its moral sanctions the CNE attempted to influence the outcome of the court proceedings. In the November 1943 issue of *Les Lettres françaises* it called on the "government of France" in place after the Liberation to create a paralegal committee made up of writers and judges charged with investigating "without prejudice" the conduct of all writers since June 1940. This committee could both regulate the profession through sanctions and "illuminate the action of the courts [*éclairer l'action de la justice*]." This advice was backed by actions since, according to Gisele Sapiro's recent study, a delegation of members of the CNE brought one version of their blacklist to the Ministry of Justice in 1944 hoping to further the prosecution of those whom the CNE labeled the major offenders [*grands coupables*].[8] *Les Lettres françaises* and the CNE had a dual effect on the literary establishment at the time of the purge. In its attempt to "save the honor of French letters," the review identified collaborationist writers, denounced their political commitments, defined treasonous acts, and set the terms for the cases of writers which would be heard before the purge tribunals. Through its attempt to define a writer's responsibility, *Les Lettres françaises* also gave a theoretical grounding to the courtroom proceedings and provided what would become one of the central points of the debate regarding literature in the years following the war.

BEGINNING IN OCTOBER 1944, while the leading political figures of the collaboration were still in exile in the German town of Sigmaringen, the courts began the trials of writers accused of treason. Indeed, it is one of the blotches on the purge that many writers who had supported the collaboration went to trial before the politicians who had implemented it. In October 1944 Georges Suarez, editor of the collaborationist sheet *Aujourd'hui* was the first writer to be tried, convicted, and executed according to Article 75.[9] Paul Chack, the author of maritime novels and a propagandist for several fascist and

---

[8]*Les Lettres françaises,* Nov. 1943. This is the conclusion Sapiro reaches in her dissertation, 483.

[9]For a thorough chronology of these trials see Assouline, *L'Epuration.*

anti-Bolshevik groups, was convicted and executed one month later. The same fate was reserved for Jean Luchaire, man-about-town and editor of the Nazi-sponsored daily *Les Nouveaux Temps*. Two radio announcers were tried and executed during the purge: Paul Ferdonnet, who worked for the German Radio-Stuttgart and came to be known as the "traitor of Stuttgart," and Jean Hérold-Paquis, a propagandist for the collaborationist Radio-Paris, who became famous for repeating the same phrase at the close of every program: "England, like Carthage, shall be destroyed." In his memoirs Henri Béraud, a writer for the fascist weekly *Gringoire*, tells of how members of the Resistance came to get him in his apartment and hauled him to Fresnes (Béraud, *Quinze Jours,* 15). Béraud went to trial at the end of December 1944, was condemned to death for treason, and was pardoned by de Gaulle after his conviction, thanks in large part to François Mauriac's action on his behalf. Lucien Rebatet, a music and cinema critic at *Je suis partout* and author of the 1942 best-selling fascist memoirs *Les Décombres,* received the death sentence in November 1946 but had it commuted to hard labor for life and ended up serving only a few years in prison. Rebatet had fled to Germany shortly before the Liberation of France, thus delaying his trial and undoubtedly saving his life. In December 1945 Abel Hermant, a member of the French Academy and a columnist at Luchaire's *Les Nouveaux Temps*, was condemned for national indignity and sentenced to life in prison. He was released in 1950 and died soon after. Two of the more prominent collaborators died before either the courts or the CNE could begin proceedings against them. Ramon Fernandez, a literary critic who, along with Drieu la Rochelle, had supported Doriot's *Parti populaire français* and the collaboration, died of an embolism shortly before the Liberation of France. Drieu, for his part, underwent what might be called a self-purge. In a short text titled "Final Reckoning" he looked back at his involvement with the collaboration. Refusing the "transitory" institutions of the purge courts, he reached his own verdict: "Yes, I am a traitor. Yes, I worked with the enemy [*Oui, j'ai été d'intelligence avec l'ennemi*]. It is no fault of mine if this enemy was not intelligent. . . . I demand the death penalty" (Drieu la Rochelle, *Secret Journal,* 73). On March 15, 1945, Drieu swallowed poison, opened the gas spigot, and ended his life. As for Céline, initially indicted for treason, he was eventually charged, convicted, and received amnesty for national indignity but never spent any time in a French prison. Of all these cases the most closely watched were those of Charles Maurras, the leader of the far right-wing *Action française*, and Robert Brasillach. Both Maurras and Brasillach were accused of treason, both were convicted, and only Maurras's age—he was 76 when his trial began—saved him from the fate of the younger writer: execution by firing squad.[10]

Whether they faced the charge of treason or of national indignity, the writers were accused of having espoused numerous elements of Nazi ideology: anti-communism; anti-Semitism; support for the *relève* (the system designed to send French workers to Germany in exchange for French POWs); support for the *Milice* (Vichy's police force); support for the German and French troops fighting the Soviets on the Eastern front; attacks against de Gaulle and the Resistance; participation in collaborationist organizations; trips to Germany during the Occupation, in particular to the International Writers' Congress at Weimar in 1941. All these attitudes and activities were proof in the eyes of the prosecution that the writers had betrayed France, even though some of the defendants rightly argued that a number of these attitudes belonged as much to France as they did to Germany.

Many of the writers brought to trial had espoused some form of anti-Semitism during the Occupation, but even while the full extent of the Shoah was revealed to the nation, the purge courts never directly addressed France's role in the deportation of Jews.[11] Vichy France bears a tremendous responsibility in the massacres of the Holocaust. In October 1940, only a few months after Pétain came to power, the government imposed a series of discriminatory laws re-

[10]Maurras was convicted of treason and crimes of collaboration, but the jury resolved that his age, 76, was an "extenuating circumstance." Maurras was imprisoned at Riom, the city where the Vichy government had put the leaders of the Third Republic on trial in 1942, then at Clairvaux. He died in November 1952.

[11]For a study of Vichy's anti-Semitic measures and policies during the Occupation see Marrus and Paxton, *Vichy France*.

stricting the private and public rights of Jews in France. Vichy then instituted a policy of deportation, which began with the internment of Jews in various camps in France, the most notorious among these being Drancy, a camp that came to be known as the *anti-chambre d'Auschwitz,* and ended with the shipment of the Jews eastward by train. Vichy was ultimately responsible for the deportation of 75,000 Jews, only 3 percent of whom, according to Michael Marrus and Robert Paxton, survived (Marrus and Paxton, *Vichy France and the Jews,* 343). Unlike the Nuremberg trials, however, *l'épuration* did not try any Frenchman for crimes against humanity. It was not that the prosecution was unaware of Vichy's racial persecution. Rather, prosecutors transferred the responsibility of Vichy's anti-Semitic policies onto Nazi Germany. During the trials of politicians as well as of journalists, prosecutors charged collaborators with anti-Semitism as a way of proving they had betrayed France. Racism was considered one more instance of a writer's adherence to Nazi ideology and treason of the French "soul."

This led occasionally to skewed indictments. Take the case of Louis-Ferdinand Céline, for instance. Céline published some of the most virulently anti-Semitic pamphlets in the years preceding the war and had had these pamphlets reprinted during the Occupation. Given his status as a literary figure as well as the strength of his writing, Céline added to an atmosphere in France where Vichy's anti-Semitic legislation was more easily accepted by public opinion. Unlike numerous other writers brought to trial, Céline had no formal ties with Vichy France or collaborationist parties. Indeed, to the extent that Céline commented upon Pétain and Vichy, it was to criticize the regime for being too lenient in its anti-Semitic policies.[12] One could argue that for Céline—and he was by no means alone—questions of politics were invariably reduced to one overarching ideology: anti-Semitism. In the list of charges brought against Céline at the end of the war, however, anti-Semitism is only one among several, including

[12]See, for example, the letter to the editor of the anti-Semitic *Au Pilori,* dated 2 Oct. 1941, in which Céline calls Pétain "the deputy of the Rothschilds" (*Cahiers Céline 7,* 123).

the unsubstantiated accusations of having denounced members of the Resistance and of having been a member of the collaborationist Cercle Européen (Céline, "Reply"), as if anti-Semitism alone was not substantial grounds for indictment. In Brasillach's case the accusation of anti-Semitism came after the accusation of anti-communism, which leads us to wonder if questions of political alignment weren't more important than the writer's responsibility in the death and deportation of Jews. While calling his anti-Semitic articles a form of "denunciation," the prosecution never linked Brasillach's anti-Semitic railings to acts of persecution (Isorni, *Le Procès*, 162).

Maurras, for his part, was the only writer, to my knowledge, whose anti-Semitism was directly tied to murder during his trial. On February 2, 1944, Maurras wrote an article in which in a light-hearted tone he asked to know the whereabouts of the Worms family, whose son, Roger Stéphane, was committed to fighting Maurras's anti-Semitism. Four days after the publication of the article in *Action française*, Pierre Worms, Roger's father, was found dead, murdered by members of the *Milice* near his home on the French Riviera. At his trial Maurras and his attorneys claimed that the dates cited by the prosecution were incorrect and that Maurras had written his article about Worms after the murder. The court received from the prosecutor's office in Draguignan a telegram stating that Worms had been killed before Maurras published his article. On the basis of this telegram the prosecution was forced to drop these charges against Maurras, even though it was revealed soon after that the telegram was a fake.[13] Of all the trials of writers this is the closest the prosecution came to establishing a direct link between words and acts. Had it not been for the forged document, they could have proved for once that an opinion had been translated into violence, that a denunciation in the press had led to the murder of a Jewish man. Unlike the Nuremberg trials, however, the trials in France were limited to crimes of treason, and it is only in the last decade that the French courts have

[13]London, *Le Procès*, 35, 213–14. See also Weber, *Action française*, 471–72. I want to thank Stephanie O'Hara for bringing the complexity of this episode to my attention.

sought to charge French collaborators with crimes against humanity. In 1945 the prosecutors knew of the horror of the concentration camps, but the postwar trials remained political trials, aimed at proving that the collaborators had betrayed France. Though certain writers and a part of French public opinion would demand that collaborationist writers be held responsible for abetting the deportation of Jews, during the trials the charge of anti-Semitism served to prove a writer's support for the Nazi political program and was never considered a crime in and of itself. This was perhaps symptomatic of the postwar period: by condemning as traitors certain French anti-Semites such as Céline, Brasillach, or Darquier de Pellepoix, the courts were transforming anti-Semitism into a foreign, specifically German, ideology and avoiding the prickly and perhaps much more damaging issue of an authentically French participation in the Shoah.

The specific charges brought against the writers varied from trial to trial, but the accusation of having betrayed what Teitgen called the French soul invariably shadowed accusations of political betrayal. The courts often charged collaborationist intellectuals with having engaged in economic and symbolic if not literal sexual exchanges with the German occupiers, and one sometimes gets the impression that, more than anything else, it is for these crimes that the treasonous writers were being pursued. Prosecutors and journalists alike claimed that a number of the writers accused of treason had profited financially from the Occupation, adding venality to the already long list of charges. The economic metaphor circulated widely during the purge as the courts repeatedly indicted writers who had been subsidized by the Nazis. Attorneys for the state readily drew upon the cliché of collaborationist writers living the high life during the Occupation, a picture that they quickly contrasted to the privations suffered by the majority of the French. In its opening statement the prosecution accused Jean Luchaire of having led a "golden existence" during the four years of the Occupation. His salary of 100,000 francs per month, the "occult allocations" he received from the Ministry of Finance, along with the "financial support" the Germans gave *Les Nouveaux Temps* all contributed, according to the court clerk, to Luchaire persevering in his "treasonous work" (*"son oeuvre de trahison"*; Garçon, ed.,

Les Procès, 357). That Henri Béraud was the highest paid journalist during the Occupation, at 600,000 francs a year, seemed to be proof enough of his treason (Assouline, *L'Epuration,* 43). A journalist describing Georges Suarez claimed that his ostentatious beige overcoat was a sign that he was one of the "nouveau riche of the treason" (35). According to the Communist party organ, *L'Humanité,* Sacha Guitry, the fashionable playwright, should have been punished precisely because he "made millions during the Occupation." Elsewhere *L'Humanité* called Abel Hermant a "traitor at 1500 francs per article."[14] In many cases the collaborationist journalists had indeed profited during the Occupation as German funds and German censure often determined whether a periodical would go to press and who would be remunerated. But the accusation of venality also provided the prosecution with an explanation for the treasonous act: greed could replace ideology as a motive for collaboration. *L'Humanité* accused Hermant of selling his articles precisely because nobody bought his "100 unread novels." In times of penury and onerous Occupation costs the rich writer's very lifestyle showed a lack of solidarity with the French nation, and for the writers at *L'Humanité* the accusation of profiteering had the added advantage of being able to cast the collaboration in terms of class. Whether purging writers, politicians, or the economic elite, the communists saw the postwar period as the opportunity to overturn economic inequalities and establish a new democratic society.[15] They were keen to draw an equivalence between economic collaborators, referred to invariably as the bosses [*patronat*], and the bourgeois writers whose taste for luxury and "apartments in the faubourg Saint-Honoré" had led them to rent their pens to the Germans. The language of the purge trials binds both the literary act and treason to a system of economic exchange. In a time of censorship and mimeographed clandestine reviews the pure writer, the Resistance claimed, had remained poor.

Accusations of economic exchange were often seconded by

[14]*L'Humanité,* 14 Nov. 1944, 17 Dec. 1944.
[15]For the relation between the communists and the economic purge, see Rousso, "L'Epuration," 99.

charges of illicit sexual exchanges, as if it were only a small step from profiteering to prostitution. During the Occupation both Resistants and collaborators had turned to the metaphor of a feminine France overrun and occupied by German virility. It is perhaps no coincidence that at the Liberation the "Loi Marthe Richard" closed the French brothels: brothels had been considered sites of collaboration and may have represented France's capitulation in the popular imagination (Novick, *The Resistance,* 139). The event that most violently combined collaboration, illicit sex, and the pent-up anger of the purge was what came to be known as *"la tonte,"* the public shearing of French women suspected of having collaborated.[16] Many of these women, though not all, were accused of having slept with the enemy, thus bringing an added dishonor to France's already besmirched reputation. The *tonte* was a public spectacle, and the condemned women were often paraded through the center of town or presented to the jeering crowds from a platform built for the occasion. If, as Rousso points out, these "shameful episodes" (Rousso, "L'Epuration," 85) rarely ended in an execution—though the condemned women were often beaten—the women were nonetheless accused of having sexually betrayed France, treated like prostitutes, and made to represent the guilt of an entire nation that had collaborated with the enemy.

The tactic of attacking the defendant's sexual mores is not new in France: the Revolutionary tribunals had accused Marie-Antoinette of having had incestuous relations with her son. While during the purge men were not victims of the *tonte*, the intellectuals who collaborated were accused of having had indecent relations with the Germans. At the forefront stands Brasillach, whose description of the Occupation in terms of sexual pleasure came to be seen during the purge trials as emblematic of a certain collaborationist mentality. On two occasions in 1943, after having left *Je suis partout*, Brasillach reflected upon what the collaboration meant to him. In an article from September 1943 he tells of running into a friend who launches into a soliloquy that Brasillach records "more or less" faithfully. A partisan of the collaboration from the beginning, the friend had changed perspectives by the

[16]See Brossat, *Les Tondues.*

end of the war: "Now I *like* the Germans [*j'aime les Allemands*]. When I meet German soldiers . . . I feel a sort of brotherly affection for them ... From a collaborator of reason, I have become a collaborator of the heart [*collaborationiste de coeur*]."[17] The following year Brasillach made the same claims in his own voice: "I've contracted a liaison with the German genius, I will never forget it. Like it or not, we have lived together; French(men) of some reflection during these few years will have more or less slept with Germany, not without quarrels, and the memory of it will remain sweet to them."[18] According to Alice Kaplan, Brasillach's declarations about an eroticized and virile friendship with German soldiers "did more than any other text or action to condemn Brasillach as a traitor" (Kaplan, *Reproductions,* 16). To be sure, the prosecutor's statement to the court is loaded with sexual innuendo and begins, appropriately enough, with a paralipsis: Marcel Reboul reads the passage where Brasillach talks about a "collaboration of the heart," asserts that he won't use these pages to obtain an "easy effect," and then, practically in the next breath, speaks of Brasillach's "almost carnal love of brute force." Reboul then accuses Brasillach of having "fornicated" with Germany in order to be released from his prisoner of war camp, an accusation that turns the writer into little more than a *fille de joie* at the service of the enemy. The question remains whether, in his phrase about "having slept with Germany," Brasillach was speaking figuratively or literally. In either case Reboul reappropriated this terminology and turned Brasillach's politics into a knavish and sado-masochistic sexual commerce (Isorni, *Le Procès,* 140, 142, 145).

As with the charge of having received money from the Germans, the accusation of sexual commerce with the enemy seemed to furnish proof of treason. Just as the traitor made money while the rest of France scrimped, the treasonous writer was accused of enjoying sexual pleasure while his countrymen experienced only pain. This logic

[17]"Naissance d'un sentiment," *Révolution nationale,* 4 Sept. 1943. I have quoted from Brasillach, *Œuvres complètes,* vol. 12, 579 (emphasis is in original text).

[18]"Lettre à quelques jeunes gens." Brasillach's article first appeared on 19 Feb. 1944 in *Révolution nationale.* This passage reappears in Isorni, *Le Procès,* 138.

was not limited to writers and intellectuals; it is the guiding principle behind the shearing of women accused of having slept with German soldiers. In Brasillach's case there is the added question of his homoeroticism, never openly declared but hinted at in his own writings and implied by the prosecution. Brasillach's sexuality has long been the subject of speculation; after all, his fascist itinerary began at the Nuremberg rallies, where he found himself surrounded by "100 nineteen year old boys" steeped in "seriousness, virility and the hard and powerful love of the fatherland," and ended with translations of erotic Greek poetry (Brasillach, *Notre Avant-Guerre*, 347–48). But for Reboul there was no doubt, nor was there for Sartre, who took his cue from the Brasillach trial and cast the collaborator as a man seeking to be sodomized by the German occupier. In 1947 Georges Duhamel drew up a catalogue of different collaborationist types: along with "losers" (*"les ratés"*), "imbeciles," "those who suffer from venality," and "ideologues," he lists the "depraved" (*"les vicieux"*) and "females in ecstasy" (*"les femelles extasiées"*) (Duhamel, *Tribulations,* 47). Upon reading this phrase, I thought Duhamel was talking about the women accused of having taken German lovers. I was wrong. Duhamel's females in ecstasy were men. One is left wondering which, in Duhamel's reasoning, was worse: traitors or men behaving like women. At the Liberation sexual deviation had become a synonym for political betrayal. Prosecutors, writers, as well as the general public willingly confused "intelligence with the enemy" with carnal knowledge. Rebuilding France, reclaiming the French soul also meant, at least for the purge courts, reconstituting normative gender roles.

The collaborationist intellectuals on trial had all been accused on the basis of their journalism rather than their literary work. Even for an author of fascist novels, such as Brasillach, the prosecution maintained that his journalism and his literary activity were two separate realms.[19] Paradoxically, however, prosecutors regularly cited a writer's prestige as proof of his responsibility, and it was a common

[19]The one exception to this rule is Céline, whose 1944 novel *Guignol's band* appears on the list of collaborationist works, but this can only be the result of the prosecution's not having read the novel.

conceit at the trials for prosecutors to claim that they admired the accused's literary talent. At Maurras's trial the court clerk reading the
accusations began by acknowledging the writer's "great talent," but,
he added, it was precisely this talent that gave Maurras such power to
sway public opinion. In the words of the clerk, Maurras by his writings "created the climate favorable to . . . the Vichy government by
making public opinion adopt in advance the political program [*les dis-
positions gouvernementales*] that followed" (London, *Le Procès*, 17). The
attorney prosecuting Brasillach made the same argument; the writer's
talent gave him the power to convince and, where necessary, convert
his readers. During the interrogation the presiding judge claimed that
Brasillach had abused his "power of persuasion and . . . the extent of
his influence as a writer over a part of public opinion." And later in
the trial the prosecutor began his arguments by underlining what he
called the "undeniable talent" manifest in Brasillach's novels (37, 54).
It was precisely because a writer had accumulated a certain literary
prestige that he bore a greater responsibility for the opinions he expressed in his journalism. De Gaulle had recourse to the same argument when he refused to commute Brasillach's death sentence. In his
memoirs he commented upon his reaction faced with Brasillach's petition, "The courts of justice condemned several notorious writers to
death. When they had not directly or willfully served the enemy, I
commuted their punishment, on principle; but in contrary cases I did
not feel I had the right to reprieve them. For in literature as in everything talent is a bond of responsibility" (De Gaulle, *The Complete War
Memoirs*, 799). For de Gaulle and the prosecutors literary talent like
excessive financial gain became corroborating evidence of a writer's
treason. To betray one's talent was to betray France. This said, it
should be added that lack of talent didn't save Paul Chack from the
firing squad.

While the writers were not on trial for their novels, plays, or poetry, literature itself was on trial, though in an indirect way. The
purge of intellectuals who had supported the collaboration was also
about the use and abuse of literary prestige. In the eyes of the prosecution the trials were meant to cleanse not just the political or jour-

nalistic milieus but to purify French literature. And it is not surprising that the Resistance paper *Les Lettres françaises* declared that its mission was "to save the honor of French letters." Purging writers became a way for the nation to recapture some of its literary prestige.

Though writers rarely testified against each other in court, the one exception is Paul Claudel's testimony in the Maurras trial. Through a written statement Claudel claimed that the success of Maurras's political theories coincided with the destruction of France and that Maurras had denounced him as a member of the Resistance in several articles in *Action française*. Maurras's answer was swift: he reproached Claudel for having written both an ode to Pétain in 1942 and a hymn to de Gaulle in 1944 and claimed that Claudel's style was not only heavy (*gros*) but that his writing seemed to be translated from a dialect of High German (London, *Le Procès*, 44). This quarrel between two writers, while taking place inside the courtroom, also points to the larger quarrels outside the tribunals in the court of public opinion. Alongside the depositions and arguments of the courtroom, alongside the pleas and verdicts of the tribunals, writers who had participated in the Resistance were denouncing, accusing, and punishing the collaborationist writers. This intraprofessional purge was carried out in the press and was less concerned with the writer's life than with his reputation. There is little doubt that the literary field and, in particular, the writers I examine in this study were affected at least as much by these polemics within the literary field as they were by the courtroom proceedings.

Of the numerous clandestine publications *Les Lettres françaises*, founded by Jacques Decour and Jean Paulhan in 1941, offers the most illustrative examples of how writers associated with the Resistance identified and denounced the intellectuals they suspected of collaboration. From its very first issue *Les Lettres françaises* announced its intent both to "save the honor of French letters" and to "thrash the traitors."[20] The purge of literature, the punishment of collaborators, is thus inscribed on the masthead of the very first issue. Paul Eluard and

---

[20]"Nous sauverons par nos écrits l'honneur des lettres françaises. Nous fustigerons les traîtres vendus à l'ennemi." *Les Lettres françaises*, Sept. 1942.

Sartre both contributed to this publication, as did Aragon, Edith Thomas, Claude Morgan, Michel Leiris, Claude Roy, Raymond Queneau, and Mauriac among others, though until the Liberation of Paris the articles and poems in *Les Lettres françaises* remained unsigned. The paper also published quotations from Lamartine and Goethe, Stendhal and Whitman, Apollinaire and Hugo, as if these figures were guaranteeing or indeed signing the clandestine review's anonymous articles. The Resistance writers divided literary history into two groups of writers: patriots and traitors, appropriating the first, denouncing the second. And while the writers of *Les Lettres françaises* remained anonymous, the paper regularly printed the names of collaborationist writers in capital letters, exposing them to public shame and beginning a process that would result in the notorious blacklists of writers published at the end of the war.

The writers at *Les Lettres françaises* combined a commitment to the Resistance with what they called a "defense" of French letters: "French letters are under attack," read the proclamation in September 1942, "we will defend them." Literature is an "instrument," a tool; indeed, in the minds of the Resistance writers literature was the ultimate tool for countering "Germanic barbarism" (*Les Lettres françaises*, Sept. 1942). For the writers at the review there was no separation between writing and resisting—the writers were equally committed to politics and to aesthetics. For many of these writers, however, poetry rather than prose was the genre responsible for "saving the honor of French letters." An article from February 1944 labeled poetry the "conscience of France," thus consecrating the genre in its fight against fascism. "She [poetry] behaved admirably [*Elle s'est admirablement conduite*]," the author of the article added, as if poetry were a woman resisting the temptation of collaboration. In April of the same year, in a eulogy for Max Jacob, who died in 1944 at Drancy, the author depicts poets as the martyrs of the Resistance: "Poets are deported, tortured, murdered because they represent good against evil" (*Les Lettres françaises*, Apr. 1944). For *Les Lettres françaises* poetry became the representative of the national spirit struggling against foreign domination and the poet embodied the suffering of the nation's martyred flesh. Poetry became the genre through which the purge of collaborators could take place.

This conception of a politically engaged literature also depends upon a criticism of escapist literature and the "art for art's sake" attitude. An article from the second issue criticizes the fascist writers precisely because they attempt to separate art from politics. Parodying the attitude of the "modern Nazi writer," who, by not talking about the war becomes an accomplice to the crime, the Resistance author writes, "Let us speak of cats and of the Xestobium plubeum. Or let's escape to the two refuges of childhood: dreams and fairy tales" (*Les Lettres françaises*, Oct. 1942). At the end of the war Vercors returned to this theme in his short story *Les Mots*: a German officer tells a French poet that by painting a landscape he has "enriched humanity with new beauty," while in the background his troops massacre the civilians of a French village (Vercors, *Les Mots*, 43). The theory outlined in the early issues of *Les Lettres françaises* is summarized in an article by Michel Leiris, dated 28 October 1944, titled "What It Means to Speak" (*"Ce que parler veut dire"*), in which the author defined what he called the prose writer's "rules of behavior" (*Les Lettres françaises*, 28 Oct. 1944). Denouncing writers who had openly supported the Nazis as well as those who during the Occupation considered their work as nothing more than literary, Leiris saw literature as a privileged art precisely because language is an instrument, "a way of acting" (*"un moyen d'agir"*) that permits the writer to influence the actions of others. In their understanding of language Leiris and the other writers of the Resistance were not far from the position taken by the prosecutors and the courts who, basing themselves on Article 75 of the Penal Code, equated a treasonous word with a treasonous act. According to *Les Lettres françaises*, collaborationist writers were as accountable for their deeds as collaborationist soldiers. This was the literary lesson of the Occupation; the writer assumes a "litigious responsibility" when he writes, and by signing his text he takes full "responsibility" for his work. In this brief article Leiris was both denouncing collaborationist intellectuals for not having understood the weight of their words, at least until they were brought before a purge tribunal, and describing the role and responsibility of politically committed writers and intellectuals in terms similar to Sartre's.

Leiris returned to these considerations in "The Autobiographer as Torero [*De la littérature considérée comme une tauromachie*]," the prefatory essay to *Manhood* [*L'Age d'homme*]. Begun before the Occupation and finished in January 1945 against the backdrop of Le Havre devastated by Allied bombing raids, this essay traces what Leiris calls the "danger" involved in writing in general and in publishing an autobiography in particular. For Leiris this danger comes from exposing oneself to the world in the same way that a bullfighter exposes himself, even if only for an instant, to the horns of the bull. However, the writer can only attain this state of danger by adopting a specific rhetoric, a rhetoric that refuses to resort to "tremolos or sobs" or to "flourishes and gilding" (Leiris, *L'Age d'homme*, 19), a rhetoric, in a word, that Leiris calls a form of "classicism" (21). Even if literature does not always participate in a struggle of life and death, Leiris tells us, it is nonetheless engaged in a fight for personal and collective liberation (*affranchissement*) (25). Perhaps still under the imprimatur of the purge authorities Leiris ends his preface to *L'Age d'homme* with the conclusion that literature's role is "to bring the supporting evidence (*pièces à conviction*) to the trial of our present society" (25). Leiris's 1945 essay is more complex and thorough than the 1944 article in *Les Lettres françaises*. Still, the two texts turn around concepts at the heart of the purge trials: literature is an act that demands the writer's honesty, engages his responsibility, exposes him to danger, and takes place in the shadow of the tribunals.

Alongside defining the conditions and the style of politically responsible literature, *Les Lettres françaises* was committed to publishing evidence of certain writers' treason of France and of French literature. Shortly after Drieu la Rochelle had taken over the *Nouvelle Revue française* and turned the prestigious literary journal into a collaborationist publication, the writers at *Les Lettres françaises* wrote a mock eulogy, denouncing him and Ramon Fernandez for having turned the review into a "rank cadaver." In the following issue an article by Claude Morgan titled "Denouncing Maupassant [*Haro sur Maupassant*]" criticized Paul Morand for having denigrated Maupassant, a writer who bore witness to the German Occupation of 1870 and who, in Morgan's terms, was an "example for French writers today."[21] Morand's book, while containing several anti-Semitic and anti-Masonic passages, was not particularly critical of Maupassant. Morand did claim, however, that Maupassant was more of an opportunist than a politically committed writer and that on the whole the depiction of Prussians officers in his stories was rather balanced. At stake in the article from *Les Lettres françaises* was a defense of Maupassant and of the honor of French letters and a clear denunciation of Morand's "complicity" with the Germans. Morand's study of Maupassant was, according to Morgan, "a way like any other of betraying [*C'est une façon comme une autre de trahir*]," thus identifying literary criticism as a genre that could be put at the service of the enemy. Another article from November 1942 condemned the writers who for the past two years had gone to the International Writers' Congress in Weimar, an accusation that weighed heavily against the treasonous writers during their trials. The partisans at *Les Lettres françaises* accumulated evidence against important French writers one after another. They accused Colette of having penned an article on the Burgundy region for the collaborationist weekly *Signal*: "by giving to the collaborationist press the slightest bit of writing, even if it isn't political, the writer plays a part in the concert of enemy propaganda orchestrated by Goebbels." They savaged Jacques Chardonne for his conversion to fascism; "he gave himself," wrote the author, "like a woman who has just been stopped." They condemned Brasillach, Rebatet, and Drieu la Rochelle for having gone to Germany in 1942. They labeled Giono a mercenary ready to publish in any collaborationist review if the price was right. They denounced Céline for claiming that almost all of France, including members of the Resistance, profited from the Occupation. They proscribed Montherlant for *La Reine morte,* the play he wrote during the Occupation. Nor did the Resistance writers limit themselves to the literary field. In March 1944 an anonymous author in *Les Lettres françaises* attacked Georges Clouzot's film *Le Corbeau* for hav-

---

[21]*Les Lettres françaises*, Sept. 1942, Oct. 1942. Morand's study of Maupassant, *Vie de Guy de Maupassant,* was published by Flammarion in 1942.

ing presented a negative portrait of the French, the same terms, it should be noted, that the Vichy government had used in its attempt to censor Clouzot's film at the time of its release. Even after the Occupation these recriminations continued: such was the case when Aragon attacked Gide for having studied the German language with a suspicious amount of "application" in June 1940.[22]

Not all the writers denounced in the pages of *Les Lettres françaises* ended up in court, nor even did they all make it onto the CNE's blacklists. The project of the Resistance intellectuals, however, coincided in several ways with the project of the purge tribunals. The writers and the prosecutors of the Resistance all sought to identify collaborationist writers, delineate their acts of treason and "intelligence with the enemy," and mete out the appropriate punishment. At the same time, they sought to ensure that writers in the postwar, renovated society would be held legally and professionally accountable for what they wrote and where they wrote it. The trials, the blacklists, the denunciatory articles were all part of an attempt to define, in Leiris's terms, "what it means to speak." Whether or not this attempt was successful would only be decided years later.

IT WOULD BE A MISTAKE to believe that the purge courts and the writers at *Les Lettres françaises* were making their claims uncontested. Though the collaborationist writers may not have been able to publish in a daily newspaper such as the conservative *Le Figaro*, they wrote defense pleas, editorials, letters, essays, novels, plays, and poems that challenged both the accusations of treason and the conception of literature proposed by the prosecutors and the Resistance writers. And though the accused writers first defended themselves on political grounds, their final arguments depended upon establishing a theory of literature that could successfully compete with the one presented by the writers calling for their punishment.

[22]These accusations, beginning with the one against Colette, are made in the following issues of *Les Lettres françaises*: Dec. 1942 (Colette); Nov. 1943 (Chardonne and Céline); June 1943 (Giono); Jan.–Feb. 1943 (Montherlant); March 1944 (Clouzot); 25 Nov. 1944 (Gide).

The first line of defense of all the accused writers was to claim that in supporting Pétain and the collaboration they had been doing their patriotic duty. This argument hinged upon two points. First, the defendants went straight to what was and remains one of the most contentious points of the purge trials: Pétain's legitimacy. Pétain went on trial in August 1945, and writers and politicians alike claimed that they should not be put on trial before the purge courts had established Pétain's guilt or innocence. Furthermore, in the view of the collaborators Pétain headed a government that had come to power legally and served the interests of the French nation. This argument figures prominently in the 1947 pamphlet against the purge written by Maurice Bardèche.[23] Before the war Bardèche had coauthored a *Histoire du cinéma* with Robert Brasillach, his brother-in-law and the man he "loved more than any other" (Bardèche, *Lettre*, 19). After the war, and after the execution of Brasillach, Bardèche continued a three-pronged career. As a literary critic he wrote biographical studies of Balzac, Proust, Céline, and other writers. As an editor he founded and directed the extreme right-wing review *Défense de l'Occident*. As a polemicist he repeatedly and violently attacked the Nuremberg trials, the purge, and France's Republican governments. In his *Lettre à François Mauriac* Bardèche upbraids Mauriac for supporting the postwar regime and condemns the purge precisely because Vichy was a legal government, voted to power by the National Assembly, and recognized by foreign governments. After signing the armistice, Vichy may have lost its "sovereignty," Bardèche argues, but it retained its "legitimacy" (24). As for the Free French, they constituted nothing more than "a meeting in a London hotel of private parties with no mandate to govern" (22). Bardèche was less interested in legal questions than in exonerating Vichy France and French fascism; his pamphlet, after all, ends with a racist declaration of faith. Still, his *Lettre à François Mauriac* presents what was clearly one of the main stumbling blocks for the Resistance and one of the primary arguments in defense of accused collaborators, from Pétain to Brasillach.

[23]Bardèche, *Lettre à François Mauriac*. For more information on Bardèche, see Kaplan, *Reproductions*, 161–88.

Fascist writers and collaborationist intellectuals understandably cast their support for the Vichy regime as a patriotic act, but within this argument there were two major variants. For a fascist writer such as Brasillach patriotism included an intimacy with the Germans. Throughout his trial Brasillach claimed that in his writings he had only defended "a certain French tradition" (Isorni, *Le Procès*, 71) and that the Gaullists who had left France in 1940 were the real traitors. In the words of his attorney, Brasillach had so thoroughly "penetrated the French soul" that he could not have betrayed France (170). The final proof of his patriotism was that, unlike some others, and here Isorni was referring to both the Gaullists in London and to the collaborators who had fled to Sigmaringen in June 1944, Brasillach had chosen to stay in France throughout the war. According to Brasillach, at least at his trial, collaboration with the Germans was a historical inevitability and the only way for France to keep its dignity and "to save . . . what could still be saved" after the defeat (188). For Brasillach, then, patriotism and an intimate collaboration with the Germans went hand in hand. At the same time, however, for Charles Maurras and other writers at *L'Action française* Nazi Germany remained anathema even while they supported the collaboration, Pétain and the Vichy regime. In his statement to the court Maurice Pujo, the codirector of *L'Action française,* who went on trial with Maurras, defined the periodical's position as a "resistance" to "German desires and demands" (Pujo, *L'Action française*, 22–23). Pujo and Maurras both claimed that their politics had always been embodied by their motto "France alone" (*la seule France*). This vision of the Occupation presented Laval as a lackey of the Germans, and Pétain as a shield protecting France against Nazi demands. Maurras, for his part, claimed that he had always maintained a mortal hatred of Germany. Though the jury was not convinced by these arguments, he seems to have been unable to mention the Germans during his trial without pronouncing the slur *Boche* (London, *Le Procès*, 53).

Along with these declarations of patriotism the defendants repeatedly pleaded poverty. Proving that one hadn't profited from the Occupation became one of the primary defense strategies of the accused writers. Maurras's attorney claimed that colleagues had to force his client to accept a raise from 4,000 to 5,000 francs a month as editor of *L'Action française*, and he still earned less than the average worker at the periodical's print shop (London, *Le Procès*, 156). There were, Maître Goncet conceded, book royalties, but that was another matter. During Brasillach's trial, his attorney, Jacques Isorni, claimed that not only was *Je suis partout* notorious for paying its employees poorly—including its editor in chief—but that when Brasillach was offered a raise to stay at the paper after 1943, he answered "You can't make me do anything for money! [*On ne me fera rien faire pour de l'argent!*]" (Isorni, *Le Procès*, 205). Jean Hérold-Paquis, the radio propagandist, claimed at his trial that during the Occupation he "made less in two months than Maurice Chevalier made in half an hour," a pointed analogy since Chevalier had been accused of collaboration but never brought to trial (Assouline, *L'Epuration*, 73). A great source of humor in Céline's final novels is his repeated claims that his impecunious state has left him living in rags, eating nothing but noodles and cooked carrots. Poverty is at the heart of Céline's postwar poetics, but at the trials themselves claims of poverty served to prove a writer's moral purity. Being poor, or "modest," to use Isorni's term, meant that the writer had not profited from the Occupation the way an industrialist, for example, might have. One of the clichés employed by the defense stated that accused writers and intellectuals had been more severely punished than the men who had profited from building the Atlantic Wall. Conversely, opponents of the purge set out to show that *all* of France, and not just the collaboration, was overrun by greed. In a 1943 letter to *Je suis partout* Céline claimed that the real "traitors" were the 30 million Frenchmen who had profited from the war and not the "idealists," that is, the collaborationist intellectuals, who had only speculated in "gratuitous thoughts" (Céline, *Cahiers Céline 7*, 190). In response to charges of having sold themselves to the enemy, the accused writers all maintained that they had remained poor, pure, and French.

François Mauriac, the catholic novelist who had supported Pétain at the beginning of the Occupation but had quickly passed to de

Gaulle's camp, was one of the first writers allied with the CNE who called for indulgence toward the accused writers. When Henri Béraud was condemned for treason, Mauriac in his front-page article for *Le Figaro* wrote that Béraud in his extreme anglophobia was guilty only of a "directional error" (*"une erreur d'aiguillage"*) and not of treason. Béraud belonged to the "cult" of French literature, and this, Mauriac pleaded, should help other writers to forget their "just rancor," an argument aimed specifically at Camus, with whom Mauriac was in the midst of a polemic (Mauriac, *Le Baillon dénoué*, 218–22). Whereas Camus called for a fast and efficient purge based on his notion of justice, Mauriac preached moderation.[24] One week after Béraud's trial ended and after de Gaulle had commuted his sentence from execution to hard labor for life, Mauriac shifted his support to Brasillach. He not only provided the defense with written statements during the trial but also petitioned de Gaulle for clemency after the verdict. Jean Anouilh, Camus, Claudel, Colette, André Derain, Jean Paulhan, Paul Valéry, and Vlaminck all signed the petition in favor of Brasillach, though Julien Benda, Simone de Beauvoir, Sartre, and Vercors refused to endorse it. The petition contained only one argument, that Brasillach should be pardoned in consideration of the fact that his father had died for France during the first months of World War I. This differs considerably from Mauriac's usual arguments for indulgence; Brasillach's supporters certainly had other weapons in their arsenal. This simple argument, however, creates a link with one of the principal claims made by collaborationist writers: in supporting the collaboration Brasillach and his ilk had been as patriotic as the Frenchmen who had given their lives during the Great War.

De Gaulle rejected this appeal, but the petition implicitly called forth the testimony of history, and this strategy returned in almost every defense plea concerned with the purge, from the trials to poems, from private journals to novels. By appealing to contemporary affairs and to previous events that had divided France, the accused

[24]Camus, *Combat* 18 Oct. 1944. Several studies have already analyzed the debate between Mauriac and Camus at this time. See, in particular, Judt, *Past Imperfect*, 68–72; Lottman, *The Purge*, 142–46.

authors attempted to minimize, even to render banal, both the horrors of the Occupation and the crimes of which they were accused. In and out of the courtrooms traitorous writers began a search for historical precedents, which they hoped would act as legal precedents. By appealing to the past, the accused hoped to find justification for recent events. Maurras put his trial under the sign of Jeanne d'Arc and André Chénier and revived a lifelong obsession when he declared, upon receiving a guilty verdict, that his conviction was "the revenge of Dreyfus."[25] In his plea Brasillach compared the Nazi atrocities to the crimes of French colonizers in Indochina (Isorni, *Le Procès*, 93), and Maurice Bardèche claimed that the partisans of Ho Chi Minh were "authentic Resistants," while the Vietnamese "faithful" to the French were loathsome collaborators" (Bardèche, *Lettre*, 123), a line of argumentation intended not so much to praise the Vietnamese insurgents as to dilute the crimes of World War II. The comparison of colonial and fascist violence would become widespread during the postwar period, appearing not only in the purge trials but in watershed texts such as Aimé Césaire's 1956 *Discourse on Colonialism*. But analogies can never be detached from their context. It hardly seems necessary to point out that the analogies made between French colonialism and Nazi war crimes have entirely different effects and ramifications whether they are used to condemn the colonialists or defend the Nazis and their French associates. The same analogy used in an accusatory mode by Césaire, for example, can, of course, become nothing more than an exculpatory utterance when pronounced by Isorni or, forty years later, by Jacques Vergès in his defense of Klaus Barbie.

The incarcerated writers liked to point to their status as political prisoners, drawing a sharp distinction between themselves and the common criminals they encountered in prison. All almost invariably mentioned, with a simulated *frisson* that comes from rubbing shoulders with the common people, that collaborators were often interned alongside thieves and murderers. This desire to retain a privileged

---

[25]Maurras supporters kept trotting out this phrase in the postwar years. It figures as the dramatic last words of a partisan account of the Maurras trial, Chandet, *Le Procès Maurras*. See also the anonymous 1948 pamphlet calling for the revision of the Maurras trial, entitled *Notre J'Accuse*.

status in the eyes of the law is also evident in the dominant historical analogy of the postwar period, the comparison of the purge of 1945 to the Terror of 1793. This analogy turned the accused writers into the victims of political excess and had the added benefit of echoing criticisms of the Revolution and its legacy (including the French Communist party) already initiated by the Vichy government and the French fascists. Texts by imprisoned writers offer a florilegium of this historical analogy: hearing the footsteps of Resistants coming to arrest him, Henri Béraud said that he almost instinctively thought of Danton, who was arrested at home, stoking his fire (Béraud, *Quinze Jours*, 15). Brasillach denounced his trial as a "Revolutionary Tribunal." Maurice Bardèche in his 1947 *Lettre à François Mauriac* claimed that the postwar trials were "dirtier than the Directoire" (Bardèche, *Lettre*, 103). And while in prison in 1945 Jacques Chardonne wrote, "since Robespierre, we know what the nation demands" (Chardonne, *Détachements*, 23). All these writers turned to the historical analogy both as a way of deflecting their own guilt and as an attempt at stigmatizing the purge. But the purge, in fact, only confirmed their political convictions. If, as they claimed, history was repeating itself, then not only was the purge as bloody as the Terror and the system of justice in 1945 as arbitrary as the law of 1793, since after all it confused political prisoners and common criminals, but also neither France nor Europe had progressed since the Revolution. Comparing the purge to the Terror served as proof for these writers that they and the Vichy government had been right all along in discrediting the Republic.

The turn to analogy is also at the core of Paul Morand's 1951 historical novel *Le Flagellant de Séville*.[26] Morand, a diplomat, travel writer, and novelist had participated in what the French called the

---

[26]Morand, *Le Flagellant de Séville*. See also Morand's *Le Dernier Jour de l'Inquisition*, another historical novel set during the inquisition of 1813 in Lima, Peru. In 1961 Morand published a biography of Louis XIV's minister of finance, Nicolas Fouquet, which resembles the book on Maupassant in its portrait of a man who is something of a trickster and an opportunist. It also recalls the purge of 1944–47, however, when Morand claims that Fouquet, imprisoned by the king, was the victim of two "merciless purgers" *("épurateurs impitoyables")*, Colbert and Louis XIV. Morand, *Fouquet*, 15.

"collaboration mondaine," the world of writers and celebrities who hobnobbed with the German high command in France. Morand had also wholeheartedly supported the Vichy regime, writing several texts in favor of Pétain and serving from 1943 until the collapse of Vichy as France's special envoy to Romania. By the end of the war Morand was in Switzerland, where he stayed in exile until 1952, and *Le Flagellant* served as his literary comeback and his commentary on the purge. Morand's novel is set during another Occupation, the Occupation of Spain by Napoléon's troops, and tells of another collaborator, Don Luis, a Spanish nobleman, who out of patriotism and an attraction to French culture, joins forces with Napoléon's brother, Joseph Bonaparte, king of Spain from 1808 to 1813. The novel is an indictment of politics in general and a demonstration of the destructive force of ideology, but it is also an attempt to rewrite the history of postwar France in terms sympathetic to the collaborators. Borrowing a standard technique of the historical novel, *Le Flagellant de Séville* mixes vocabulary from two periods. To describe the war in Spain, Morand repeatedly uses terms such as *occupation army, reprisals,* and *partisans,* which automatically send the reader back to occupied France. When Don Luis commits his first act of treason, a handshake with a French officer, we are hard pressed not to think of the celebrated encounter between Pétain and Hitler at Montoire. And when Don Luis returns to his native Seville, he comes close to being brutally murdered by partisans of the "white terror," in a scene meant to make the reader think of the atrocities that took place in France during what came to be known as *"l'épuration sauvage."* After reading the novel, we are left with a series of questions designed to lead us not only toward an indictment of war but also to an apology for the collaboration. Isn't Don Luis, the collaborator, a righteous man? Aren't the Spanish loyalists as violent and as cruel as the Bonapartists? Is it any worse to support Joseph Bonaparte and the French than to acquiesce, as did the loyalists, to an English occupation? Published the same year that the National Assembly considered passing a law on amnesty for crimes committed during the war, *Le Flagellant de Séville* is an appeal to public opinion to acquit both Don Luis and Morand, an author

who had been blacklisted by the CNE and expelled from his position in the Ministry of Foreign Affairs.[27]

Morand was not the only writer to borrow the example of Napoleon's conquest of Europe to condemn the purge. In 1947 Claude Jamet, a high-school teacher turned journalist, sought to exonerate himself and other collaborators by writing that for him Hitler was "another Napoleon" (*"Hitler pour moi, c'est Napoléon bis"*), a statement that is less a condemnation of the emperor than an acquittal of Nazism (Jamet, *Fifi Roi,* 253). Jean Galtier-Boissière, the editor of the satirical review *Le Crapouillot*, wrote in his journal of the immediate postwar period that "Napoleon, before Hitler, had put Europe to fire and the sword" (*"à feu et à sang"*) and that at the end of his reign his troops, "like the SS today," were denounced throughout the land (Galtier-Boissière, *Mon Journal,* 223). Leaving his apartment one afternoon, Drieu la Rochelle overheard his concierge proclaim, "Hitler is repeating Napoleon" (*"Hitler refait Napoléon"*) (Drieu la Rochelle, *Journal 1939–1945,* 403). Even ten years after the end of the war *Ecrits de Paris*, a right-wing monthly almost entirely devoted to worshiping Pétain and rehabilitating the collaborators, published an article revealing to its readers that one of history's greatest and least-known victims of a purge was none other than "Napoleon himself" (Roux, "Un Epuré," 97). All of these historical analogies, whether calling upon the Hundred Years War, the Terror of 1793, the Napoleonic conquest, or French colonialism serve the same function: the recourse to historical precedents is a way to minimize the crimes of the war. The collaborationist writers and their supporters all argued that there was nothing new under the sun and that, in condemning the traitors, the judges were committing the mistakes of previous generations who had given way to political violence and revenge. The argument by historical analogy attempted to transform the collaboration into a matter of historical contingency; accused writers recast their political commitment as simply the wrong choice in a conflict

[27]For more on Morand's itinerary and in particular his candidacies to the French Academy see Rousso, *The Vichy Syndrome,* 66–68. See also Verdès-Leroux, *Refus,* 478–80, and Andrea Loselle, "The Historical Nullification of Paul Morand's Gendered Eugenics," in Melanie Hawthorne and Richard J. Golsan, eds., *Gender and Fascism in Modern France,* 101–18.

where both sides had sinned and neither side could claim the moral high ground. Furthermore, this form of historical relativism, while calling attention to the past, also turned the reader's gaze away from the horrors of the war that had just ended. Speaking about Jeanne d'Arc or the Terror or Napoleon's war in Spain was a way for the collaborationist writers not to speak directly about Oradour or the concentration camps. When the collaborators spoke of the concentration camps, it was only within the confines of this rhetoric of analogy. The purge, they claimed, had transformed them into pure victims. Jamet, recalling the death of a Jewish friend executed by the Germans, goes on to say that where the Jews had once been interned at Drancy, it was now the turn of the collaborators. The fascists, the argument went, were the Jews of the postwar years. But they didn't stop there. Thinking through analogy led opponents of the purge to compare the concentration camps to the bombing of German cities, not only in order to condemn the Allies but also to exonerate the individuals held responsible for the massacres of the Shoah. It was only a small step from there to outright Holocaust denial.

One of the strongest arguments against the excesses of the purge was made by a leader of the intellectual Resistance, Jean Paulhan. Paulhan, who had founded *Les Lettres françaises* and participated in the early days of the CNE, was convinced by 1945 that the purge of writers had gone too far. His pamphlet *De la paille et du grain,* published in 1948, attacks *Les Lettres françaises*, the CNE, and its blacklists.[28] The short text begins with a standard historical analogy that compares the purge to a "(small) revocation of the Edict of Nantes" (Paulhan, *De la paille,* 57), but then Paulhan turns to the examples of Romain Rolland and Rimbaud, two writers who were glorified by the Communists during the Occupation but who, Paulhan warns us, were not so different from the accused writers of 1945: both "betrayed" France, Rolland in 1914, Rimbaud forty years earlier. Paulhan

---

[28]Paulhan, *De la paille*. References are in the text. Paulhan reiterated his claims a few years later in *Lettre aux directeurs de la Résistance*. See Mehlman's use of Paulhan's essay in his analysis of the reception of deconstruction in America, "Writing and Deference," 1–14. See also the subtle reading of Paulhan's purge texts presented in Michael Syrotinski, "Some Wheat," 247–63.

cites Rimbaud's 1872 text calling for the German occupation of his native Ardennes, and Aragon's 1927 defense of Rimbaud, to prove that the CNE blacklists and sanctions of 1944 are, at best, arbitrary (88). Furthermore, Paulhan argues that the Communist writers who filled the ranks of the CNE and who were so intent upon judging crimes of collaboration were themselves nothing more than collaborators of the Soviets. Paulhan avers that it is only by chance (*"un hasard de l'histoire"*) that Brasillach and Rebatet were on trial rather than Aragon and Claude Morgan (121). By a twist of fate France was almost ruined by men who prayed every morning to the Goddess France (*"la déesse France"*) and was saved by men who every day thrashed the French army (124). Paulhan sees the CNE's blacklists as the equivalent of what Morand in his historical novel calls the "white terror," a form of political revenge that replaced justice.

Paulhan's analogies exemplify the complex and often contradictory positions taken by intellectuals during the purge. As founder of a clandestine publication, Paulhan had not only established impeccable Resistance credentials, but he and his team of writers had also set up one of the principal instruments for purging collaborationist writers. *Les Lettres françaises* was after all dedicated to bearing witness against France's treasonous intellectuals. By the end of the war, however, Paulhan's reversal was so complete that he adopted the arguments systematically made by precisely the writers the Resistance had been intent upon denouncing. The declaration that the French Communists were traitors, for example, could be found in almost every text defending Vichy and the collaboration. And in many cases the communist writer Aragon became the collaborators' favorite target. While Paulhan claimed that it was only the vicissitudes of history that kept Aragon out of jail, Alfred Fabre-Luce, a journalist with ties to Vichy and the collaborationist milieu, delighted in reminding his readers in 1945 that Aragon had made numerous antipatriotic and "collaborationist" declarations during World War I (Fabre-Luce, *Au nom des silencieux,* 89). Indeed as early as April 1940 Drieu la Rochelle had told Paulhan he believed that Aragon was an "international agent" at the service of a foreign power (Drieu la Rochelle, *Journal 1939–1945,* 178). If the same arguments had not appeared in Paulhan's

important 1948 essay, we might simply dismiss them as a case of juridical wrangling in a period when the lines between friend and foe,
between enemy and ally were not always distinct. Paulhan, however,
held a position of moral authority in the postwar years, and as Jeannine Verdès-Leroux recently noted, his pamphlets furnished the accused collaborators with an important weapon (Verdès-Leroux, *Refus*, 418). Here was a seemingly impartial arbiter who pointed out the
injustice of the CNE blacklists and condemned without quarter the
purge of writers and intellectuals. Paulhan's pamphlets must have
been all the more comforting for the collaborators since he simultaneously exaggerated the number of victims of the purge and argued
against assigning responsibility to a writer for the deportations, torture, and massacres during four years of German occupation.[29]

It may very well be that Paulhan's political position during the
purge derived from his conception of literature, for responsibility as
understood by the purge courts and by many Resistance writers was
not part of Paulhan's literary vocabulary. Or rather, if Paulhan understood the necessity and the difficulty of making political choices, he
was convinced that literature should not be subjected to the same
constraints. Much of his work as an editor in the postwar years seems
to have been dedicated to protecting literature from a social and political responsibility imposed by forces outside the literary field.
When Paulhan founded *Cahiers de la Pléiade* in 1946, he aimed to use
this publication as a response to the CNE and Sartre's *Les Temps modernes*.[30] Paulhan systematically published writers who had had what
the French euphemistically call "*ennuis*" at the Liberation. Texts by
Céline, Chardonne, Giono, and Jouhandeau appeared in the pages of

---

[29]In the original edition of his *Lettre aux directeurs de la Résistance*, Paulhan
claimed that the purge was responsible for the summary execution of "more
than 60,000" French men and women. Since then historians have established
that there were approximately 9,000 summary executions in the years following
the Occupation. An editor's note at the end of the 1987 edition of *Lettre aux directeurs de la Résistance* rectifies Paulhan's claims.

[30]*Cahiers de la Pléiade* did not entirely escape questions of the writer's responsibility. In the very first issue Roger Caillois published an article in which
he condemned certain writers' intellectual frivolity and postulated that writers
are "infinitely responsible" (*"responsables infiniment"*). Caillois, "Des excès," 130.

the *Cahiers de la Pléiade*, often alongside texts by certified writers of the Resistance such as Camus, René Char, Malraux, and, of course, Paulhan himself. In an introductory note to the winter 1948 issue Paulhan identified his new literary magazine as "a place . . . where men and words (and books) can be cleansed of the filth accumulated during years of war, Occupation and deliverance" (Paulhan, "Note," 9 [my translation]). To go beyond the politics of the war, beyond the violence of the purge, this is Paulhan's aim. In this sense the project of the *Cahiers de la Pléiade* continues what *Les Lettres françaises* had begun: to fight against censorship; to create a space where literature might express itself free from the shackles of politics; to publish texts that, in Paulhan's words, "other reviews and periodicals might neglect" (9). This neglect could only come, in Paulhan's mind, from the censorship imposed by the CNE.

Paulhan was a writer with a taste for the paradoxical. When engaging in quarrels with other writers, Julien Benda was a privileged sparring partner, he delighted in pointing out the logical inconsistencies of their arguments. His articles and books often take readers through circuitous paths where, as he himself claimed, "The best arguments are upended" (Paulhan, "Lettre sur la paix," 409–10), but Paulhan's rhetorical brio in *De la paille et du grain* as well as in his *Lettre aux directeurs de la Résistance* also mirrored the complexity and the paradoxes at work during the purge. Paulhan's defense of literature and freedom of expression led him to defend writers who during the Occupation routinely denied this right to others. His argument against censorship led him to ignore the most damaging texts by writers accused of collaboration. He attacked intellectuals sympathetic to one totalitarian regime, the Soviet Union, only to support writers who had lent their talents to another. His use of analogy ended up in a sort of ideological scrambling in which white was black, black was white, and both terms were neutralized. This was one of the standard defense practices of the accused collaborators: making everyone guilty seemed to lessen the collaborators' guilt. Paulhan's arguments were not presented in bad faith. His pamphlets honestly and intelligently attempted to answer the legal and moral questions posed by the purge. And yet when Paulhan entered the ring, when he attempted to question certain attitudes, his texts turned out to be less a resolution of these questions than a reproduction of the difficulty the author, as well as the French nation, had in resolving them.

For Paulhan the postwar purge of intellectuals had turned into the misplaced trial of literature, and in its rush to judgment the CNE made one crucial error: the purgers failed to distinguish between a hack such as Paul Ferdonnet and genuine literary creators such as Henry de Montherlant and Céline (Paulhan, *De la paille*, 157). Paulhan's final argument against the purge was the defense of the collaborationist intellectual as a persecuted artist, and this too was one of the keystones of the defense during the purge trials. This type of barely veiled plea consistently reappeared in the literary texts as well as the juridical documents that constitute the purge archive. Take, for example, Morand's 1951 novel *Le Flagellant de Séville*. We already saw how Morand used the example of the Napoleonic wars as an analogy for World War II. After telling the tale of Don Luis, the novel ends by evoking Francisco Goya's exile in France. Like Don Luis, the Spanish painter had welcomed the arrival of Joseph Bonaparte in Spain and had had to flee to Bordeaux when Ferdinand VII ascended to the throne. Like Morand, Goya was an artist, a witness to the horrors of war, but somehow absent, distant from the impurity of politics and ultimately, the text implies, innocent of all charges. Marcel Aymé also mobilized the myth of the artist as innocent but in an even more troubling way. During the war Aymé had published fiction in collaborationist periodicals such as *Je suis partout* and *La Gerbe*, though he never openly declared his sympathy for the Vichy regime or the German Occupation forces. At the end of the war, however, Aymé came out as an acerbic critic of the purge. He published several articles, one play, and one novel all violently hostile to the purge. In his novel *Uranus*, published the same year as Paulhan's *De la paille et du grain*, Aymé paints a satirical portrait of postwar France, a society governed, in his view, by personal interests presenting themselves as political commitment. Of all his characters, however, Maxime Loin, the hunted fascist, seems the most sincere, precisely because his faith in politics is genuine and grew out of an artist's sensibility. Loin, Aymé would have us believe, is a Brasillach type, a delicate soul who wears a Lavallière, the ribbonny cravat of artists, and has a penchant for poetry (Aymé, *Uranus*, 55). In the construction of the novel this poetic sensibility is not just a personal quirk; it comes to us in Maxime Loin's self-defense plea and acts as a sort of extenuating circumstance for the fascist's political commitment.

What Paulhan, Morand, and Aymé presented as the cultural exception of the writer had, in fact, been one of the main arguments of the purge trials. While Morand turned to Goya as his predecessor, other accused writers repeatedly referred to André Chénier, the poet guillotined during the Terror of 1794, who was presented with increasing frequency during the purge as an artist victim of political excess. Mauriac may have been the first to use this analogy to admonish his peers when he claimed that Chénier was condemned for his moderation and that "history does not forgive" the execution of philosophers and poets (Mauriac, *Le Baillon dénoué*, 178). Imprisoned in Fresnes, Sacha Guitry started writing verse and commented that it made him feel "very André Chénier" (Guitry, *60 Jours,* 245). Céline ended his 1946 defense brief by claiming that his fate was no different from that of Lavoisier, Chamfort, and Chénier, all of whom had been "punished"—the word is Céline's—during the Revolution (Céline, "Reply to Charges," 539). Among all the accused writers, however, none identified more with Chénier than Robert Brasillach, who while in prison wrote an essay on the poet, in which, drawing on the resemblance between 1944 and 1794, he cited Chénier's "exemplary attitude" (Brasillach, *Chénier*, 12). For Brasillach the two periods were similar in their violence; like the purge, the Revolution was a time when murderers and thieves called themselves patriots. Most importantly, the two periods resembled each other in their prosecution of writers of great talent. No wonder then that Brasillach's attorney claimed that his client had inherited Chénier's mantle (Isorni, *Le Procès,* 17–18).

Beyond the historical analogy the references to Chénier lead us in two other directions. First, by referring to Chénier, the writers were attempting to distinguish themselves from both the politicians and the common criminals who often surrounded them in their prison cells. Just as the prosecutors and the editors of *Les Lettres françaises* had argued that the writer's talent brought with it an even greater responsibility, the collaborationist writers attempted to turn their literary prestige, their "intellectual splendor" into what Maurras's attorney called an "extenuating circumstance" (London, *Le Procès,* 153). The writer, they argued, had a special status in France. He benefited from a prestige that should exempt him from the retribution of partisan politics. Brasillach's defense included several quotes from prominent writers—Aymé, Claudel, Mauriac, Valéry—claiming that, in Claudel's words, "Brasillach's talent honors France." The talented writer, according to this logic, could not be a traitor because his writing embodied the very prestige of the nation. Counting on this combination of patriotic and literary arguments, Isorni concluded his plea for Brasillach by asking the jury, "Do civilized nations execute their poets?" (Isorni, *Le Procès,* 174, 177). The answer in Brasillach's case was yes, but in his trial we see the deployment of an argument for the redemptive power of literature. Claiming the status of poet became a way of both adumbrating one's political writings and exempting the writer from the law.

As they developed the myth of the collaborationist intellectual as persecuted artist, these writers simultaneously denounced the purge as the lowest form of popular entertainment. To be sure, the purge had its carnivalesque aspects; pictures taken during the shearing of women suspected of collaboration often show a riotously festive crowd. In the months following the Liberation the purge seemed to be governed by a popular justice run amok. Opponents of the purge quickly seized on this impression of uncontrolled violence to denounce the entire enterprise of postwar justice. Aymé and Céline frequently represented the postwar period as nothing more than a horror show—gouged eyes, burnt genitals, lingering death—perpetrated on collaborators to appease a bloodthirsty public.[31] The purge, in Céline's words, was a "Grand Guignol," a blood-and-guts spectacle in which legal formalities and the very idea of justice had given way to

---

[31]Citing Aymé's *Uranus,* Georges Bataille sees the torture of collaborators during the purge as a meeting in contemporary France of violence and eroticism (*L'Erotisme,* 107).

an imperative to entertain a vengeful French populace. Imprisoned in Fresnes, Henri Béraud compared his jail cell to the 1930 movie *The Big House* and believed that the Resistance authorities who had put him there were under the spell of what he called "*hollywooderies*" (Béraud, *Quinze Jours,* 59–60). Concluding from Béraud's trial that all men have a passion for blood, the usually mild François Mauriac compared the trials of intellectuals to bullfights, in which the writer played the fateful role of the sacrificial beast (Mauriac, *Le Baillon dénoué,* 219). In the last days before his suicide Drieu la Rochelle called the purge an "unbearable comedy" (Assouline, *L'Epuration,* 26). Maurras labeled his trial a "sinister farce" (London, *Le Procès,* 120). Claude Jamet also denounced the purge as a "farce" and a "guignol," and borrowing from Alfred Jarry, claimed that "Fifi" (the F.F.I.) "is playing Ubu Roi," Jarry's absurd and imbecilic "doctor in pataphysics" (Jamet, *Fifi Roi,* 110). In Aymé's 1952 play, *La Tête des autres,* where we see a jazz musician condemned by a system that wholly profited from the Occupation, one of the characters compares the prosecutor Maillard's summation to the work of an "artist" and gushes, "I had to restrain myself from applauding" (Aymé, *La Tête,* 21). From these statements we can begin to gauge the extent to which writers and their sympathizers were investing in literary form. To condemn the purge trials as bad theater was to recast the purge as a series of political and aesthetic oppositions: what Brasillach called the "unique work" of Chénier versus the popular entertainment of the "Grand Guignol"; the excellence of pure poetry against the degeneration of farce; the conviction of talent against the madness and injustice of the crowd. Not without some success, at least in postwar literary circles, the collaborators managed to portray the purge as low comedy and themselves as the keepers of a pure and aesthetically "high" literary form.

The cult of the politically pure artist leads us to a final consideration on the status of literature during the purge. Along with a defense of their political commitments, many writers accused of treason began to argue for the autonomy of their literary enterprise. Again, a series of examples illustrates the point. Awaiting his trial, Maurras embarked on a translation of Horace's poetry, as if this, rather than his reactionary politics, had been his primary concern all along.[32] Though in Brasillach's case the relation of politics to poetry is complex, he nonetheless spent his last days in jail translating Greek poems, as if he too had already left the world of postwar politics. Rebatet, the notorious author of the best-selling 1942 *Les Décombres*, his violently anti-Semitic and collaborationist memoir, devoted his time in jail to maniacally correcting the proofs of his novel *Les Deux Etendards* and searching for what he called the *"mot propre"* (Rebatet, *Les Mémoires . . . II*, 257). Robert Poulet, a collaborationist journalist, writing his journal in the Fresnes jail, found himself in the throes of what he called a "movement that is more musical than intellectual" and concluded, "I am dancing and singing my thoughts" (Poulet, *L'Enfer*, 104). And in his defense of Brasillach, Jamet went so far as to say that even his anti-Semitic, anti-democratic, and anti-communist articles contained the "music" (*"petite musique"*) of the great writer (Jamet, *Fifi Roi*, 207). In all these cases writers who had put their literature at the service of anti-Semitic, collaborationist, and fascist propaganda now seemed to be arguing in favor of the pure pleasure of their texts, even in their most politically repugnant writings.

Several things are at work here. Fascism had already, in the words of Walter Benjamin, aestheticized politics, and many of the imprisoned writers had previously argued that their fascism had come out of their cult of aesthetics. Describing Brasillach's itinerary from graduate of the Ecole normale supérieure to editor of *Je suis partout*, Rebatet claimed in 1942 that "Brasillach had come to fascism through poetry" (Rebatet, *Les Décombres*, 44). Indeed, the American scholar David Carroll has recently claimed that the nationalist, fascist, and anti-Semitic politics of these writers was incontrovertibly tied to their conception of the organic work of art.[33] This attitude was often used against them: fascist writers were condemned for their irresponsible "art for art's sake" attitude well before the end of the war. Still, the ar-

---

[32]H. Maurras, *Souvenirs*, 40. The author relates how in jail Charles Maurras gave a freshly composed ode to Léon S. Roudiez, writing his doctoral thesis on Maurras before *L'Action française* at Columbia University.

[33]For the relation between poetics and fascist politics see Carroll, *French Literary Fascism*.

gument for stylistic autonomy took on an additional significance during the purge. By focusing on the literariness of their work, the writers accused of treason began to argue for an inoculation, of sorts, of their other writings. At the moment when writers at *Les Lettres françaises* were proclaiming that literature is engaged in the world and that, in Mauriac's words, "to speak is to act," the collaborationist writers were seeking to disengage from any type of political significance (Mauriac, *Le Baillon dénoué*, 218). Literature, they claimed, is not litigious and cannot be held up to the same moral and legal standards as political action. The collaborationist writers became the proponents of a modernist conception of literary language, a language that is self-referential and about nothing but its own musicality. The most dangerous authors, the authors who had abused their privilege as intellectuals, were attempting to transform themselves into totally gratuitous writers. Not all the writers accused of collaboration used this argument in a simplistic manner. During his trial Brasillach refused to renounce any of his wartime writings. Still, this did not prevent his attorney from arguing that because he was also a poet Brasillach did not deserve the same fate as the Vichy minister Pierre Pucheu. The collaborationist writers put the argument for literary autonomy to varying uses. But all at one time or another implied or explicitly argued that since they were poets, since they were "very André Chénier," their journalism, their speeches, their political commitment, and indeed their very bodies should benefit from the same immunity granted to the literary work.

Behind these claims of literary gratuity lurks a defense of freedom of opinion. To be sure, France's tradition of free speech is different than that of the United States. French governments regularly pass laws forbidding certain types of speech. In April 1939, for instance, on the eve of the war the Daladier government had passed the Marchandeau decree outlawing racist slander in the press. A year later Vichy came to power with its own, very different imperatives to censor. Still, the accused writers and their defenders often claimed that they were being put on trial not for political acts but for their opinions. Brasillach's attorney claimed that his client's trial was nothing more than a "trial of opinion" — *"il s'agit uniquement d'un procès d'opinion"* — and that this type of trial is contrary to Republican ideals (Isorni, *Le Procès,* 183). With the irony that made him a postwar celebrity of sorts, Isorni adds that, if he didn't know better, he would think the prosecutor in the Brasillach case was simply trying to eliminate his political enemies, and concludes that he naturally quickly rejected this hypothesis (194). This argument against "trials of opinion" also frequently appeared in attacks against the excesses of the purge. In a 1950 article published in *Le Crapouillot* and arguing that amnesty be granted to all accused collaborators, Aymé made two points: the Vichy government was strictly legal, and the purge had been created to punish unpopular, that is, extreme right-wing, political opinions (Aymé, "L'Epuration"). Through the purge trials the Gaullists had punished what Aymé called "crimes of opinion" (*"délits d'opinion"*) and not acts of treason as they claimed. Aymé's article is brief, but the point is clear. While Resistance intellectuals were proclaiming that "to speak is to act," collaborators and their supporters, at least in some cases, were distinguishing opinions from actions. To have written in favor of the collaboration was an opinion, not an act, and the postwar governments could not punish opinions without betraying their commitment to a democratic process.

On the one hand, then, arguments for a writer's responsibility, on the other hand, claims that the writer was exempt from the law of the land. On the one hand, literature — understood as both fiction and journalism — is an act, and therefore, actionable; on the other, literature is gratuitous, without consequences. We are free to question the motives of both sides. To proclaim the responsibility of the writer was perhaps, as Tony Judt suggests, nothing more than a seizure of power by the communists, a way of "staking out a larger territory for themselves" (Judt, *Past Imperfect,* 61). When Aymé or Isorni argued for freedom of expression, it may have been nothing more than a legal ruse put forth by men who had no interest in guaranteeing the free speech of their political enemies. And as we read these differing opinions, we realize that both sides were arguing in favor of the prestige and the exemplary status of the writer. Still, the purge planted the seeds for two competing theories of literature that return, in various forms, sometimes diametrically opposed, sometimes intertwined in the works of several of postwar France's most important writers.

Never before in the history of French letters had theories of literature been so massively mobilized to serve a political end. Perhaps it is not surprising that the writers who were being purged should have claimed that their literature had always been pure. Nor should we be led to believe that these arguments about the status of literature appeared *ex nihilo* during the purge trials. Proponents of aesthetic autonomy and the advocates of committed art drew their respective lines in the sand well before 1940: the debates around French socialist realism, the splits within the surrealist camp, and Valéry's essays on poetics can be seen as rehearsals within the literary field for the debate about literature during the purge. But the trials of the purge also adapted and crystallized the opposition between committed literature and "art for art's sake." The debates and arguments at the end of the war reveal that this opposition could also directly affect the lives of men and women as well as the rebuilding of a nation. In so doing, the purge trials laid the foundation for literary studies in the second half of the twentieth century.

CHAPTER 2

Sartre:
Sentencing Literature

In 1969, as he approached the end of his career, Sartre wrote a letter to his bibliographers, Michel Contat and Michel Rybalka, using a curious juridical metaphor to compliment them on the thoroughness of their work:

> I not only found in [the bibliography] all the writings, without exception, that I remembered; you also resurrected the ones I had forgotten. I rediscover them with a certain astonishment, and at times a feeling of uneasiness. Most of them are witnesses for the prosecution.[1]

Sartre's use of the phrase "witnesses for the prosecution" also leaves the reader with a feeling of uneasiness and a number of questions. To what articles, we wonder, is Sartre referring? For what crimes does Sartre imagine himself on trial? Who constitutes the prosecution in this trial? And why, finally, does Sartre cast this bibliographic discovery in juridical terms? What might be considered nothing more than an offhand remark to two scholars can perhaps be explained by Sartre's commitment to juridical interventions. Throughout his career he had engaged in courtroom proceedings, ad-

---

[1]Contat and Rybalka, eds. *The Writings of Sartre,* xi.

vocated causes, mimicked a legal vocabulary, borrowed from the courts, and performed much of his work in relation to the tribunals of the state. Whether it was in defense of Jean Genet or the communist sailor Henri Martin, whether he was condemning the United States for genocide in Vietnam at the 1967 "Russell Tribunal" or lending his support to Basque separatists during the so-called Burgos trial, Sartre consistently assigned to himself the roles of attorney, judge, and jury. Even the three authors about whom Sartre published book-length studies—Baudelaire, Genet, and Flaubert—were all the subjects of celebrated court cases. The trial remained at the heart of Sartre's work until his death. But if Sartre saw literature as a tool that could be used to defend certain causes, he also understood it as a trace that could return to lead the writer before the tribunal. As his letter to his bibliographers makes clear, Sartre considered writing, even his own, to be a site of litigation.

There is, of course, precedent for the intellectual's commitment to court cases. On several occasions during his career Sartre mentioned Voltaire's defense of Jean Calas and Zola's plea in favor of Alfred Dreyfus. As Christophe Charle has shown, the birth of the intellectual in the 1890s coincided with the development of the petition as a weapon directed against the state and its courts (Charle, *Naissance*, 116–37). No one embodied with more fervor and conviction than Sartre the role the French intellectual created for himself as an advocate for the downtrodden who used the courts as an intermediary to attack an abusive power structure. Still, if a juridical rhetoric was crucial to Sartre's thought, if his writing consistently returned to the space of the tribunal, it is perhaps because his development as an intellectual was determined less by tradition than by an event: the purge of collaborationist writers at the end of the Second World War. Several critics have pointed to the possible ties between Sartre's work and the postwar period, most notably Alice Kaplan, for whom "existentialism was in large part a response to the 1944–1947 purge."[2] Sartre's theories

[2]Two recent studies comment on Sartre's participation in the purge trials. This chapter found its impetus in Kaplan's assertion in "Literature and Collaboration," 971. See also Judt's criticism of Sartre in *Past Imperfect*.

of literature in the postwar years mobilize the themes and rhetoric of the purge though not without contradiction. After 1945 the author for whom literature had once been inextricably tied to an overwhelming feeling of nausea, linked literature to an irrepressible need to purge.

Understanding existentialism's "response to the purge" begins with an investigation of one of the most ballyhooed terms of the trials: *responsibility*. Prosecutors, attorneys, and writers from both sides of the ideological divide cited responsibility as the key to judging suspected political and intellectual collaborators. For the proponents of the purge the term *"les responsables"* became a mantra of sorts that designated both the politicians who had led France to its demise and more generally anyone who had collaborated.[3] In February 1945, at the time of Brasillach's execution, the Resistance weekly *Carrefour* devoted a special issue to this theme and sent a questionnaire to a number of writers. Among the numerous respondents Vercors set the tone. According to the author of *Le Silence de la mer*, "a published writing is an intellectual act [*un acte de la pensée*]. The writer is responsible for the consequences of this act."[4] Restating what had become one of the central tenets of the Resistance, Vercors equated language to an act. Just as Mauriac and Leiris had done the previous year, the respondents to the *Carrefour* survey claimed that a violent word was the equivalent of a violent act. But Vercors also made explicit what had often remained implied in the debates about the responsibility of writers. For Vercors a text had consequences, a claim that forced the writer to answer, to respond before a court of law not only for his own writings but for the violence and the oppression, the murder and the persecution that resulted from policies he had supported.

A year after Brasillach's trial Simone de Beauvoir turned this type of responsibility into the very definition of modern man. Justifying her refusal to sign the petition Mauriac had circulated in favor of Brasillach, de Beauvoir claimed that responsibility for one's acts lay at the

---

[3]See, for example, Camus's article calling for the purge, in which he opposed the French who were "unaware" (*"inconscients"*) of the national interest during the Occupation to the *"responsables,"* who had to be tried and condemned. *Combat*, 18 Oct. 1944.

[4]Vercors in *Carrefour*.

core of our existence: "In order for the life of a man to have a meaning, he must be held responsible for the evil as well as for the good he does" (de Beauvoir, "Oeil pour oeil," 813–30 [my translation]). Only responsibility, as determined by others—colleagues, peers, judges—can confer this meaning on the individual; only responsibility can grant us an existence. Throughout his trial Brasillach had indeed admitted his responsibility: "I have always felt the responsibility of the leader . . . and it is for this reason . . . that I am here and not elsewhere, in other foreign countries" (Isorni, *Le Procès,* 111). Brasillach's remark was an allusion to both Resistants who had spent the Occupation in London and to collaborators, including Pétain and Laval, who had fled France to Germany at the Liberation. De Beauvoir wrote that she was "touched" by Brasillach's attitude, especially his desire to "courageously assume his life" (de Beauvoir, "Œil pour œil," 829). He had, she said, admitted his responsibility for the consequences of his intellectual acts. Curiously, in one of postwar France's first definitions of the existentialist life, it is a collaborator, Brasillach, who embodies the values de Beauvoir and the existentialists were promoting. This paradox would return to haunt Sartre's works.

If Sartre emerged from the war as one of France's leading intellectuals, his sometimes ambiguous position in Occupied France has become the focus of an important controversy today. Sartre's politics have recently been the target of a major reevaluation by academics and journalists alike. And if, as Claude Lanzmann has recently claimed, attacking Sartre has become "the fashion of the day," it is nonetheless no longer possible—if it ever was—to believe in the legend of a Sartre wholeheartedly dedicated to resisting the German Occupation.[5] Sartre's war began in September 1939, when he was mobilized, and continued through the phony war, the debacle of June 1940, his imprisonment along with the rest of his division in a German POW camp, and in March 1941 his release, and his return to Paris. Back in the capi-

[5]The two principal biographical sources for Sartre's activity during the Occupation, other than Sartre's own statements, are Cohen-Solal, *Sartre,* and Beauvoir, *The Prime of Life.*

tal Sartre helped form the Resistance group Socialisme et Liberté with, among others, Maurice Merleau-Ponty and in the summer of 1941 attempted to enlist the assistance of André Gide and André Malraux, who were both in a state of semiretirement in the South of France. Having met with no success, he disbanded Socialisme et Liberté in December 1941, continued his teaching at the Lycée Condorcet, and dedicated himself to his writing, publishing numerous articles, his philosophical treatise *Being and Nothingness,* and two plays, *The Flies* and *No Exit.* The facts of Sartre's life at the time are not disputed, but certain critics have denounced what one has called Sartre's "complicity" with the Occupation forces (Joseph, *Une si douce occupation,* 157). Already during the Occupation the French communists had claimed that Sartre had been released from the prisoner of war camp because the Germans looked favorably upon this disciple of Heidegger and Hegel. And one critic asserts that the Christmas play Sartre wrote in the prison barracks used anti-Semitic caricatures to amuse the Nazi officers (84). Furthermore, Sartre's resistance group, his critics contend, was nothing more than a facade, a make-believe Resistance of little or no consequence. Sartre regularly published texts during the Occupation, but his choices of where to publish were not always as pure as it might have seemed at the end of the war. To be sure, Sartre wrote in Resistance publications such as *Cahiers du Sud, Les Lettres françaises,* and *Combat,* but he also published two articles and one interview in *Comoedia,* a collaborationist weekly backed by German funds. It was Jean Paulhan who recommended that Sartre publish in *Comoedia,* but to do so in 1941 was, at the very least, what Sartre's biographer has called a "serious mistake" (Cohen-Solal, *Sartre,* 177). Finally the publication of *Being and Nothingness* and the staging of *The Flies* were made possible only with the approval of the German censors. In order to publish his work, the argument goes, Sartre did not hesitate to make certain "dishonorable concessions," including drinking champagne with Nazi officers on the night of the premiere of his play (Joseph, *Une si douce occupation,* 234). The degree of Sartre's "complicity" with the Germans was certainly less than some of his more virulent critics suggest. The degree of his commitment to the Resistance was perhaps less than he himself implied at the end of the war. Readers today seem less generous toward Sartre than those who had lived through the war and were reading the author in 1945. Still, there is little doubt that even during the most painful moments of the Occupation, Sartre was single-mindedly devoted to furthering his literary career, and this ambition led him to adopt certain ambiguous positions.[6]

If by the end of the war Sartre had positioned himself as one of the representative voices of the Resistance, his wartime work doesn't always warrant such an interpretation. His use of the term *responsibility*, which became one of the keystones of the purge, is a case in point. To see how Sartre's understanding of the term responsibility shifted from 1939 to 1945 is also to see how Sartre repositioned himself during the postwar purge. Sartre initiated his reflection on responsibility in *Being and Nothingness*. After a section where he states that freedom is man's fate, Sartre concludes that total freedom leads to total responsibility: "[man] is responsible for the world and for himself as a way of being." In his habit of illustrating his demonstrations with examples from his environment, Sartre turns to the war: "If I am mobilized in a war, this war is *my* war; it is in my image and I deserve it" (Sartre, *Being and Nothingness,* 708). In 1943, according to Sartre, war has become the test case of man's responsibility.

There are, however, two ways to read this passage. The first is as a philosophical allegory of France during the German Occupation. *Being and Nothingness* is an ontological essay seeking to found the subject on the basis of liberty and responsibility. Published at a turning point in the war, Sartre's essay seems to be warning his reader that it is no longer possible not to be committed, that the reader is now politically responsible. The text is loaded with terms that belong to both political and philosophical registers. In 1943 the word *freedom* (*liberté*) has precise political connotations in Occupied France, referring explicitly to the French Republic's motto "*liberté, égalité, fraternité,*" which Vichy had erased and replaced upon seizing power. Other

---

[6]This is the conclusion drawn by Martinoir in her essay on the literature of the Occupation, *La Littérature occupée,* 143.

terms such as *reprieve (sursis)* and *recess (suspension de séance)* (709), which Sartre uses as examples of irresponsibility, could be read as referring to France's ambiguous status lying somewhere between war and peace during the Occupation. Through such a reading, then, the essay would be creating a resistant subject, a subject who could assume his full responsibility only by resisting Vichy and the German Occupation. At the same time, however, we cannot read the passage solely as a treatise on Occupation and Resistance. The references to war can easily be seen as nothing more than examples from quotidian life Sartre uses to illustrate his theses, alongside the too-eager waiter, for example, or the paper cutter. The specific referent of the passage remains indefinite: Sartre refers to *a* war *(une guerre)* rather than *the* war *(la guerre),* and, as opposed to his postwar essays such as "What Is Literature?" he never names the Occupation as such. When a little later in the text he quotes Jules Romain or Raymond Radiguet, both of whom wrote important novels set during World War I, Sartre seems to be drifting from 1943 back to 1914. Furthermore, his discussion of coercion in this passage does not refer to the Occupation, as one might imagine, but rather to his enlistment into the French Army before the invasion of France.[7] Even *responsibility* is used, as Sartre himself says, in its "banal" sense, that is "the consciousness of being the originator [*l'auteur*] of an event or an object" (707). So, as Sartre encourages a political reading, he also denies it. Responsibility in 1943 remains caught between an ontological lexicon on the one hand and on the other the political or juridical meaning given to it at the end of the war. One could argue, as Sartre himself did after the war, that the reader of 1943 knew very well what he was talking about, and that, as with his play *The Flies,* allegory was the best way of avoiding censorship.[8] Yet precisely because they are allegories, the play and the philo-

---

[7]Years later, speaking about the change he underwent during the war, Sartre says, "at that time they had turned me into a soldier against my will. I had therefore already experienced something that wasn't my freedom and governed me from outside." Sartre, *Situations IX*, 99.

[8]"Why make the Greeks speak ... if not to disguise one's real thinking under a fascist regime?" Quoted in Contat and Rybalka, eds., *The Writings of Sartre,* 87.

sophical treatise avoid the determinacy of meaning that Sartre's post-war politics require. As allegories *The Flies* and *Being and Nothingness* can never be more than only partially committed to the historical situation in which he was writing. Ultimately these texts leave the reader between two states, as if they were reproducing the ambiguity they sought to dispel.

Sartre himself sought to dispel this ambiguity at the end of the war by becoming the theorist of the purge. While the essays that he wrote for Resistance publications can be read as a continuation of the work initiated in *Being and Nothingness*, they are also a series of corrective readings of the wartime philosophical treatise. In February 1943 Sartre began participating in the meetings of the National Writers' Committee, the group whose primary role very rapidly became the purging of collaborationist writers. He also published in the clandestine Resistance review *Les Lettres françaises* and followed its editorial policy of identifying and denouncing French authors who collaborated or associated with the enemy. In April 1943 he upbraided Drieu la Rochelle for being a representative of what he identified as Nazi self-hatred. In July of the following year Sartre criticized Marcel Aymé for having written a play, *Vogue la Galère*, that reflected fascist despair.[9] In this article Sartre claimed that Aymé was less guilty than Robert Brasillach or Alphonse de Chateaubriant; he not only used his articles to denounce, he established degrees of culpability. In April 1944 Sartre wrote an article for *Les Lettres françaises*, where he set the tone for his postwar literary theory. Equating literature to liberty, Sartre wrote, "Literature is not an innocent and facile lyric capable of accommodating itself to any sort of regime, but by its very nature confronts us with the political problem: to write is to demand that all men are free."[10] Literature is not innocent. By its very nature, Sartre tells us, it is not only political but linked to a rhetoric of judgment. Literature demands that we judge it and the writers who produce it. By the following year Sartre had founded *Les Temps modernes,* and in his intro-

[9]Sartre, "Drieu la Rochelle ou la haine de soi"; "L'Espoir fait l'homme."
[10]Sartre, "La Littérature, cette liberté." The translation is from Contat and Rybalka, eds. *The Writings of Sartre,* 94.

ductory essay to the journal he returned to the problem of responsibility, this time adapting it to the political circumstances in which he found himself.[11] Just as Voltaire was engaged in the Calas trial and the Dreyfus affair inspired Zola's commitment, the Occupation taught the writers of Sartre's generation their responsibility: "Each of those authors, at a particular time in his life took stock of his responsibility as a writer. The Occupation taught us ours" (Sartre, *What Is Literature?* 252). Responsibility has now shifted from an ontological category to a juridical procedure intended specifically to measure the legal and moral liability of the writer. Tony Judt has suggested that Sartre's emphasis on a writer's responsibility was an attempt to "deculpabilize" himself for his ambiguous position during the war (Judt, *Past Imperfect,* 40). Whatever Sartre's psychological motive, we are tempted to argue that it was less the Occupation than the purge that taught Sartre and the existentialists about responsibility. In his articles denouncing Drieu and Aymé, in his theoretical considerations on a writer's responsibility, Sartre was preparing his readers for the upcoming trials of collaborationist authors and redefining himself as France's theorist of the purge.

By the end of the war, then, Sartre had transformed responsibility into an ethical and juridical category, thus realigning his thinking with the tenets of the purge authorities. The essays Sartre wrote after 1944 add to his existential investigations the question of what to do with intellectuals who were accused of having betrayed France. Equating responsibility to the literary project, as he did in his introductory essay to *Les Temps modernes,* became a way of both tracing what Sartre saw as the future of literature and justifying the sanctions against writers of the recent past. "Introducing *Les Temps modernes*" begins with a denunciation of irresponsible writers: "All writers of middle-class origin have known the temptation of irresponsibility" (249), writes Sartre, assailing writers who have attempted to separate their writing from their income. The irresponsible writer does not acknowledge that his art is his source of revenue; he refuses to admit that he writes for a

---

[11]Sartre, *What Is Literature? and Other Writings.* Page numbers are given in text.

wage. Sartre links writing, responsibility, and remuneration for two reasons. First, he announces the socialist and class-based literary analysis of his new review. The writers at *Les Temps modernes* know that they are committed (*engagés*) because they acknowledge their place in a society of wage (*gages*) earners, no different, Sartre would like to think, than a worker on the assembly line. At the same time Sartre is recalling one of the principal accusations of the purge trials: as in the case of Jean Luchaire, the courts often tried to prove an author guilty of treason by claiming he had accepted German money. During the purge trials economic exchange was akin to an exchange of "intelligence" with the enemy. Sartre reiterates this accusation in the second paragraph of his essay when he evokes the writers who were being punished "for renting their pens to the Germans" (251). The collaborationist intellectual, according to Sartre, was a *vendu*; he had sold out or at the very least rented himself to the enemy and, worse yet, didn't acknowledge this debt. Precisely because he is economically irresponsible, the collaborator is politically irresponsible. Faced with the accusation of treason, the collaborator in Sartre's essay naively declares, "What do you mean? ... Does the stuff someone writes actually commit [*engage*] him?" (251). In order to seal his demonstration, Sartre travels back to the nineteenth century. Abandoning the collaborators of 1940–44, he turns his prosecutorial gaze on three writers from a previous generation: "I hold Flaubert and the Goncourts responsible for the repression that followed the Commune because they didn't write a line to prevent it" (252).

In "Introducing *Les Temps modernes*" Sartre is playing several chords at once. His definition of a new, responsible literature depends, first of all, upon rejecting the model of the collaborationist intellectual. To do so he relies on caricature, turning the collaborator into the mealy-mouthed buffoon of a political cartoon whose understanding of his responsibility is, in fact, the opposite of what Brasillach actually said when he was on the stand. If we compare Sartre's 1945 article with de Beauvoir's 1946 "Oeil pour oeil," we find two diametrically opposed portraits of the collaborator. While de Beauvoir praises Brasillach's almost heroic attitude, Sartre transforms the collaborator on trial into a timorous defendant. Both these articles, however, reveal the importance of the purge trials for the theorists of existentialism as both authors locate the purge at the center of their reflection on literature and philosophy. But it is precisely at the moment when Sartre admits the importance of the purge that he changes the subject and conflates the French collaborationist intellectual and the nineteenth-century aesthete on the grounds that they are equally irresponsible. Sartre's essay merges two time periods; it denounces a literary tradition associated with Flaubert's aestheticism while at the same time asking the reader to reflect upon the postwar trials. Only, and this is where the difficulty arises, after "Introducing *Les Temps modernes*" Sartre will no longer speak about the purge directly. His existentialist biography of Charles Baudelaire, first published in May 1946, and the essay "What Is Literature?" released the following year, represent Sartre's major theoretical statements about the status of literature. And while they were written at the height of the purge, while they continue the author's reflection on responsibility and judgment, they no longer refer explicitly to the trials occurring while Sartre was writing. Nonetheless, these essays give us a number of clues that encourage us to read them allegorically as a reaction to, a reflection on, and, at times, a justification of the purge of fascist and collaborationist intellectuals.

Sartre's major literary statement after the war is, of course, "What Is Literature?" in which he argues in favor of politically committed prose. The essay expands and clarifies the ideas of "Introducing *Les Temps Modernes*" by classifying different literary periods and systematizing different literary forms. Sartre's first step in the essay is to dismiss poetry from his considerations: "Poets are men who refuse to *utilize* language" (29). One answer to the question "What is literature?" is that it is *not* poetry. Sartre modified his conclusions several years later in "Orphée noir," where he defines the poetry of *négritude* as "the most authentic revolutionary plan" of his day (330). Still, to dismiss poetry from the political field in 1947 is problematic. Sartre is not only returning poetry to a traditional, depoliticized aesthetic space, he is also attacking a specific poetry: the poetry of the Resistance, and the communist Resistants in particular who considered poetry the "honor" and the "conscience" of France. Through the voices of Aragon and Eluard, among others, and in the pages of *Les Lettres françaises* poetry had traced for itself a major role not only in the Resistance but in the postwar literary reconstruction of the nation. Political poetry at this time is the domain of the Communists, and what Denis Hollier has called Sartre's "resistance to poetry" is also a response to a rival form of committed literature.[12] By denying poetry the possibility of commitment, Sartre is also denying these Communist poets a role in postwar politics: to claim that poets refuse to utilize language as a political tool is to consolidate the "supremacy" of *Les Temps Modernes* as postwar France's literary and political review.[13]

The ambiguity and indeterminacy of poetry, then, have no place in Sartre's considerations. Literature, at least as he defines it in "What Is Literature?" is a prose text engaged in revealing the injustices of the world through what he calls "action by disclosure" (37). By simply naming the evils of colonialism, for example, or racism in America, literature commits itself to a process of contestation and change. But for literature to reveal the world, style must remain invisible. To use language in this sense is to surpass language; it means going from the realm of the word to the act—"to speak is to act" (36), "words are action" (37). Sartre, again, seems less to be creating concepts than reiterating a series of theoretical arguments circulating at the time. In October 1944 Leiris had defined literature as "a way of acting," and Mauriac had stated that "to write is to act," two claims that can be traced to the definition of treason given in Article 75 of the French Penal Code. Article 75 rests on a hermeneutics that defines language as a form of direct representation, no more open to the poetic principle of indeterminacy and ambiguity than an act would be. For the purge courts language was invisible. An article denouncing a Communist or a Jew was a denunciatory act, a speech praising the Milice, the equivalent of bearing arms. The courts' reading of texts by the likes of Brasillach and Maurras was classicist in a sense. Radically opposed to Claude Jamet, for example, who made the obscene claim that he could hear music in Brasillach's anti-Semitic articles, the prosecutors of the purge courts

---

[12]"After the poets of the Resistance, the Liberation was initiating a resistance to poetry." Hollier, *The Politics of Prose,* 9.

[13]Boschetti. For Sartre's positioning in relation to the French Communist party see Boschetti, *The Intellectual Enterprise,* 106–10.

saw straight through the style to the content. They read for the signi-
fied, not for the signifier. So too with Sartre. Even though Sartre's
style is instantly recognizable, even though he claimed to rewrite some
of his texts maniacally, the first parts of "What Is Literature?" are intended to evacuate the question of style or rather, to focus the reader's
attention entirely on the content the style is vehiculating. By the end
of the war Sartre transferred onto his critical vocabulary a system of
argumentation and an understanding of literature borrowed from the
trials, which, assuming he was writing at the Deux Magots, were taking place some 500 yards away. Sartre rarely commented upon the trials; his brief mention of the collaborationist writers in "Introducing
Les Temps modernes" is the one exception. And though he refused to
sign the petition in favor of Brasillach's clemency, it was Simone de
Beauvoir and not Sartre who justified this refusal. Sartre's "response
to the purge" consisted in giving a theoretical voice to the claims and
arguments made by the Resistants and the purge authorities.

"What Is Literature?" holds still more clues for reading Sartre's
critical theory in relation to the purge. This title calls to mind "What Is
a Collaborator?" an essay Sartre published in 1945 in the periodical *La
République française* and in which he draws a psychological portrait of
the collaborationist intellectual (Sartre, *Situations III*, 43–61 [my
translation]). The similarity of the two titles underscores a likeness in
purpose in the two essays: to identify and purge undesirable elements
from postwar France. Though not strictly biographical, both essays
contain sketches of what Sartre would later term his "existentialist
biographies," and both rely upon the construction of subjects—
whether writer or collaborator—whom Sartre makes carry the full
weight of responsibility. Sartre uses his essay "What Is Literature?" to
give a synoptic history of French literature in which he portrays the
nineteenth-century aesthete as a solitary, marginalized, selfish, and effeminate being, in a word, the foil for the committed writer of 1947. In
a curious amalgamation, however, Sartre transfers onto this irresponsible writer precisely the "social and psychological laws" he identified
and denounced in the collaborator two years earlier.

What is a collaborator? What is literature? The questions echo
each other, and so do the answers. One of Sartre's ambitions at the

end of the war was to create a sort of social cohesion around the working class, and in these two essays he identifies the collaborator and the nineteenth-century aesthete as agents who disrupt social harmony. The similarities between them begin in their irremediable isolation. In his 1945 essay Sartre maintains that the collaborator, and here he is thinking of Drieu la Rochelle and Alphonse de Chateaubriant, is a solitary creature; he refuses to join society and submits to what Sartre calls "rigorously individual realities" (57). Collaboration, like suicide, is a "phenomenon of disassimilation" (46) and remains in Sartre's mind, a marginal event. This, of course, may have been wishful thinking on Sartre's part since acceptance of Pétain and the collaboration was widespread in France, at least until 1942 (Laborie, *L'Opinion*). Sartre's attempt to marginalize the collaboration and minimize its extent surprisingly resembles de Gaulle's claims that the "majority" of writers "had taken France's side" during the war (De Gaulle, *The Complete War Memoirs,* 798). In "What Is Literature?" Sartre also describes the nineteenth-century aesthete, the producer of what Sartre calls "bourgeois art," as a loner, a marginal individual. Barbey D'Aurevilly, Flaubert, even George Sand—all these writers play the part of the forlorn individual and cultivate their loneliness: "[the nineteenth-century aesthete] was fond of speaking of his *solitude*" (Sartre, *What Is Literature?* 113). In his 1946 essay on Baudelaire, Sartre denounces the poet's individualism and ridicules his cult of solitude. Even in his childhood, "[Baudelaire] already thought of his isolation as a *destiny* . . . he felt and was determined to feel that he was unique" (Sartre, *Baudelaire*, 18).

If Sartre's foils are isolated, it is because all of them, with the possible exception of Hugo and Zola, have rejected their class of origin, the bourgeoisie, without subsequently turning to the proletariat. Again, the similarity between Sartre's portrait of the collaborator and his sketch of the nineteenth-century writer is startling. The collaborator, such as Marcel Déat or Luchaire, is most often found "among the intellectuals who abhor the bourgeoisie, their class of origin, without having the courage or the possibility of joining the proletariat" (Sartre, *Situations III,* 46). As for the nineteenth-century writer, he has torn himself from his class, though by refusing to write for the masses, he remains at the service of the bourgeoisie (Sartre, *What Is Literature?* 166). In Baudelaire's case Sartre examines his status as a dandy and concludes that the poet is a *déclassé* who rejects bourgeois values, is rejected by the aristocracy, and makes the mistake of not finding his "justification" in the proletariat (Sartre, *Baudelaire,* 139). As Alice Kaplan writes, for Sartre, "fascists are outsiders" (Kaplan, *Reproductions,* 14), and so, it turns out, is the nineteenth-century aesthete. The collaborator and the nineteenth-century writer become marginal figures, "internal emigrants" (Sartre, *Situations III,* 48), who, in Sartre's view of the postwar world, must be purged from society and from the renovated literary scene.

This inability of writer and collaborator to integrate themselves into society is matched by their incapacity to situate themselves in their own times. The collaborator judges his acts not according to his situation but from the perspective of a "far-off future" (54). He is infected by an "intellectual disease" Sartre calls "historicism" (52) which permits him to justify his crimes in the present by putting them in a historical perspective. In this light the collaborator considers Vichy's partnership with the Nazis as nothing more than a "reversal of alliances" (54), one of the many that can be found throughout history. Sartre's criticism is pertinent, for historical relativism was one of the main arguments used by collaborators not only during the Occupation but also at the purge trials: Pétain's supporters could just as easily compare him to Saint Louis as to de Gaulle, all in the interest of lessening his guilt. Having denounced the collaborator's recourse to false analogies and historical relativism, Sartre turns to literary history. The nineteenth-century writer is equally incapable of living in his own times: he looks back to win approval of the great poets of the past and forward to the readers of the future: "as for the past, he concluded a mystic pact with the great dead; as to the future, he made use of the myth of glory" (Sartre, *What Is Literature?* 116). Even more significantly, the nineteenth-century writer dreams of his future glory in juridical terms. Calling the desire for posthumous fame a "mechanism of overcompensation," Sartre states that the nineteenth-century writer cannot help but repeat to himself: "I shall win my trial on appeal" (115), a quote he revives from Gide's *Le Journal des Faux-Monnayeurs* to show how certain writers ignore their *situation* and transform their lives and work into courtroom drama. The writers' appeal to posthumous fame is, for Sartre, a manifestation of their bad faith precisely because these writers attempt to skirt a trial by their peers. Their irresponsibility allows their work to "escape judgment," and they claim not to "come under the jurisdiction of the collectivity." The nineteenth-century writer believed his role was to provoke scandal and that "his inalienable right was to escape its consequences" (121). The confusion of the collaborator and the irresponsible writer is so complete that Sartre concludes this part of the essay by stating that the nineteenth-century aesthete has "betrayed literature" (131). Just as the purge tribunals had judged and punished collaborators, Sartre is ready in the immediate postwar years to judge and condemn his literary precursors. The essay on Baudelaire makes this clear. Retracing Baudelaire's childhood, Sartre claims that from his earliest days the poet needed to define himself through the judgment of those who surrounded him: "What he wanted was neither friendship, love, nor relations on equal terms. . . . He wanted judges" (Sartre, *Baudelaire*, 56). Statements such as this may, however, tell us more about Sartre than about Baudelaire. What the text presents as the poet's desire for judgment must also be read as Sartre's need to judge. This judgment, to be sure, is an echo of *Being and Nothingness*: "The Other looks at me and . . . holds the secret of my being" (Sartre, *Being and Nothingness*, 473). But it is also further indication that through his literary criticism Sartre is rewriting the purge trials.

Sartre's trial of the nineteenth-century aesthete and his essay on the collaborator have one final point in common. In his portrait of the collaboration Sartre claims that a number of its "brilliant recruits" came directly from the homosexual milieu. Collaborators, according to Sartre, often represented relations between France and Germany as a sexual union where France played the implicitly passive role of the woman (Sartre, *Situations III*, 58). Though metaphors of the Occupation as a sexual exchange were common enough, Sartre certainly had in mind Brasillach's infamous phrase from 1943, in which he claimed that "Frenchmen of some reflection" had slept with Germany.[14] Though Brasillach's lines specify neither the gender nor the roles of either partner, for Sartre the collaborator is the passive subject of foreign domination, just as in his imagination the male homosexual can only be the passive partner in sodomy, an association that leads Sartre to define the spirit of the collaboration as a curious blend of masochism and homosexuality (58).[15] Sartre's motivation for making this association seems twofold. First, homosexuals, according to Sartre, are the ultimate guilty party. Sartre had already described them in *Being and Nothingness* as avatars of bad faith and the subjects of an "intolerable feeling of guilt" (Sartre, *Being and Nothingness*, 107), and this supposed guilt seems to be reincarnated in the collaborator at the end of the war. Second, "What Is a Collaborator?" paints the portrait of men who are fundamentally antisocial and, therefore, anti-French. In identifying the collaborator as sexually other, Sartre can again isolate him from the renovated postwar society he is proposing. As we might have anticipated, Sartre returns to this characterization in his portrait of the nineteenth-century writer. In "What Is Literature?" Sartre's writer remains (relatively) heterosexual, though he considers love a "useless passion" disconnected from procreation and production. But throughout his other essays Sartre repeatedly denounces certain writers from previous generations as homosexual aesthetes. In "Introducing *Les Temps Modernes*" he attacks Proust not only for having "made himself into an accomplice of bourgeois propaganda" (259) but also for trying to erase the differences between heterosexual and homosexual love. These charges fall somewhere between the outrageous and the incomprehensible, but Sartre's point is that the homosexual remains a radical element, an outsider incapable of being incorporated into society even when he tries to pass as bourgeois. In 1946 Sartre describes Baudelaire as a dandy who, while not a practicing homosexual, nonetheless "sometimes looked like a woman" in his dress and was "femininity" incarnate (Sartre, *Baudelaire*, 152–54). In his essay on

[14]Brasillach's article was published on 19 Feb. 1943 in the review *Révolution nationale* and was quoted by the prosecution at his trial. See Chapter 1.

[15]For a discussion of the metaphors of femininity in Sartre's literary criticism see Halpern, *Critical Fictions*.

Mallarmé, begun in 1952 and published years later, Sartre returns to the sexual metaphor and the desire of nineteenth-century writers. In this text he claims that if the Romantics weren't gay, they certainly acted the part: "Their outbursts [*effusions*], their swoons, their affectations of purity, their delicacy, their sentimentality, all this fuss, would make one think they were queens [*des tantes*]" (Sartre, *Mallarmé*, 32 [my translation]). And in *L'Idiot de la famille* Sartre identifies Flaubert's sexuality as feminine, passive, and homosexual: Gustave wants to be a woman, and "feminine desire is passive anticipation" (Sartre, *L'Idiot*, 685 [my translation]). Should we conclude with David Carroll that, when Sartre labels the collaborator a sexual and social outsider, he is making "the same accusation that Barrès and others made of Dreyfus . . . and the identical claim that the anti-Semitic fascists and collaborators had made against the Jews" (Carroll, *French Literary Fascism*, 150)? Is Sartre's vision of postwar society as homophobic and normative as that of the extreme right? This type of analogy is more misleading than helpful and results in the deflection of guilt the collaborators themselves sought at the end of the war. Still, in 1947 Sartre is arguing for social cohesion and against deviance, eccentricity, and marginalization—his own as well as that of other writers. His statements about the collaborators' effeminacy most closely resemble claims made by the purgers of postwar France who asserted that during the Occupation the traitorous writers had "fornicated"—figuratively speaking—with the enemy. Sartre's argument against the homosexual aesthete is unfair and unjustified, but it serves as one more indication that his postwar essays are staging a massive purge of French literary history in which the culprits, most notably the nineteenth-century *hommes de lettres*, have become identical in their habits and desires to the men on trial for betraying France. Solitary, marginal, and effeminate, Sartre's nineteenth-century writer and his World War II collaborator have become partners in crime.

From Brasillach's trial to his essay on Flaubert, from the tribunal to the pages of *Les Temps modernes*, Sartre has continued the process of the purge by redefining the role of the literary critic as judge, the role of the writer as the accused, and the role of literary texts as witnesses for the prosecution. Sartre's theory of responsibility is not without its paradoxes though. Judt, for example, points out that Sartre's manifestos for responsibility were accompanied by an equally "irresponsible" political attitude when it came to the crimes of the Soviet Union (Judt, *Past Imperfect*, 307). Less intent upon contesting Sartre's political choices, Hollier has argued that while in his essays Sartre was constructing his theory of a *littérature engagée*, his plays seem to be doing quite the opposite. Thus, according to Hollier, while Sartre attempts to make language an act, the characters of plays such as *The Flies* and *Dirty Hands* use action as a way of escaping language (Hollier, *Les Dépossédés*, 37–53).

There is, however, another paradox at work in Sartre's literary essays. While modeled on the laws and verdicts of the purge tribunals, these texts only mention the postwar trials as such on one occasion. The essays are a response to the trials in the form of literary theory and biography, but at the same time they seem to obfuscate the trials themselves. We are thus faced with a series of articles that, while propounding the situation of the writer in history, while creating a theory from a specific moment in history, ignore, or rather suppress, an important part of their own historical and political situation. Sartre, it seems, can only speak of the purge through indirection, allegorically. It is almost as if Sartre refused to acknowledge the purge, as if the very event that led him to formulate his theory of literature had to be excluded from literary considerations. The purge is a process of elimination that Sartre has eliminated from his text by removing all explicit references to the trials. To be sure, one could argue that in his essay Sartre is simply extrapolating a universal lesson from a local event. But it is almost as if he had not learned one of the lessons he was teaching his readers about the importance of the local event. We can only speculate as to Sartre's motive. His ambivalence toward the purge may have been a reflection of his own ambivalence during the Occupation. Judt has spoken of Sartre's need to deculpabilize himself, but this interpretation of Sartre's motives relies on the belief that Sartre felt a conscious or unconscious culpability, which is not at all certain (Judt, *Past Imperfect*, 40). France may have felt guilty for the collaboration, Sartre probably did not. Another, and to my mind more plausible explanation, may come from the fact that by 1947, when Sartre was writing *What Is Literature?* the mood in the country had changed, and much of the enthusiasm for the purge had died down. Sartre's rhetorical strategies at the time included an appeal to the widest possible audience. By hiding the purge, by veiling the attacks, he may have been attempting to avoid an event that had become distasteful to many. This avoidance of an explicit rhetoric of revenge also had the added benefit of demarcating Sartre from the communist intellectuals, one of the last groups to continue its calls for a violent purge. Whatever the motivation, Sartre's obscuring of the trials, his purge of the purge, turns out, in subsequent works, to be much more difficult than even Sartre could have imagined. When he comes to celebrate a true writer of modern times, Jean Genet, the terms on which he draws turn out to be startlingly close to those he had used in order to define and condemn the collaborator.

Published in 1952 as a 578-page introduction to the Gallimard edition of Genet's complete works, *Saint Genet* presents to the postwar reading public an authentic contemporary writer, an existential hero.[16] Sartre's stated goal in this voluminous introduction is to go beyond the limit of psychoanalytic interpretation and Marxist explanation and recount the story of one man's freedom, and the choice of Genet was prescient—he remains one of postwar France's strongest and most intriguing writers. Sartre first met Genet in 1944, and his defense of the writer began with a petition he and Cocteau composed and circulated in July 1948 requesting that French President Vincent Auriol pardon Genet on the grounds that he was, as they wrote, a "very great poet" (White, *Genet,* 386–88). The resemblance of this petition to Mauriac's efforts in favor of Brasillach is uncanny; members of the literary community banded together and appealed to the head of state in order to save a writer sentenced by the French courts. Not only did they argue that Genet's talent was an extenuating circumstance, but many of the same writers who had signed for Brasillach now joined Sartre in signing for Genet. Aymé, Claudel, and Colette all signed, though Aragon, Camus, Eluard, and the once clement Mauriac, who even wrote an es-

---

[16]Sartre, *Saint Genet* (my translation).

say in 1949 condemning Genet to silence, did not (Mauriac, "Le Cas Genet," 7).

The petition succeeded, Genet was released from prison, and Sartre continued his defense of the writer by embarking on his study. At first glance Genet is worlds apart from the nineteenth-century writer and the collaborationist intellectual Sartre had condemned at the end of the war. What separates him from these avatars of bad faith is his acceptation of his *situation* in the present. The collaborator and the nineteenth-century aesthete were escape artists; both lived in the distant past or some far-off future from which they justified their choices: "I shall win my trial on appeal." Genet, on the other hand, is a realist: "He wants to win or lose in this world" (Sartre, *Saint Genet,* 70). He not only accepts his situation, he claims it as his own, and it becomes a source of "pride," the means through which Genet transforms his passivity into an "active revolt" (69). Whereas in Sartre's thinking Brasillach or Baudelaire had sought to escape his responsibility, Genet refuses all forms of escapism, from physical pleasure to drunkenness (71). Genet, Sartre tells us, is the very opposite of the irresponsible artist: "he intends to pay for his work." And if Sartre has chosen Genet as the embodiment of modern times, it is precisely because he knows that his literature "is an act" and that it is working to "undermine the foundation of our society" (539).

Sartre's Genet, then, categorically rejects the "temptation of irresponsibility." And yet this subject Sartre creates and names "Genet" resembles, like a twin brother or a reflection in the mirror, the collaborationist subject Sartre had constructed seven years earlier. Like the collaborator, Genet is a loner; his status as an orphan results in a child who was never "socialized" (19), and his destiny of isolation is sealed when society brands him a thief. Solitude is his fate; Genet belongs to a category of marginalized individuals, whom Sartre labels "products of disassimilation" (41), a phrase we can compare to the expression "phenomenon of disassimilation" Sartre had used when describing the collaboration. This similarity might begin to suggest that the study of Genet is, at least in part, and with a radically revised conclusion, a rewriting of the earlier essays on literature and the collaboration.

Genet's marginalization continues in his relation to politics. He remains classless, and though he rejects the bourgeoisie, he is never in solidarity with the proletariat. Or rather, his solidarity is only aesthetic and eroticized. Genet wants to ignore the "disconcerting existence of the proletariat" (351), and when he sees a worker in the street, he transforms the worker's movements into an attractive gesture. Even among the members of his homosexual milieu there is no solidarity. It is precisely Sartre's identification of Genet as gay, however, that recalls his earlier portraits of outsiders. For Genet too displays a curious blend of masochism and passivity. Sexually Genet is "an object for others," and to describe his behavior Sartre evokes Simone de Beauvoir on feminine sexuality. More than anything, Genet's sexual relations resemble "feminine eroticism" (48), and this sexual passivity determines every aspect of his behavior with others: as during the sexual act, in his quotidian actions Genet submits to others whether they be cops or judges (135). Solitary, marginal, and sexually passive, Genet seems to be a 1952 transposition of the treasonous subject Sartre had condemned in his earlier essays. Indeed, Genet's distinguishing characteristic is that he is a traitor. Sartre locates treason at the very heart of Genet's aesthetics: "If poetry risks becoming treason, treason . . . certainly becomes poetry" (206).

In 1952 Sartre takes the terms he had previously used to condemn the collaborator and the nineteenth-century aesthete and turns them inside out like a glove. Now solitude, "disassimilation," aestheticism, sexual passivity, and treason have become the author's weapons. Genet has become an existentialist hero, according to Sartre, precisely because he is marginalized, because he embraces his solitude and his sexuality. The reversal in Sartre's essay is so complete that he characterizes Genet's *art poétique* as a celebration of impurity. Genet is an untouchable: "I could not touch him without dirtying my hands" (51), writes Sartre. He equates beauty to purity, and beauty in Genet's fiction can only be seen through "excrements" (433); "the art of making you eat shit," writes Sartre, quoting the author (433). In his literary theory, Sartre has gone from providing theoretical support for the purification (*l'épuration*) of French society to the defense of an author who befouls this society. From the purge of the' republic of letters, Sartre is now writing in favor of an author who refuses to be purged.

Sartre's choice of Genet as a model for postwar literature might nonetheless surprise us, especially considering Genet's credo that, as Leo Bersani has written, "*betrayal is an ethical necessity*" (Bersani, *Homos*, 151). In trying to unpack Sartre's relation to Genet, we might be tempted to distinguish the treachery Genet lauds in his novels from the forms of treason debated in purge courts. After all, one of the first traitors we meet in Genet's prose, the pimp Mimosa in *Our Lady of the Flowers*, is a double-crosser who sells his friends and colleagues to the police but does not betray his nation. Still, Genet's 1947 novel *Funeral Rites* explores precisely the type of crime that had traumatized the nation: the betrayal of France by young men during the Occupation. *Funeral Rites* is an ode to Jean Décarnin, Genet's lover, who, as a member of the Communist Resistance, was shot and killed during the Liberation of Paris. From this event Genet creates a scenario of eroticism, which includes, for example, when Genet imagines Hitler participating in a gay orgy, some of the most extreme scenes in postwar French literature. During his mourning, during the funeral rites of the title, Genet imagines and describes Décarnin's assassin, spotted for the first time on a movie theater newsreel. The murderer is a member of the Milice, who were at the service of the Nazi occupiers and who, more than anyone else, embodied treason in the eyes of the French public at the end of the war. Riton, the militiaman who shot Décarnin, is for Genet two times a traitor, once because he betrayed France and again because he killed Genet's lover. And yet in spite of this betrayal, or perhaps because of it, Riton becomes the object of Genet's fascination and his love. Confronted with this "little traitor," Genet writes, "My hatred of the militiaman was so intense, so beautiful, that it was equivalent to the strongest love. No doubt it was he who had killed Jean. I desired him" (Genet, *Funeral Rites*, 54). Genet's eroticization of the traitor participates in both his aesthetics of Evil and his constant reversal of society's values. His portrait of a member of the Milice transforms his novel into the glorification of precisely the type of political treason Sartre had condemned in 1945. It is as if

Genet's literature had reactivated in Sartre the trauma of the purge, forcing it to come out once again in an indirect form.

A year after the publication of *Saint Genet*, Vincent Auriol, the president who had granted Genet clemency, promulgated an amnesty for the men and women condemned of crimes of collaboration. It is difficult not to see Sartre's 1952 essay as another type of reevaluation of the purge trials in France. Sartre, of course, was by now less interested in national reconciliation than was Auriol; his essay is also meant as a denunciation of the dominant ideology in France. Still, in *Saint Genet* Sartre has given us the portrait of a writer who claims as his own precisely the traits Sartre had denounced in other writers and intellectuals a few years earlier. The reversibility of Sartre's arguments about literature leaves us with a paradox: it points to the force of the purge in Sartre's thought but at the same time begins to hint at the instability of this process. Sartre's 1952 study tells the tale of putting literature on trial, but Sartre has gone from prosecutor to defense attorney, and his defense plea turns out to be a rewriting of the literary criticism he had submitted during the purge. *Saint Genet* cannot be said to invalidate Sartre's earlier incriminations of Drieu and Brasillach, or of Flaubert and the Goncourts; nothing in his writing suggests he ever advocated a revision of the purge trials. *Saint Genet* is less a revision than a *détournement*, a metamorphosis of the trials. Genet's work irremediably blurs the categories of guilt and innocence Sartre had patiently constructed from 1944 to 1947. And if Sartre never specifically mentions the purge in France, he nonetheless concludes his book by comparing Genet to Nikolai Bukharin, the victim of the Stalinist purge, tried and executed for treason in 1938. "Genet is the Bukharin of bourgeois society," writes Sartre (656). Genet, the unrepentant traitor, Genet the mirror of our own guilt (662), this Genet is also the writer who seems to have taught Sartre that it is only at the moment when his foundations for judging begin to shift, only when the laws he writes start to waver, that he can set literature free.

CHAPTER 3

Blanchot: Rebuttals

Critical interest in Maurice Blanchot can be divided into two distinct approaches. Blanchot was central to a generation of critics who looked to his theories of textuality and vertiginous undecidability in an attempt to get beyond the calls for responsibility and judgment Sartre formulated in the postwar years. In this sense Blanchot was the single most important critic for readers searching for an antidote to existential models of literary criticism. At the same time certain scholars have read Blanchot's essays and novels for their often cryptic and encoded historicism, thus engaging the author in what Steven Ungar has called the "aftereffect" of the Second World War in France.[1] As a result, Blanchot, as much as any other writer, embodies the aspirations, blindspots, and controversies of literary modernism. Two articles on Blanchot, written at an interval of almost 20 years, crystallize the paradoxical reception of this enigmatic writer.

In his 1966 study "Impersonality in Blanchot" Paul de Man acknowledges Blanchot's importance for his own critical itinerary. It is

---

[1]Ungar, *Scandal*. Borrowing Freud's concept of *Nachträglichkeit*, Ungar analyzes Blanchot's work in terms of the return of a repressed political past.

hard not to be struck by both the theoretical and biographical similarities between the two critics.[2] Not only do the major themes of de Man's criticism, and in particular his deconstruction of subjectivity, derive directly from Blanchot's postwar work, but also both authors followed a startlingly similar path from an engagement with fascist politics in their youth to the radical disengagement of literature from political reality. Given this, it is not surprising to find that de Man's essay on Blanchot opens with an attack on Sartre. "Since the end of the war" (de Man, *Blindness and Insight,* 60), de Man writes, a certain trendiness has dominated French literature, and the prime offender is Sartre and his "frantic attempt" to keep in touch with "fashionable trends" (61). The reference to Sartre is astute not only because Blanchot's work is emphatically not part of a trend, according to de Man, but because Blanchot's critical essays of the postwar period are, to a great extent, a response to existentialist themes. In his essay de Man points to what separates Blanchot from the intellectual fashion of modern times: "In reading Blanchot, we are not participating in an act of judgment, of sympathy, or of understanding" (63). If Blanchot's work moves us beyond judgment, the keystone of Sartrean literary analysis, it is precisely because his writing dissolves the subject. Author and reader, in de Man's words, "co-operate in making each other forget their distinctive identity and destroy each other as subjects" (64). Turning to Blanchot's reading of Mallarmé, de Man examines what he calls "impersonality" in Blanchot's criticism, an impersonality that one can achieve only through what de Man first calls "askesis": "Blanchot must eliminate all the elements derived from everyday experience, from involvement with others, all reifying tendencies that tend to equate the work with natural objects" (78). Impersonality involves a very personal work, a rigorous self-discipline that results in an "extreme purification" (78). Only after this process can Blanchot go on to his real concern, the "temporal dimensions of the text" (78). De Man's article on Blanchot was originally published in French in the review *Critique,* and the French version of the text

[2]De Man, *Blindness,* 60–78.

leads us to a startling discovery. The word de Man used was not *puri-fication*, as in the English version, but *épuration* (De Man, "La Circularité, 547–60). It is hard to imagine that de Man could have used such a word, even as late as 1966, without thinking of the political and historical weight it carried. Certainly the use of this word tells us something about de Man's own desire to purge the political from his literary criticism. At the very least the word *épuration* hints that, while avoiding "fashionable trends," Blanchot's work is perhaps not all that far from the concerns that had preoccupied Sartre "since the end of the war."

The second reading indicative of a trend in the reception of Blanchot is Jeffrey Mehlman's 1983 article "Blanchot at *Combat*: Of Literature and Terror," published as the first chapter of his *Legacies: Of Anti-Semitism in France*.[3] In his study of Blanchot, Mehlman sets out to reveal the extent to which political ideologies and their legacies are reinscribed in theoretical and literary texts. Mehlman begins by identifying the main themes of Blanchot's political writings of the 1930s: an allegiance to the Bernanos of *La Grande Peur des bien-pensants*; a violent criticism of the Blum government and of Republican institutions; a call for insurrection, and indeed terrorism, against democracy. Far from disappearing, these themes return, in Mehlman's view, as some form of repressed trauma throughout Blanchot's later work. Take, for example, the theme of terror. In 1942 Blanchot published a review of Jean Paulhan's 1941 *Les Fleurs de Tarbes*, a complex and paradoxical essay on "terrorism" in letters. Paulhan's text is a polemic of sorts against "terrorist" writers who since the Romantic revolution have struggled to free themselves from clichés, platitudes, and the rules of rhetoric. It is, at least on the surface, a plea for a return to the conventions of classical rhetoric. Under this plea, however, Blanchot discovers a second, more radical form of reading that makes Paulhan the herald of a "Copernican revolution" in which language no longer revolves around thought, but thought around language (Blanchot, *Faux pas*, 101). Forty years after its publication Mehlman returns to this essay and sends it in two directions. The se-

[3]Mehlman, *Legacies*, 6–22.

cret revolution Blanchot discovered in Paulhan echoes Blanchot's political articles from a not so distant past, the "calls to terrorism" issued by Blanchot when he was still at *Combat* (Mehlman, *Legacies,* 13). At the same time Mehlman projects Blanchot's essay into the future, by affirming that the second reading of Paulhan it proposes "is perhaps best understood in terms of contemporary deconstruction, the heritage of the style of reading Blanchot was then initiating" (12). Mehlman concludes this portion of the article by stating that Blanchot's 1942 study on Paulhan "may thus be read simultaneously as a discreet inauguration of French literary modernity and a coded farewell to plans for a French fascism of the 1930s" (13). Mehlman is thus making Blanchot's texts speak of a political commitment they apparently seek to repress. He is extracting a confession from the author of *Faux pas*.

Read today, these two articles are chillingly prescient. We can no longer approach de Man's laudatory review of Blanchot's work without thinking about the purges he went through: the one he put himself through by turning to deconstruction and the trials his work underwent after his death when his past as a journalist for the pro-Nazi paper *Le Soir* was revealed. A few years after having published his article on Blanchot, Mehlman became a major voice in the controversy surrounding the revelations about de Man and elaborated his thesis that deconstruction is irremediably tainted by the fascist past of several of its main practitioners (Mehlman "Prosopopeia," 137–43). And though Mehlman has been reproached for his "prosecutor's" zeal[4] and accused of erasing fundamental questions in Blanchot's text,[5] his finely tuned study prevents us from reading Blanchot, or his legacy, without reconsidering the relation between fascist politics and liter-

---

[4]Mesnard, "Blanchot," 103–28. See also Verdès-Leroux, *Refus,* 101.

[5]"The essential question raised in Blanchot's text [*La Folie du jour*] by the 'collision' and eventual undoing of the specular relationship between the metaphysical (light, clarity, reason, theory) and the empirical (a true event) is itself erased in Mehlman's attempt to reattach them in a metaphorical genealogy that would account for a certain form of 'French literary modernity'—read deconstruction, Derrida, de Man . . .—by turning it into a direct and easily recognizable offspring of 'French fascism in the 1930's.'" Newmark, *Beyond Symbolism,* 177.

ary modernity. What interests me here, however, is not so much Mehlman's divergence from de Man and deconstruction as the convergence of their readings of Blanchot. Both critics, for entirely different reasons, see Blanchot's work as having undergone a purge process—de Man calls it an *épuration*; Mehlman, an "obliteration." Whether they attribute it to the work of the unconscious or to a stylistic discipline, both locate this purge as a turning point in Blanchot's work. Neither critic, however, has considered the extent to which Blanchot's postwar criticism constitutes a reflection on the postwar purge itself. Blanchot never, to my knowledge, mentioned the trials as such, and though his name appeared on a letter supporting his publisher, Gallimard, he was never directly involved in the accusation or defense of writers.[6] To comment directly on the trials would have meant, after all, to subordinate literature to politics. Still, Blanchot's literary essays not only initiate a form of literary modernity, they present a series of allegories that force us to reflect upon what it means to judge writers and to put literature on trial. It is not unreasonable to conclude that Blanchot does indeed engage his work in the intellectual fashion of the day, and in particular through their dialogue with Sartre and their considerations on judgment and responsibility his essays constitute an important reevaluation of the purge.

If Blanchot's writing gives rise to both passionately apolitical and aggressively historical readings, it is perhaps because his own trajectory is laced with ambiguities and paradoxes. Before the war Blanchot wrote some 100 articles for far-right publications such as *Combat* and *L'Insurgé*, two reviews linked to *L'Action française* and characterized by a revolutionary tone, calls for insurrection, and a pronounced nostalgia for the fascist-inspired riots in Paris on 6 February 1934.[7] Blan-

---

[6]Blanchot's name appeared on a cover letter written on behalf of Gaston Gallimard when the publishing house was being investigated in November 1945 by the Commission for the Purging of Publishing. The letter reads, in part, "[Gallimard] founded the Pléiade Prize with a panel made up mostly of Resistance writers: Arland, Blanchot, Bousquet, Camus, Eluard, Grenier, Malraux, Paulhan, Queneau, Sartre, Tual, and the Gestapo became alarmed at this and demanded the addresses of all the members of the panel." Quoted in Assouline, *Gallimard*, 315.

[7]Holland and Rousseau, "Blanchot: Bibliographie I," 224–45; "Blanchot:

chot's political voice fades in 1938, when he undergoes a conversion of sorts from political commentator to literary critic and author of quasi-mystical novels and *récits*. During the Occupation Blanchot published numerous articles in the *Journal des débats*, most of them reviews of literary works which were later collected in *Faux pas*, published by Gallimard in 1943. It is difficult to situate Blanchot's wartime criticism on the political spectrum for several reasons. Blanchot undeniably argues for the autonomy of literature from historical and political forces, and this might seem to tie his work to certain writers, including some of the very ones he reviews, who both upheld the autonomy of art and were favorable to the collaboration.[8] In his review of Henry de Montherlant's *Solstice de juin*, for example, Blanchot quotes the author precisely when he warns writers against too much involvement in the daily business of politics: "Today's newspapers and reviews, when I open them, I hear rolling upon them the indifference of the future, as one hears the sound of the sea when putting certain shells to one's ear."[9] Montherlant's quote, which gained notoriety in recent years when Jacques Derrida used it as the title of his defense of Paul de Man, can be read as a warning against excessive political involvement issued by a writer who supported the Vichy regime and admired Nazi strength. Montherlant's advice against a politically committed literature is also an acceptance of the *status quo* in Occupied France. At the very least Blanchot's reading of *Solstice de juin* is a far cry from that of the National Writers' Committee, who branded Montherlant a traitor in 1944. Similarly, we can see the distance separating Blanchot from the writers of the Resistance in their respective commentaries on Jacques Chardonne. Whereas Blanchot appreciates Chardonne the moralist and criticizes his work on purely formal

---

Bibliographie II," 124–32. For the relation of these two publications to Maurras and *L'Action française* see Verdès-Leroux, *Refus,* 40–89.

[8]In her essay on Paul de Man's wartime journalism, Kaplan points out that the argument for the "autonomy of literary forms doesn't conflict with transcendent Nazi doctrines of race and spirit" ("de Man," 276). Carroll's *French Literary Fascism* also claims that literary autonomy could be used to uphold doctrines of racial or cultural purity.

[9]Blanchot, *Faux pas,* 352.

grounds, thus maintaining a separation between the writer and the propagandist, the anonymous critic at the clandestine journal *Les Lettres françaises* accuses Chardonne of having accepted Nazism and of having "offered" himself to the victors. The critic thus describes Chardonne's conversion to Hitlerism: "You have to see how he [Chardonne] enters into joyous ecstasy to celebrate the beauty of the young victors. He gave himself, like a woman who has just been slapped, with sweet cooing."[10]

Situating Blanchot is never simple. While he wrote reviews of many authors favorable to the collaboration—Chardonne and Montherlant, but also Ernst Jünger and Thierry Maulnier—he never made the political pronouncements that might lead us to suspect that, as a critic, he accepted the Occupation. Furthermore, Blanchot also wrote positive reviews of works by writers engaged in the Resistance: Paulhan's *Les Fleurs de Tarbes*, Eluard's *Poésie involontaire*, Sartre's *The Flies*, and Camus's *The Myth of Sisyphus*. Critical of Camus's lack of philosophical rigor, Blanchot nonetheless opens the door to reading *The Myth of Sisyphus* as "an attempt to explain our times" (Blanchot, *Faux pas*, 66). His review of Sartre's play is typically ambiguous; he says it is a work of "exceptional value and significance" (72) yet claims that Orestes lacks the strength to destroy the "titanic world" in which he acts. Still, through his use of terms such as *liberation, liberty,* and *reprisals*, Blanchot hints that he has understood the play as an allegory of Resistance.

By the end of the Occupation Blanchot's name is associated with Resistance intellectuals such as Eluard, Sartre, and Paulhan also published by Gallimard. We know relatively little about his Resistance activities even though several of his *récits* can be read as revelations about the author's involvement in the Resistance. Philippe Mesnard sees *The Madness of the Day* as an account of the day when Blanchot narrowly escaped execution at the hands of the Germans (Mesnard,

---

[10]"Chardonne s'est converti à l'hitlérisme. Il faut voir dans quelle allègre extase il entre pour célébrer la beauté des jeunes vainqueurs. Il s'est donné, comme femme après une gifle, avec des roucoulements dans la gorge." From "Jacques Chardonne et *Mein Kampf*," *Les Lettres françaises*, 11 Nov. 1943, 2 (my translation).

"Blanchot," 110). In a recently released short story, *L'Instant de ma mort*, which takes place between D-Day and the end of the war, Blanchot tells the story of a young man—himself?—who, on the verge of being executed, hears the far-off gunshots of his "comrades of the Maquis" (Blanchot, *L'Instant*, 11 [my translation]). Where, then, are we to situate Blanchot politically? Does his trajectory reveal a change of political commitment or simply opportunism? By reviewing Camus and Chardonne, Montherlant and Sartre, is he trying to keep both parties sweet? Blanchot's itinerary, from supporter of Maurras to Resistant, may be exceptional, but it is not unique; Claude Morgan, the editor of *Les Lettres françaises,* and Claude Roy are two prominent examples of writers who seceded from the far right during the Occupation. Unlike these two, however, Blanchot does not go over to the opposite extreme; Morgan and Claude Roy both joined the Communist party during the war. What is particular in Blanchot's itinerary is not so much his separation of literature from politics but rather his constant interrogation of the very points at which literature and politics intersect.

Like Blanchot's life, his texts remain elusive, and any attempt to situate them in relation to an event such as the postwar purge risks ending up in a spiral of ambiguity and equivocation. Still, an attempt to situate Blanchot amid the position taking of the purge might lead, it seems to me, to an understanding of what is at stake in his work. My starting point is Blanchot's relation to Sartre, who from 1943 on occupied the position many French intellectuals used to navigate through the French literary field.

In 1943 Blanchot published a study of Sartre's play *The Flies.* That year Sartre returned the favor by publishing a review of Blanchot's novel *Aminadab* in the Resistance journal *Cahiers du Sud* (Sartre, *Situations I*, 122–42). In spite of concluding that Blanchot is a "quality writer" (Sartre, *Situations I,* 142), Sartre points to what he sees as a paradox in this author. *Aminadab*, a novel in the fantastic literature genre, relies heavily upon the mood and style of Kafka's novels while the author himself, Sartre tells us in a footnote, was at one point in his career a disciple of Charles Maurras. While Sartre reminds us that Blanchot claims not to have read Kafka before writing *Aminadab*, it is nonetheless significant, in Sartre's view, that an adept of Maurras's "French thought" (*penser français*) doctrine should encounter in the realm of fantastic literature "a writer of Central Europe" (123–24). In a paradoxical and provocative move Sartre puts Blanchot under the dual sign of Franz Kafka and Charles Maurras. Blanchot uses the same "meticulous and courteous style" as Kafka, the same "polite nightmares," the same "vain quests," the same "sterile initiations" (123). Clearly Sartre's comparison and his stated preference for Kafka over Maurras is a jab at the nationalist and anti-Semitic cultural politics of the Vichy regime. But it is also a blow at Blanchot, for though Sartre does not probe Blanchot's politics, he nonetheless concludes his essay with an implicit comparison of Blanchot and Maurice Barrès and a claim that *Aminadab*, in its quest for transcendence, is "tainted with Maurrasism" (140). Sartre's review is startling, especially since *Aminadab* is not explicitly political and since Sartre himself seems at least initially more interested in defining the parameters of fantastic literature than in denouncing Blanchot. Still, his statements tell us that even as late as 1943 Sartre remembered Blanchot's political past to the point of seeing Maurras's influence in his literary work. In a reaction similar to the type of commentary performed at *Les Lettres françaises*, Sartre is implicating a literary work in the political field. He is using Blanchot to attack Vichy's "*penser français*" credo, and this in spite of the fact that Blanchot has turned to literature and away from the politics of the Occupation. But at the same time Sartre may be exonerating Blanchot; it is precisely his Kafkaesque writing that will save him from the influence of Maurras. Sartre's review is less an attack than a lesson. He is ushering Blanchot away from "Maurrasism" and into the fold of another type of political thought. In the postwar years, however, Blanchot would turn this lesson inside out by using Sartre to disengage the literary work from the realm of political commitment.

By the end of the war Blanchot had sufficiently distanced himself from Maurras to participate in the early issues of *Les Temps modernes*. He also became closely associated with *Critique*, however, a review that Anna Boschetti has defined as an antithesis to Sartre's monthly (Boschetti, *Intellectual Enterprise*, 159–66), and it is in the pages of

Critique that Blanchot begins to formulate the basis of his postwar literary theory in essays that are often driven by a desire to contest existentialist doctrines. Using Sartre's own terminology, Blanchot refutes Sartre's theses, disputes his claims, and attempts to undermine his analyses. Words such as *commitment, bad faith, liberty, existence, revolution,* and *judgment* constantly reappear in Blanchot's essays but with a meaning often antithetical to Sartre's. The essays reprinted in *La Part du feu* as well as the studies in *Lautréamont et Sade*, both published in book form in 1949, constitute a major revision of Sartre's postwar criticism and a challenge to the arguments of the purge that Sartre's postwar theories of responsibility and commitment were supporting.

That *La Part du feu*, a collection of articles from *Critique*, should open with two essays on Kafka, serves perhaps as a first indication that Blanchot is indeed responding to Sartre.[11] The dialogue begins in earnest, however, with his reviews of Sartre's novels *The Age of Reason* and *The Reprieve,* the first two volumes of the *Roads to Freedom* trilogy. Blanchot poses the problem of the relation between literary text and political ideology in the novel, and in the *roman à thèse* in particular. Sartre's works present themselves as an illustration of the philosopher's thesis on man's liberty, but in attempting to decipher this thesis, according to Blanchot, we must first confront the problem of literary forms. Blanchot begins by stating that Sartre's novels were originally published without their final volume, a lacuna that denies the work the possibility of ever arriving at a concluding recommendation. The paths of the novels never attain the freedom announced in the title. Their narrative structure, far from following any road at all, resembles a whirlwind, an "aberrant cyclone" (Blanchot, *La Part,* 202) with a multitude of centers, so that, Blanchot concludes, we are left with nothing but a series of fragments that lead only inward. The *roman* prevents us from reaching the *thèse*. For Blanchot the novel responds to its own laws, which include an ethics of "ambiguity and equivocation" (203). It has its own truth, "which forces it to affirm nothing without seeking to take it back and to attain success without

[11]Blanchot, *La Part* (my translation).

preparing for failure, so that if ever a thesis triumphs in a novel it ceases to be true" (203). Blanchot is thus using Sartre against Sartre. He is demonstrating precisely the opposite of what Sartre defined as the role of literature in contemporary society and this by way of *The Roads to Freedom*. Where Sartre had seen Maurras's influence in the fantastic novel *Aminadab*, Blanchot transforms the politics in Sartre's novels into a formal and technical experiment, a reading that is all the more startling given that Sartre's last novels are terribly conventional. And while Sartre defined the writer's responsibility to society and history, Blanchot attempts to prove that the writer's only engagement is with the ambiguity of literary form.

The review of *The Roads to Freedom* challenged Sartre the novelist. "Literature and the Right to Death," Blanchot's major theoretical statement in the immediate postwar years, argues against Sartre's 1947 critical essay "What Is Literature?" Blanchot begins his essay, which Hollier has called an "anti-Sartrean manifesto" (Hollier, *Les Dépossédés*, 14), with the same question Sartre had posed, "Why write?" but concludes that writing does not necessarily have an end, that it may lead nowhere, and that the impetus for writing may be the most trivial of circumstances: a magazine order, for example, or a chance occurrence (297). For Blanchot the Sartrean question reveals nothing about the nature of literature and only leads to what he calls "a trial of art" (*"un procès de l'art"*), "a trial . . . of its powers and its ends" (294). To ask the question "Why write?" is to put literature on trial, to question its intent. It is to participate in the very process of the purge. With this phrase we thus arrive at what may be the crux of Blanchot's response to Sartre in the immediate postwar years. To respond to Sartre is to respond, albeit allegorically and through indirection, to the forces that are putting not only writers but also the "powers" and "ends" of literature on trial.

With an eye to the purge tribunals Blanchot sets out to revise the verdicts proposed by Sartre in "What Is Literature?" by rewriting Sartre's vocabulary. Sartre used the notion of "bad faith" to try and convict both the collaborator and the nineteenth-century aesthete who refused to accept their historical and social situation. For his part Blanchot transforms "bad faith" from a condemnable inauthenticity to the essence of literature: "in literature, as soon as probity enters the equation, imposture is already there. Here, bad faith is truth" (300). Furthermore, because literature is the language of ambiguity, treason and dishonesty (*tromperie*) (302) are the stuff of literature, and Blanchot's writer remains irresponsible to the core (*"un irresponsable sans conscience"*) (303). Such is the writer's duplicity that politicians can only regard him with distrust and defiance. The literary work always has an aesthetic ideal, according to Blanchot, and writers, even while making political statements and supporting a cause, are also engaged (*"ont pris parti"*) in literature. Literature "denies the substance of what it represents" (301). Politically disengaged, committed only to its own form, literature cannot support the theses necessary to a political program.

We would be mistaken to situate Blanchot too closely to the purge trials. Blanchot never openly took a position on any of the trials. He never publicly took a stand on Brasillach's trial, for example; his name does not appear on the petition circulated in favor of the author by Mauriac, nor do we know that he refused to sign it. We cannot reduce Blanchot's theory of literature to an attempt at self-exculpation; he never had any of what the French euphemistically called *"ennuis"* at the Liberation. Furthermore, Blanchot is situating his ideas in literary history and not in the political events; his references in arguing for a writer's irresponsibility are Valéry and Mallarmé, not Rebatet and Céline. Still, Blanchot is connecting with a discourse generated by the purge. When he denounces the "trial of art" and praises irresponsibility, Blanchot is unmistakenly working not only against Sartre but against an entire literary field that included the purge tribunals, Resistance intellectuals, and the National Writers' Committee blacklists. Without ever displaying indulgence for collaborationist writers, Blanchot is bucking a trend that had dominated French letters since the end of the war. Blanchot's 1949 essay subtly undoes or at least puts into question the credo of a writer's responsibility, a credo that had spread in the months following the Liberation of Paris and become a dogma by the end of the decade. Blanchot has not only stripped himself of fashionable trends, he is deeply committed to revising them. Herein lies the paradox. The more Blanchot distances himself from these trends, the more they seem to reappear in his work. On the literal level he is committed to declaring literature's autonomy from the political field. Allegorically, however, the essay is a coded reflection on precisely the historical event from which Blanchot is retiring. The movement of Blanchot's text is the exact opposite of Sartre's in "What Is Literature?" Sartre had called for literature's commitment to the historical event while ignoring or forgetting the very event—the purge—that generated his theory of committed literature. Blanchot claims to obviate the event and yet never stops asking his reader in 1949 to reflect upon the theories of literature inspired by the purge. In this sense Blanchot's essay is as much a response to the postwar purge as was Sartre's.

Every time Blanchot moves away from history, it seems to pull him back. Shortly after having declared literature's autonomy from politics, he paradoxically turns to a political event in order to illustrate his theory. Literature, he writes in "Literature and the Right to Death," is akin to the French Revolution and the Terror of 1793. Both literature and revolution represent the moment when everything is possible, when absolute freedom reigns, when law, faith, and the state all slip into the void. These are "fabulous moments," Blanchot writes, when the boundary between reality and fable blurs and the writer, like the revolutionary, needs only a few words to change the world. Blanchot's enthusiasm reaches its peak when he claims that the Terror of 1793, because it transformed everyone into a suspect, because it gave to the citizens the right to death (*"le droit à la mort"*) also opened up the possibility of total freedom. "The Terrorists are those who, because they want absolute freedom, know that they want their death" (310). One writer at the time embodied the total freedom of the Revolution and the Terror: the Marquis de Sade, an aristocrat incarcerated in the Bastille, "perpetually imprisoned and absolutely free, a theoretician and symbol of absolute liberty" (311).

What are we to make of Blanchot's historical analogy? How can we interpret his example of an imprisoned writer to illustrate literature's absolute freedom? At the beginning of this chapter we saw how Jeffrey Mehlman traced the links between the rhetorical terror in Blanchot's 1942 essay "How Is Literature Possible?" and his calls in the prewar articles for a political terrorism against the left-wing government of Léon Blum. Steven Ungar has also established a genealogy from Blanchot's political writings to his criticism. According to Ungar, Blanchot's January 1937 article titled "De la Révolution à la littérature," published in the right-wing journal *L'Insurgé*, is Blanchot's "initial draft of the theorizing of literature and culture" (Ungar, *Scandal and Aftereffect,* 113). Literature for Blanchot is self-contained, but it is also revolutionary by "its oppositional force" (114). Ungar claims that in 1937 Blanchot "seemed still to privilege politics—associated . . . with reactionary nationalist revolution—over literature," but at the same time, Blanchot "set literature apart . . . from the short-term events associated with politics" (114). As for "Literature and the Right to Death," published in the late 1940s, Ungar concludes that it "transposed onto literature the capacity to negate and change that Blanchot had ascribed a decade earlier to revolution in the name of a new French nation" (123).

As convincing as this retroactive reading is, an analysis of Blanchot's essay in relation to its contemporary intertexts provides us with another clue to understanding this complex essay. From the beginning of "Literature and the Right to Death" Blanchot has hinted at the importance of Sartre's "What Is Literature?" and if we keep this text in mind, we discover that Blanchot may again be proposing a revision of Sartre. In "What Is Literature?" Sartre praises the "revolutionary" writers of eighteenth-century France, draws a comparison between Rousseau and Richard Wright, and ends with an exhortation to writers in 1947 to join the socialist cause and write for the proletarian revolution: "we must militate, in our writings, in favor of the freedom of the person *and* the socialist revolution" (Sartre, *What Is Literature?* 223). Sartre puts forth this conclusion only after having established a system for judging the reactionary literary work; in the sequence of his essay the political commitment of the revolutionary writer in 1947 follows the purge of the irresponsible intellectual. Sartre was not alone in associating literature, revolution, and the purge. From *L'Esprit* to *L'Humanité* writers called for revolution. By the end of the war this association had become one of the favorite themes of

French intellectual life, at least among left-wing activists. As one observer noted, the success of a socialist revolution depended upon the success of the purge: "we felt from the early days of the Resistance that the purge was intimately linked to the success of this revolution that liberated France had to accomplish (Domenach, "La Justice," 184–93). While leftist commentators consistently rewrote the postwar years as a new Revolution, opponents of the purge answered these calls to revolution in postwar France by comparing the purge to the Terror of 1793: writers from Maurras to Marcel Aymé used the analogy of the Terror to denounce what they saw as the arbitrary justice and escalating violence of the purge. The French Revolution and the Terror, then, were references that circulated from text to text as authors recast the ideological struggles of the purge in historical terms.

It is my contention that these contemporaneous associations are also at work in Blanchot's references to the Revolution and the Terror. Read in this light, Blanchot's assertions both echo and dismantle the postwar revolution Sartre and a number of Resistants were promoting, for the revolution Blanchot proposes negates the possibility of any real political action, it is "negation itself" (Blanchot, *La Part,* 311). Literature does not militate for the revolution, rather, "literature contemplates itself in the revolution" (311). In Blanchot's postwar essay revolution and terror are part of literary rhetoric. At the very moment when literature names reality—and thus attempts to alter it— literature also eliminates reality: "The word gives me what it signifies, but first it eliminates it" (312).

One of the pitfalls of reading Blanchot's criticism as the neurotic repetitions of an initial traumatic encounter with fascism is that it ignores Blanchot's commitment to the debates of postwar France. Claims that Blanchot is rewriting his prewar articles in his postwar literary theory must take into consideration the fact that he is also propelling himself into the arguments surrounding the status of literature in 1949. Far from ignoring the fashion of the day, Blanchot's essay constantly returns to the issues that are haunting postwar French intellectuals. The lesson he draws from the Occupation, however, is radically different from the one presented by the Resistance writers. By associating literature and revolution, Blanchot is disarming both and denying them the capacity to change the world.[12]

"In 1793, there is one man who identifies perfectly with the Revolution and the Terror. He is an aristocrat, attached to the crenels of his medieval castle, a tolerant man, rather timid and of an obsequious politeness: but he writes" (Blanchot, *La Part*, 311). This writer is Sade, and with Blanchot's reference to Sade we are once again in the world of paradoxes and aporias. As Blanchot tells it, Sade is free in his chains, incarcerated because of his freedom, and thrown into prison by the disciples of liberty. Along with these paradoxes there is an accumulation of intertextual resonances. Blanchot's fascination with Sade echoes that of other writers such as Paulhan, Georges Bataille, and Pierre Klossowski, who saw the author of *Justine* as the embodiment of the transgressive spirit. Though many of these writers had discovered Sade before the war, his work benefited from renewed interest in the postwar years, an interest that may have found its impetus in Jean-Jacques Pauvert's decision to begin publishing Sade's complete works in 1947. For these writers Sade offers a counterexample to Sartre's eighteenth-century ideal, Voltaire, for if Voltaire defended Jean Calas and inspired Danton, Sade had a much more problematic relation to justice, to the Revolution, and to its calls for freedom. For all these writers, Blanchot included, Sade represents a freedom from moral judgment and the juridical gaze at the moment when he is condemned and incarcerated. Freedom is no longer an escape from political tyranny; it is now a transgression through writing that situates itself in opposition to repressive state apparatuses.

At a time when France is still resonating from the execution and incarceration of writers, Blanchot is arguing for the absolute freedom of the writer, a freedom that neither censors nor judges can suppress. The writer remains free in spite of the verdict imposed upon him, for writing responds to a principle of ambiguity that defies the law. One

---

[12]See Allan Stoekl's reading of Blanchot's novel *Le Très-Haut* as a "forgetting" of the revolutionary and totalitarian state in both its fascist and Stalinist forms. Stoekl, *Politics*, 22–36.

often has the impression of Blanchot as a lone voice, crying in the wilderness. His declarations about the writer's freedom, however, coincide with an important editorial direction at *Critique*: an absolute and total defense of the artist's right to expression and a condemnation of all forms of censorship. A few months after the liberation of France Bataille, the founder of *Critique*, had published an article in *Combat* defending Nietzsche's work against accusations of fascism: "[Nietzsche] claims to be distant from all political parties of his time and refuses in advance appropriation from all sides . . . the domain of Nietzsche's thought is located beyond the necessary and common worries that determine politics" (Bataille, "Nietzsche est-il fasciste?"). Two years later Bataille wrote an editorial for *Critique* defending Henry Miller, who had recently been condemned for obscenity by the French courts (Bataille, "L'Inculpation d'Henry Miller"). In another article of the same year Benjamin Goriely issued a strong condemnation of the "recent purge" of writers in the Soviet Union (Goriely, "La Politique," 475–80). During these years *Critique* editorialized in favor of a literary freedom that, in fact, is closer to American models of freedom of opinion than to the rights French writers have traditionally enjoyed. A case in point: in 1946 at *Critique*'s rival literary journal, *Les Temps modernes*, Sartre was actively supporting the penalties brought against collaboration writers and did not denounce Soviet purges until much later.

An article on Nietzsche, another on Henry Miller, a third on Soviet literary policy all argue on behalf of writers and texts facing censorship and some sort of purge. But what of Blanchot, Sade, and the postwar purge in France? Again Blanchot does not directly refer to the trials and blacklists, the debates and accusations of the purge, but his essay "Literature and the Right to Death" may be speaking of these events through indirection. Sade's comeback, as it were, in the immediate postwar years is tied not only to Pauvert's edition of his complete works but to a reflection on the relation between Sade and fascist violence. Klossowski, one of Sade's champions before the war, made precisely this connection when, in a footnote to the 1947 edition to his work *Sade, mon prochain*, he writes that the "Nazi experience" systematized the crimes of Sade's lawless world (cited in Hol-

lier, *The College of Sociology*, 417). In November 1945 Raymond Queneau described Sade's world as a "hallucinatory precursor to the
world of the Gestapo, of its tortures and its camps" (Queneau,
Bâtons, 199). Pier Paolo Pasolini had the same link in mind when in
his 1975 film *Salo* he turned Sade's *120 Days of Sodom* into a model for
the last days of Italian fascism. Blanchot's Sade is not Pasolini's.
Nonetheless, the terms he uses to describe the writer, his claim that
Sade is "negation itself" and that he has an unrelenting capacity to
"deny others, deny God, deny Nature" (Blanchot, *La Part,* 311)—
these are terms usually reserved to characterize fascist writers in the
postwar years. One need only consult Sartre, who spoke of the
"universal conflagration" (Sartre, *What Is Literature?* 163) in the novels of Drieu la Rochelle or the "collective suicide" he saw in Céline's
works (Sartre, "Portrait de l'antisémite," 462). It seems clear that
Blanchot's essay is not an apology for fascist violence. Blanchot is not
resurrecting Sade out of some sort of nostalgia for his own past involvement with the far right. Blanchot uses Sade to make a theoretical
point, that all literary acts bring us closer to ambiguity, silence, and
death. Sade is the writer who reminds us that literature is "an endless
rehashing of words without content" (Blanchot, *La Part,* 320). But
the choice of Sade as a literary model also serves to reintegrate Blanchot's texts in the debates of his time and to undermine certain values
that are at work in the French literary field during the purge. In
claiming that Sade "denies others," Blanchot negates Sartre's definition of literature as the meeting of two subjectivities. In claiming that
Sade represents absolute freedom, Blanchot is also positioning himself on the side of the writers at *Critique* who are engaged against
forms of censorship. In making Sade the centerpiece of his thought in
1949, Blanchot is writing an allegory that serves to dismantle any understanding of literature as an event that can be regulated by censors,
sentenced by tribunals, or judged by critics.

For Simone de Beauvoir, Sade "approves of the vendetta but not
of the tribunals: one has the right to kill but not to judge" (de Beauvoir, *Faut-il brûler Sade?* 79). The same might be said for Blanchot,
whose long essay on Lautréamont, published in 1949 by the Editions
de Minuit, develops his critique of judgment. *Lautréamont et Sade*

begins with a point-by-point refutation of different critical approaches to the literary text; what Blanchot calls textual commentary has the disadvantage of fixing the work's meaning and suspending its textual play (Blanchot, *Lautréamont et Sade,* 10); source studies all too often destroy the obscurity necessary to the literary work (20–25). For Blanchot none of these approaches misses the mark quite as seriously as Sartre's, who, in his *Baudelaire,* had described Baudelaire's life and poetry as a quest for a judgment the critic all too readily provides. According to Blanchot, as the critic illuminates the literary work, he is also revealing his own torments, a striking conclusion from the champion of impersonality:

> The critic is obviously implicated [*en cause*] in the work he contemplates, and the translation of the work that he gives, the secret he seeks, the meanings he avoids are all signs that he is not transparent to himself and that the daylight he has generously thrown on the tormented writer is also the reflection of his own gloom and an alibi for his torments (Blanchot, *Lautréamont et Sade,* 31).

Criticism, Blanchot tells us, must be read on at least two levels: literally, as the critic sheds light on the text, and allegorically, as a reflection of the critics own "torments." The critic's commentary is as much a reflection of his own subjectivity as it is of the text's workings, and this self-reflection has, for Blanchot, a practical effect: it nullifies his capacity to issue decisive judgments on the literary work. The critic finds himself in the untenable position of being both an objective witness (*"le témoin hors de cause"*) and an impassioned suspect (*"un accusé plein de passion"*) (33); he is both accuser and accused, victim and executioner. The reader who tries to pass as a judge, or even as a witness for the prosecution, is thus caught in a revolving door that confuses critic and writer, prosecutor and defendant. His attempt to claim moral purity casts shadows on his own morals, and any attempt to judge has the contrary effect: "to aspire to justice, is to assume the power to judge with which injustice begins" (32). What began as an essay on Lautréamont has turned into a critique of Sartre's *Baudelaire.* The essay that proposed a decisive reading of *Les Chants de Maldoror* has turned into a declaration of the text's undecidability. Or rather, according to Blanchot, the act of judging always includes an injustice. In a move intended to nullify any "trial of art," Blanchot has radically separated the role of the critic from the function of the judge. He has attempted to liberate literature from the tribunal Sartre constructed for it in 1947.

Blanchot's conclusion that Sartre "judges too much" (33) fills only a few pages of a 200-page study, but its significance reaches far beyond the essay's introductory remarks. Blanchot seems once again to be responding to the purge trials, and his comments are akin to those made by critics of the purge who reproached self-declared "responsible" writers for having donned the judge's robe. Among these critics Jean Paulhan stands out for his attacks against the proponents of a literary purge. In *De la paille et du grain*, published in 1948, Paulhan attempts to nullify the judgments of the purge courts by arguing for historical relativism. The collaborators of the Nazis, he writes, are being judged by collaborators of the Soviets (Paulhan, *De la paille*, 121). Their judgment is based on hypocrisy, on a singular injustice. Several years later Paulhan reiterates these claims when he states that the entirety of the purge, from start to finish, was an injustice; the collaborators, in his words, "were never judged," and the trials of the purge showed nothing so much as a singular "contempt for Law and Justice" (Paulhan, *Lettre aux directeurs*, 12–13). As for the writers of the CNE, Paulhan uses the same terms employed by Blanchot: Aragon, Eluard, Sartre, and Vercors "judge too much" (48). For the occasion Paulhan coins the term *surpeser*, to overweigh, to overevaluate. *Soupeser* means to ponder, to weigh judiciously; *surpeser* means that the writers who have constructed a tribunal for literature judge too much. Blanchot's attacks are less direct than Paulhan's; they remain within the confines of the literary space. And yet his argument against judgment, his exploration of what he calls "the Sartre case," inevitably reinscribes itself in opposition to the judge of the "Baudelaire case" and within the debates and divisions of the purge archive.

Just as Blanchot may have used Sade as a riposte to Sartre's Voltaire, we are led to think that he may have chosen to write on Lautréamont, the poet who follows and to a certain extent rewrites Baudelaire, in order to respond to and to rewrite Sartre's study of the author of *Les Fleurs du mal,* published just three years before. Indeed, in the first part of his essay Blanchot pretends to put Lautréamont on trial according to the criteria of Sartre's *Baudelaire.* Predictably Blanchot is unable to obtain a verdict, which leads him to cast Lautréamont as a writer who both stages and disrupts the possibility of judgment. When in *Les Chants de Maldoror* Lautréamont feigns to distance himself from his text and judge it, this judgment does not so much illuminate the text as form an integral part of the writing. The distances (*écarts*) Lautréamont establishes in commenting upon his work are part of the textual performance; as Blanchot puts it, "the distances . . . are the work itself" (Blanchot, *Lautréamont et Sade,* 18). Furthermore, whereas Sartre's Baudelaire compensates for his fascination with evil by seeking the judgment of authority figures—his parents, his mistress, the bourgeoisie, the courts—Lautréamont remains morally ambiguous. In Blanchot's terms Lautréamont naturally tends toward good (*"une tendance naturelle à la bonté"*) (44), yet it is precisely at the moment when he struggles against evil that he suddenly throws himself into its embrace (45). Any attempt to judge the character Maldoror on moral grounds encounters an irresolvable ambiguity: Maldoror is both cruel and kind, aggressive without intention, passive without consent, attracted to evil, and repulsed by it (48). Above all, Lautréamont's work defies judgment as Maldoror's every act has its moral counterpart and each verdict is undermined by the poet's irony. In Lautréamont's poetry and in Blanchot's essay literature both performs and neutralizes the critic's role as judge.

The second movement in Blanchot's reading of Lautréamont comes near the end of his essay. Blanchot recalls how, near the end of his brief life, Lautréamont turned the judgmental gaze on himself and in 1870 attempted to radically change directions. Once again the events are put under the sign of the trial: Lautréamont's editor feared being brought to court by the state and heard the distant footsteps of the "prosecuting attorney" (198). Due to this and to the commercial failure of *Les Chants de Maldoror,* Lautréamont decided to transform himself. Blanchot quotes a letter from Lautréamont to his banker in which the poet promised to stop singing about sadness, melancholy, death, *ennui*—all the themes that make up *Les Chants de Maldoror*—

and to devote himself to the new themes of hope, calm, and happiness: "I have completely changed methods, and I only sing *hope, expectation*, Calm, *happiness*, Duty" (199). Through his study of Lautréamont, Blanchot has led us to a confession. Under the surveillance of the prosecuting attorney, faced with a hostile public, the poet has begun to expurgate his own work, replacing sadness, melancholy, and death with what Blanchot calls a "clear classical vision" (201). The classic writer meets the censored poet as Lautréamont vows to his banker to purify his writing. Blanchot shows us a Lautréamont who, spurred by his publisher's fear of litigation, has rid his texts of their "negation" (200). Blanchot shows us a writer who has undergone a purge.

As we might have anticipated, it is precisely at the moment when Lautréamont reaches this new, purified state that his resolutions begin to go awry. Behind the confession that Blanchot hears, and asks the reader to listen to, Blanchot also distinguishes what he calls a "mocking voice" (204) that subverts the proclaimed conversion and disrupts the confession. As soon as Lautréamont commits himself to a new path, "the path begins to oscillate strangely" (204), and order gives way to chaos. The judgment Lautréamont bears on his work reveals itself to be false and only serves to reassert the principles the poet seemingly was repudiating. The text reasserts its ironic principle at the very moment it seemed most sincere, and this then is one of the final lessons of Blanchot's essay on Lautréamont: even when the text makes the most heartfelt plea, it escapes the order, rigor, and stability of judgment.

In his essay on Lautréamont, Blanchot wrote that a work's obscurity is often protected by the ignorance of its sources (20). One of the sources of Blanchot's work is the postwar purge of fascist and collaborationist intellectuals. If Sartre's postwar literary theory is a response to the purge, Blanchot's work is that of a double agent of sorts, who asks us to reflect on the historical event while veiling this event from his work. Rather than being read as the repetition of an earlier trauma, however, Blanchot's texts benefit from being recontextualized and situated in relation to the different positions adopted in the late

1940s. If the "purge" is in Blanchot's work, as de Man claimed, it is not because he eliminated all political concerns from his thinking but because, at least in the immediate postwar years, he constantly returned to this point of intersection between the space of literature and the site of the tribunal.

CHAPTER 4

Eluard:
Purging Poetry

Paul Eluard's war poetry has fallen out of fashion today, at least among readers in the United States. It is considered less provocative than the work of the Communist poet Louis Aragon, less complex than the poetry of René Char, less of a modernist exercise than Francis Ponge's *Soap*. While his surrealist poetry still finds its way into anthologies and critical studies, Eluard's political poems appear too naïve to generate much passion. Even among scholars of Resistance poetry Eluard is more apt to elicit admiration for his stance than interest in his work. Yet throughout World War II Eluard's poems were among the most celebrated in Europe. They were set to music by various composers, including Francis Poulenc, published in all the Resistance journals, read and sung on the BBC, and dropped by British planes into the awaiting hands of Occupied France. By 1941 Eluard had converted from surrealism to a politically committed poetry, and his voice became synonymous with the struggles of the French Resistance. Eluard's poetry of the time glorifies and glamorizes the themes and goals of the partisans fighting on mainland France: revolt, sacrifice, collective action, nationalist fervor, a denunciation of the horrors of the Occupation, a renewed faith in the Communist party, and a rediscovery of what Eluard called "freedom of expression."[1] Eluard saw his poetry as both testimony and direct action, a necessary and heroic step in the struggle to liberate France from Nazi oppression. According to his friend and political ally Aragon, at the time "nothing infuriated Eluard more than the concept of *art for art's sake*" (Aragon, *L'Homme communiste*, 130). But while a poem such as his 1942 "Liberty" reconciles political action in the form of "freedom of expression" and the poetic act, Eluard also wrote a set of darker, more foreboding poems dedicated to the purge, which shatter the image of the gentle, humanist poet and still today pose a series of problems in the relation between poetry and the political event. The importance of the purge in Eluard's thought can be seen in the articles he published in *Les Lettres françaises;* in the poems collected in *Au rendez-vous allemand*, a slim volume first published by the Editions de Minuit in 1944; and in the 1946 poem *Uninterrupted Poetry*, a 687-line text that plays with the tradition of epic narrative, incorporates several voices, borrows from a number of different poetic techniques, and has been called the apogee of Eluard's work as a poet.[2] Of all the writers in this study Eluard is the most enthusiastic about the purge. His calls for revenge reveal an author who, like the party he belonged to, considered that the punishment of treasonous writers was a necessary step in the transition from Resistance to Revolution. Eluard's purge poetry mobilizes the different themes and lexical registers, the sentiments and objectives of the Communists at the end of the war. But these poems are not only a response to the purge; they also force us to think about how the purge, like acid etchings on a metal plate, inscribed itself onto the very form of poetic discourse in the postwar years.

[1]In a 1952 speech Eluard stated that the goals of his Resistance poetry were "to rediscover, in order to harm the Occupiers, freedom of expression." Quoted in Seghers, *La Résistance*, 181.

[2]Vernier, *"Poésie ininterrompue,"* 10. Eluard, *Au rendez-vous allemand* and *Poésie ininterrompue*. The texts I refer to as the "purge poems" include the following: "Les Belles Balances de l'ennemi"; "Un Petit Nombre d'intellectuels français s'est mis au service de l'ennemi"; "Tuer"; "Comprenne qui voudra"; "Les Vendeurs d'indulgence"; "Noël, les accusés de Nuremberg sont en vacances." Unless otherwise indicated, I have used the English translations of these poems in *Uninterrupted Poetry*.

Eluard's interest in political poetry and what André Breton disparagingly called *"poésie de circonstance"* dates from before the war. In a December 1937 issue of *L'Humanité* Eluard published the poem "November 1936," a protest against Franco's seizure of power in Spain. With the war came a heightened commitment to poetry as political action. In September 1939 Eluard, a veteran of World War I, was drafted, narrowly escaped being captured during the battle for France, and returned to Paris shortly after the armistice in June 1940 to continue his writing. In 1941 he published a collection of poems, *Sur les pentes inférieures*, with a preface by Jean Paulhan, whom he had met in 1918. These poems were the first Eluard wrote under the Occupation, and though they are not all political poems, they are nonetheless the beginning of Eluard's intensive activity as one of the intellectual Resistance movement's most prolific authors. During this period Eluard published well over 100 poems, most of which appeared, sometimes many times over, in Resistance publications. Under a variety of pseudonyms Eluard published in *Fontaine*, *Cahiers du Sud*, *Cahiers de la Libération*, Pierre Segher's *Poésie*, *La France Libre*, *L'Humanité*, and *Les Lettres françaises*. In the spring of 1942 he joined the Communist party, and in February of the following year he strengthened these ties by attending the meetings of the CNE, the National Writers' Committee, along with Aragon, François Mauriac, Raymond Queneau, Sartre, and Edith Thomas. His renewed political commitment was supported by a new friendship. In 1942 Eluard was reconciled with Aragon, whom he had stopped seeing, ironically enough, when Aragon had left the surrealists and joined the party in the early 1930s.[3]

Eluard participated in two major publications of the Resistance, the Editions de Minuit, the clandestine publishing house responsible for bringing out Vercors's *Le Silence de la mer* and the review *Les Lettres françaises*, and he brought to both his literary talents and a re-

[3]For Eluard's activities as a member of the Resistance see Seghers, *La Résistance*. See also the preface and the chronology by Lucien Scheler in Eluard, *Œuvres complètes*, vol. 1.

newed faith in the Communist party.[4] It was in his position as literary director at Minuit that Eluard edited the famous volume of Resistance poetry *L'Honneur des poètes* (*The honor of poets*), which was released on 14 July 1943 and which included works by writers such as Aragon, Robert Desnos, Eugène Guillevic, Ponge, Lucien Scheler, Thomas, and Vercors.[5] Though in his introduction to the collection Eluard writes that "poets have come to us from every region of France," most of them were associated with either the Communist party, the Editions de Minuit, *Les Lettres françaises*, or all three.

As a member of the National Writers' Committee, Eluard also began publishing in *Les Lettres françaises*. His first contribution, the poem "Courage," dated 1942 and published in 1943, tells of the hardship of the Occupation in Paris during the winter of 1941–42 and laments the miseries of the city and its inhabitants. "Paris is cold Paris is hungry" (*"Paris a froid Paris a faim"*) begins this celebrated text. The poem also sketches the basic movement of many of Eluard's poems during the war: a reversal, or even a revolution, from night to dawn, from misery to triumph, from slavery to emancipation, from oppression to freedom.[6] Near the end of the poem Eluard writes, "And once again it is morning a Paris morning/The point of deliverance [*Et c'est de nouveau le matin un matin de Paris/La pointe de la délivrance*]".

Very quickly Eluard's contributions to *Les Lettres françaises* turn to the specific concerns of the purge. First his occasional articles, then his poetry begin to reflect the review's claim that "saving the honor of French letters" was indissociable from "thrashing" the French writers who were at the service of the enemy. An article published anonymously by Eluard with Claude Morgan and Edith Thomas during the summer of 1943 denounces Drieu la Rochelle and Ramon Fernandez, the editors of the *Nouvelle Revue française* (NRF), which, in their

---

[4]According to Anne Simonin, Eluard was at least in part responsible for bringing the Editions de Minuit into the Communist fold. Simonin, *Les Editions de Minuit,* 121.

[5]Eluard, ed., *L'Honneur* (my translation).

[6]"Courage" was published anonymously in *Les Lettres françaises,* Jan.–Feb. 1943.

words, existed solely to demonstrate that "French culture has adapted itself well to the Nazi regime." Another article from the same issue attacks Bernard Fay, the anti-Semitic and anti-Masonic professor at the Collège de France, for having claimed that an excess of women readers disturbed the serious scholars in the Bibliothèque nationale.[7] When in the following issue Eluard chastises a group of "so-called intellectuals" for opposing the poetry of the Resistance, he is again referring to Drieu and the NRF and to collaborationist literary circles. Of Eluard's articles in the early issues of *Les Lettres françaises*, only one, a condemnation of the treatment of French women at Auschwitz, is not a direct attack on the intellectuals engaged in the collaboration.[8] But even this text, which is one of the first in the clandestine press to mention Auschwitz, serves to establish a poignant contrast between the French women who have been deported and those who are entertaining the enemy troops in their literary salons. On the whole Eluard's prose pieces in *Les Lettres françaises* target the literary establishment, and in their eagerness to accumulate charges against the collaborationist intellectuals, these short editorials offer a vivid preview of the denunciations and sanctions brought against Vichyite writers by the CNE at the end of the war.

If, during the first years of the Occupation, Eluard had been concerned with proclaiming poetry's freedom, starting in 1943 his poems begin to participate, through both their themes and their form, in the process of purging the collaborators. Many of the poems Eluard wrote from 1943 to 1945 are accusatory texts of a surprising violence, more belligerent by far than his celebrated Resistance poems such as "Liberty" or "Courage." These poems continue the attacks on the collaborators begun in the editorials for *Les Lettres françaises*, and as they draw upon the accusations of treason and deviance leveled against the Vichyites, they also transform themselves into tribunals, mimicking a juridical rhetoric in an attempt to supplant the trials.

Perhaps more than any other writer of his generation Eluard was a

[7]Eluard, Morgan, and Thomas, "L'Agonie"; "L'Esprit de la maison." For more information on Bernard Fay, see Ory, *Les Collaborateurs,* 148.
[8]Eluard, "L'Esprit de suite"; "L'Etendard."

poet of desire. Throughout his career he tied writing to a reflection on love and sexuality and, in a sense, his wartime poetry is no different. But in the poems of *Au rendez-vous allemand* this writing of desire intersects with what became one of the main themes of the purge, namely, the understanding of the collaborators' treason in terms of sexual infidelity and deviance. From the very title of his collection Eluard draws upon the links between patriotism and sexuality in the discourse of the time. What indeed is this *German rendezvous*? *Rendezvous* connotes an appointment, in the sense of a challenge, which Germany has set and which France, or at the very least Eluard, is answering in the form of the Resistance. At the same time, however, *rendezvous* invariably carries the meaning of an assignation, an illicit sexual meeting between France and Germany, which was one of the widely circulating metaphors for the Occupation. In this case the Resistant poet sees his role as interdicting this *rendez-vous galant* and saving not just the "honor" of France but her sexual reputation as well. In choosing the title *Au rendez-vous allemand,* Eluard is assigning to himself a double role: to meet the challenge of the Occupier and to interrupt the collaboration.

The poems in this collection constantly draw on sexual metaphors in their fight against the Nazis. In "Seven Love Poems at War," published in 1943, love and sensuality assure the triumph of the martyrs of the Resistance:

> But we have always been in love
> And because we are in love
> We want to free others
> From their icy solitude.

> *Nous nous sommes toujours aimés*
> *Et parce que nous nous aimons*
> *Nous voulons libérer les autres*
> *De leur solitude glacée.*

In "Dawn Dissolves the Monsters" (*"L'Aube dissout les monstres"*) written the same year, the night of terror imposed by the Nazis gives way to a new dawn and the "kiss of the living [*le baiser des vivants*]." Throughout his wartime poetry Eluard presents a historical dialectic in which women, desire, and sensuality guarantee access to freedom, harmony, and equality. The rediscovery of love and the eroticized image of women—albeit a safe eroticism—permits the transition from Occupation to Liberation, from oppression to freedom. Eluard is, in part, repeating a cliché of his party; communist writers of the postwar period liked to cast political commitment in terms of sexual desire. In Aragon's novel *Les Communistes*, for example, secret political meetings often have the erotic charge of a tryst. Indeed, the plot of this multivolume work is built around the illicit romance of two characters who together discover love . . . and communism. For Eluard sexual and political solidarity remain closely tied to the issues of the purge. *Uninterrupted Poetry*, the 1946 poem, is in part a narrative that traces the progression from Occupation to Liberation and from Liberation to Revolution. In the last strophe the narrative voice returns to the metaphor of desire that is present from the very beginning of the poem: "The two of us live only to be faithful/To life [*Nous deux nous ne vivons que pour être fidèles/A la vie*]." The poem culminates in a declaration of fidelity, a term that draws upon both the political and the sexual lexicons. "Faithful to life," the couple is also faithful to the revolution the poem has just prescribed. For all the pathos and emotion of this poem, however, for all its sentimentality and Communist kitsch there may be something else in Eluard's decision to end the poem on this note. "Faithful" almost invariably calls to mind its opposites: unfaithful or even treasonous. It is as if Eluard's *Uninterrupted Poetry* could reach neither closure nor the final stage in its march forward without closing the book on the trials of treasonous Frenchmen. The traitors in their infidelity are, Eluard tells us, emotional deviants.

If love and fidelity are the metaphors through which Eluard proclaims the triumph of the Resistance, hate and sexual deviance are his privileged terms for denouncing the Nazis and their collaborators. We saw how for many antifascist intellectuals as well as for the purge courts *collaboration* and *infidelity* became synonymous terms. From the *tonte* of women accused of having had German lovers to Sartre's claims that collaborationist intellectuals often came from the "homosexual milieu," the purge irremediably tied politics to sex (Sartre,

Situations III, 58). In the eyes of the *épurateurs*, wandering outside the borders of prescribed sexuality was tantamount to betraying France. Eluard's poetry, so tied to desire, denounces both the Nazis, because of their sadistic impulses, and the collaborators, because they are traitors, as emotional and sexual deviants. In "The Hostile Poem" (*"Le Poème hostile"*) Eluard denounces the Nazis—the "master"—who in 1944 are fleeing France and have fallen prey to the one emotion they know: hate. "The master in his turn takes flight / Devoured by hate [*Au tour du maître de s'enfuir / Dévoré par la haine*]." In "Dawn Dissolves the Monsters" Eluard writes that the collaborators "found a heart only at the end of their rifles [*Ils ne trouvaient de coeur qu'au bout de leur fusil*]." At the core of the Nazis' and the collaborators' political commitment, Eluard tells us, is hatred. But this isn't all. Eluard's ideal of fidelity is invariably straight, at least in his poems. Betrayal, for him, is always twisted. In "Seven Love Poems at War," while the Resistance is characterized through the metaphor of a reciprocated love affair, the "executioners" are accused of self-love: they are "the same lovers of themselves [*Les mêmes amants d'eux-mêmes*]." Certainly this phrase that turns back on itself, that ends up biting its tail, designates the Nazis and the French collaborators as egomaniacs, incapable of the kind of altruism, solidarity, and fraternity Eluard considered a constitutive part of the Communist Resistance. But through this somewhat twisted line, Eluard's poem also designates the "executioners" as practitioners of a perverted sexuality. "Lovers of themselves" can signify either that they are homosexuals—they love the same sex—or that they are onanists. They love each other, they love themselves. In either case Eluard designates the political enemy as someone who turns away from what he sees as social and sexual solidarity. In grammatical terms the intercourse of the Resistance is transitive. The eroticism of the collaboration is intransitive. For Eluard, as for the purge tribunals, trying the collaborators meant purging what they considered a dangerous sexuality. But this charge that the fascists and collaborators are "the same lovers of themselves" also repeats the claims of the tribunals, which tied sexuality to ethics and which saw the purge as an occasion to set straight the sexuality of the nation. Encountering this proliferation of sexual metaphors, one wonders if Eluard and the purge authorities were not as anxious to eliminate what they considered deviance as they were to purge what they saw as treason.

For all his enthusiasm in denouncing the Nazis and their collaborators, Eluard was horrified by the spectacle of the tonte, the shearing of French women accused of "horizontal collaboration." In the poem "Understand Who Will" (*"Comprenne qui voudra"*) he speaks of his "remorse" at seeing a woman victimized by this carnivalesque form of retribution.[9] The poem is full of pathos and sympathy for the victim:

> The poor girl left lying
> On the pavement
> The reasonable victim
> With a torn dress
> With the look of a lost child
>
> *La malheureuse qui resta*
> *Sur le pavé*
> *La victime raisonnable*
> *A la robe déchirée*
> *Au regard d'enfant perdu*

Eluard clearly identifies the girl as a prostitute and sees in her not a traitor but a victim of love. Eluard's denunciation of this aspect of the purge should not be confused with a plea for clemency. His poem is also about what he considered another major injustice of the purge. As he writes in the poem's epigraph: "At that time, in order not to punish the guilty, they maltreated prostitutes." If Eluard denounces the sheering of women, it is also in order to set things right, to do what "they" — the purge authorities — were not doing and "to punish the guilty."

The first poem Eluard wrote explicitly calling for the purge of treacherous intellectuals is the rather prosaically titled "A Small Number of French Intellectuals Have Put Themselves at the Service of the Enemy" (*"Un Petit Nombre d'intellectuels français s'est mis au service de l'ennemi"*), which appeared in the October 1943 issue of *Les*

---

[9]In his study *Les Tondues* Alain Brossat quotes and discusses this poem, 68–73.

Lettres françaises.[10] Written for the most part in octosyllabic verse, the twelve-line poem announces the end of the treasonous intellectuals' "reign" and calls for vengeance upon these lackeys of the Nazis:

Terrified terrifying
The time has come to count them
For the end of their reign is near

They praised our executioners
They sold us evil piecemeal
They said nothing innocently

Beautiful words of alliance
They veiled you with vermin
Their mouths open onto death

But now the time has come
To love and unite
To vanquish and punish them

The very first line of the poem shows the collaborators as somehow betrayed by their own treachery. They are "Terrified terrifying" (*"Epouvantés épouvantables"*) as if they had horrified themselves. Eluard's line is a reprise, of sorts, of the *arroseur arrosé* motif, as if the collaborators' terror had turned on themselves. "The same lovers of themselves" have become victims of their own hatred. They know that the end is near and now foresee their imminent punishment for the intellectual crimes, the crimes of language, they have all committed: "They praised our executioners/They sold us evil piecemeal [*Ils nous ont vanté nos bourreaux/Ils nous ont détaillé le mal*]." Just as Sartre will claim six months later in *Les Lettres françaises* that literature is not an "innocent fable," Eluard writes that the collaborators' words were not innocent: "They said nothing innocently . . . Their mouths open onto death [*Ils n'ont rien dit innocemment . . . Leur bouche donne sur la mort*]." Like most of what appeared in the pages of *Les Lettres françaises*, Eluard's earliest purge poems are directed against intellectual collaborators, those who have betrayed France, and the poem relies upon precisely the same conception of intellectual treason as the

[10]My translation.

purge courts: the collaborators' words were directly responsible for the torment of France and the death of French partisans. For Eluard, as for other intellectuals sympathetic to the Resistance, to write, to speak is to act. Writing for the collaboration, "praising the executioners," carries the same weight as performing an execution. And there is little doubt that Eluard also grants his poems the authority to secure victory and avenge France's losses.

"A Small Number of French Intellectuals ..." also activates the sexual metaphors that are constitutive of Eluard's poetry. The third tercet evokes the "Beautiful words of alliance" that the collaborators have "veiled with vermin." The collaborators are parasitic rather than productive and have betrayed both the ideal of brotherhood between two states—when Eluard speaks of alliance he may be referring to a union between France and Germany consummated under the guidance of the Communist party—and the ideal of a sexual union. Pétain's collaboration, Brasillach's alliance with the Nazis is a sort of *mésalliance*, one that can only, according to Eluard, end in death. Eluard's answer to the false alliance offered by the collaborationist intellectuals is an alliance based on love. He calls upon his readers "to love and unite" (*"s'aimer et s'unir"*) in order "to vanquish and punish" the collaborators. Love, it seems, is all you need. But the question of how Eluard's poems participated in the purge remains. What role did they define for themselves? In what way did they support Communist calls to action? To what extent did these poems engage in or retreat from political action in the form of the imprisonment, the indictment, and the execution of "a small number of French intellectuals"?

To answer these questions, we must turn to the context in which Eluard is publishing. Several of his poems first appeared in *Les Lettres françaises* and had an organic relation to this review, not only because the poet himself participated in its publication but also because the poems and the articles rely on one another for their full meaning. The very title of Eluard's poem "A Small Number of French Intellectuals ..." reads like a newspaper headline; it is descriptive, prosaic, and weighty as if the work were denying, however momentarily, its status as poem. We know that this title was dear to Eluard since he showed his displeasure when editors of the Resistance review *Fontaine* changed it to the more manageable *"Ils . . ."* (Eluard, *Œuvres complètes*, 1254). The lengthy title ensures the transition between the verse of the poem and the prose of the journalism that surrounds it. Furthermore, while Eluard's poem never names the collaborators in question, an article on the same page of the October 1943 issue fills in the blanks. This article, titled "Fear in Their Gut" (*"La Peur au ventre"*), details how Robert Brasillach, Paul Morand, and Ramon Fernandez, three of the writers constantly denounced by *Les Lettres françaises*, are all beginning to distance themselves from the collaboration—Brasillach by breaking with *Je suis partout*, Morand by taking a safe diplomatic position in Bucharest, and Fernandez by resigning from Doriot's fascist Parti populaire français. Here then are some of the intellectuals who "have put themselves at the service of the enemy." The poem and the article complement each other. One presents the crimes and pronounces the sentence, the other provides the names of the accused and the corroborating evidence. One claims that the collaborators are "terrified," the other that they have "fear in their gut." Eluard's poem thus belongs to a chain of texts and actions intended to identify, denounce, and ultimately punish the treasonous writers. As a poem it maintains the prestige of poetic language: while its title is prosaic, its status as a poem is almost overdetermined by Eluard's use of octosyllabic verses, though this, of course, does not necessarily mean that it is good poetry. At the same time this poem is part of a strategy against the collaborators that includes the pages of *Les Lettres françaises*, the blacklists published by the CNE at the end of the war, and the legal action taken by the purge courts against Vichyite intellectuals.

Unlike other members of the CNE, Eluard kept his distance from the purge tribunals; though he signed a manifesto in September 1944 asking for the "swift punishment of the traitors" (*Les Lettres françaises*, 9 Sept. 1944), he never publicly denounced specific writers once the trials were under way. After the Liberation he never editorialized about the purge, nor was he ever a member of the jury during a trial. Still, Eluard links the poetic act to the act of purging the nation. When in "A Small Number of French Intellectuals ... " he writes that "the time has come" to punish the traitors, the punishment he calls for is immediate. The word Eluard uses, *"voici"* (here and now), suggests that the poem, rather than the tribunal, might be the site where the sentences will be carried out. Another poem from the same period illustrates Eluard's conception of poetry as action. First published in *L'Honneur des poètes* and reprinted in both *Les Lettres françaises* and *Au rendez-vous allemand*, "The Beautiful Balances of the Enemy" (*"Les belles balances de l'ennemi"*) evokes the scales of justice and is constructed around the French expression *"faire justice de,"* which means to refute, to reject, and to punish. The poem's first lines tell of the oppression wrought by the Nazi occupiers: "Salutes punish our dignity/ Boots punish our walks/Imbeciles punish our dreams [*Des saluts font justice de la dignité/Des bottes font justice de nos promenades/Des imbéciles font justice de nos rêves*]."[11] Dignity, quotidian pleasures, and dreams have been destroyed by the forces of tyranny. In the last two verses, however, we witness a reversal and the prediction of both the liberation from this oppression and the punishment of its agents: "And we have retrieved our strength/We will punish evil [*Et nos forces nous sont rendues/Nous ferons justice du mal*]." Eluard appropriates the expression *"faire justice de"* and turns it against the enemy. The historical reversal to which the French Resistance was dedicated, from the Occupation to the Liberation, is inscribed into the syntagmatic reversal of the text. Liberation is now inseparable from revenge, as the balances, the scales of justice, announced in the title have been set aright. "The Beautiful Balances ... " makes clear something we sensed in earlier texts: Eluard's purge poems have become an idealized site to deliver verdicts and issue sentences. What is more, *"faire justice de"* is linked, through etymology, to the poetic act itself. At poetry's root we find *poiésis,* which gives us both *poetry* and more generally *creation,* and the French poetic tradition has long played on the pun linking the verb *faire* to the act of writing poetry.[12] Writing and doing justice become inseparable in the poems of *Au rendez-vous allemand.* Eluard's purge poetry reflects a quest for action, a desire to continue the Resistance

---

[11]My translation.

[12]One need only think of the liminary poem of Hugo's *Les Contemplations.* Standing on the shore, the poet hears the voice of God who tells him: "Poète, tu fais bien!"

credo that to speak is to act. But this act is no longer simply recapturing a freedom of expression; it is about turning this expression into a *sentence*, in the sense of both a judgment and a grammatical phrase. For the poet of the Resistance writing was doing; writing now means doing justice. While Eluard himself stayed away from the tribunals, his poems enact a judgment, let fall a verdict, and deliver the sentence.

Eluard's attempt to make his purge poems the very site of justice depends upon the use of symmetrical structures within the poems themselves. The first part of Eluard's purge poems outlines the crimes committed by the Nazis and their collaborators; the second reverses the situation and stages the punishment of the criminals. This structure is at work in "A Small Number of French Intellectuals ... " and in "The Beautiful Balances of the Enemy." This structure also governs, though in a somewhat more complicated way, the poem "Kill" (*"Tuer"*). First published in May 1944 in the second volume of *L'Honneur des Poètes*, "Kill" is both a violent and a melancholy work, which, while describing the numbness that accompanied the days leading up to the Liberation, also takes the reader from suffering to revenge:

> Tonight there falls
> A strange peace over Paris
> A peace of blind eyes
> Of dreams without color
> That hurl themselves against the walls
> A peace of useless arms
> Of vanquished faces
> Of absent men
> Of women already faded
> Pale cold and tearless
>
> Tonight there falls
> In the silence
> A strange glow over Paris
> Over the good old heart of Paris
> The muffled glow of crime
> Savage premeditated and pure
> Crime against butchers
> Against death.

As we begin to read, we immediately encounter several difficulties. What is this "strange peace over Paris"? Who are the men and women Eluard evokes in the first strophe? Do the "vanquished faces" belong to the Resistants or to the Nazis at the end of their reign? Are the "absent men" the Germans and Collaborators who have fled France or the Frenchmen who have been deported? The reader is faced with the type of ambiguity constitutive of the poetic text. And yet this ambiguity serves to introduce into the poem the principle of reversibility that is at the heart of Eluard's purge poetry. We are in May 1944, one month before D-Day; those who were once the victors will soon be vanquished, and the downtrodden are about to rise up in victory. The historical reversal is reinforced in the second strophe, when the poem appropriates the language of the enemy. Eluard had used this technique in the 1943 poem "Warning" (*"Avis"*), which not only denounces the warnings placarded by the Germans to announce the execution of hostages but turns into a warning against the Occupation forces. In "Kill," when Eluard qualifies "the muffled glow of crime" as "savage premeditated and pure," he is again adopting a strategy of redressing wrongs and of turning the tables on the oppressors. It is perhaps unusual for the Resistance to refer to its acts as "crimes," nor, of course, were the partisans in the habit of describing their acts as "savage" or "premeditated." Both these terms, however, do figure in Nazi and Vichy propaganda to condemn acts of the Resistance, and *savage* in particular became the adjective most commonly used to denounce the excesses of the purge.[13] By the time we reach the word *pure,* we realize that Eluard is lauding crimes committed in the name of the purge. By borrowing terms from the fascist register, by appropriating and redirecting their vocabulary, Eluard is not only calling for an uprising against the executioners, he is announcing a complete reversal of the historical situation. The repetition of the line "Tonight there falls [*Il tombe cette nuit*]" at the beginning of the first and second strophes calls to mind the juridical phrase *"le verdict est tombé,"* issued when the court has reached a ver-

[13]See, for example, the very title of Philippe Bourdel's recent study *L'Epuration sauvage 1944–1945.*

dict. "Kill" in this sense is a staging of the purge several months before the tribunals have begun to operate. The "muffled glow of crime" is, in fact, an act intended to cleanse France of the occupiers and their consorts, and if, after having read the last line, we return to the title we realize that the infinitive *tuer* is also an imperative pronouncing the collaborators' death sentence.

Several of Eluard's purge poems directly refer to the tribunals and express a deep-seated mistrust of the courts. In one of these poems, "Noël, the Accused at Nuremberg Are on Vacation" (*"Noël, les accusés de Nuremberg sont en vacances"*),[14] Eluard lists the horrors committed by the Nazis in order to condemn not only the war criminals but what Eluard sees as the laxity of the judges conducting the trials. The poem, probably written in December 1945, shortly after the beginning of the Nuremberg trials, attacks judges who are trying to delay the proceedings: "They want to stall / Forgetfulness will come dust / will cover the disorder [*Il leur faut gagner du temps / L'oubli viendra la poussière / Recouvrira le désordre*]." In another poem from this period, "The Sellers of Indulgences" (*"Les Vendeurs d'indulgence"*), first published in the 17 March 1945 issue of *Les Lettres françaises*, Eluard uses the structure of reversal to denounce the intellectuals who called for clemency during the purge: "Those who have no heart preach pardon to us," writes Eluard (the French original *"Ceux qui n'ont pas de coeur nous prêchent le pardon"* is a perfect alexandrine), and we cannot help but think that through this line, and through a title that recalls the Catholic Church's practice of "selling" forgiveness, Eluard is targeting Mauriac, who at the time had made several appeals for quarter, based on his conception of Christian charity. Indeed, accusing intellectuals and the provisional government of being "indulgent" toward the collaborators was a standard practice at *Les Lettres françaises*.[15] Later in the poem Eluard incorporates some of the arguments he is criticizing. "Listen to them they preach aloud," he writes, and then in a strophe composed of octosyllabic lines and set off by italics, to mark

---

[14]Published in the 1946 edition of *Au rendez-vous allemand*, this poem does not appear in subsequent reprints of the volume.

[15]See, for example, Morgan, "Les Indulgents."

its distance from the poet's voice, he reproduces these arguments, which begin with a case for historical and moral relativity so common during the defense of accused collaborators and degenerate into an apology of slavery:

> *Whether he resists or surrenders*
> *One general is worth another [...]*
> *And the more slaves the master has*
> *The more reasons to be master*

The poem answers this appeal for "indulgences" by evoking (in alexandrine) the forgotten victims of Vichy and the Nazis: "The women of Auschwitz the little Jewish children / Terrorists with a sharp eye the hostages [*Les femmes d'Auschwitz les petits enfants juifs/Les terroristes à l'oeil juste les otages*].*" The poem's final image is a call for vengeance:

> There is no stone more precious
> Than the desire to avenge the innocent
> There is no sky more brilliant
> Than the morning of a traitor's death
>
> *Il n'y a pas de pierre plus précieuse*
> *Que le désir de venger l'innocent*
> *Il n'y a pas de ciel plus éclatant*
> *Que le matin où les traitres succombent*

Vengeance is a gem, a precious stone, writes Eluard, adopting a metaphoric register at the moment when his poem seems most anchored in political reality. Rejecting arguments for charity and reinterpreting Christian terminology, Eluard presents the purge as a sort of secular redemption—he uses the term *salut*—that can only be accomplished through the punishment of the executioners: "There is no health [*salut*] on earth/While the butchers can be pardoned." "The Sellers of Indulgences" was published in March 1945, one month after Brasillach's execution, and it is impossible not to hear echoes of that trial in the poem. Not only did Mauriac petition de Gaulle in an attempt to save Brasillach's life, but the poem's line about Auschwitz and the Jewish children may also be a direct reference to Brasillach, who, in an infamous phrase, had called for the deportation of Jewish children from French soil.[16] To Mauriac's petition for clemency Eluard answers with a call for vindication, to his call for indulgence, he replies "vengeance." It might be an overstatement to say that "The Sellers of Indulgences" opens itself to a dialogue between the accusers and the accused. Rather it quotes the apology of collaboration in order better to refute it. Still, the poem stages a purge trial; it lets us hear the defense, reformulates the arguments of the prosecution, and calls for punishment. It is one of the most violent of Eluard's purge poems but also one of the most direct in its anticipation of courtroom proceedings.

As we read Eluard's purge poems, we begin to see the emergence of a pattern. Certainly this pattern reproduces Eluard's faith in a historical dialectic: oppression gives way to liberation, tyranny cedes to revolution, with "vengeance" playing a crucial role in assuring this transition. Nazi oppression has been overturned, and the balance of justice has been set aright. Eluard's poems constantly stage a reversal, a *renversement*, which, as Peter Novick remarked, dominated the Resistance mentality at the end of the war.[17] The trope equivalent to this *renversement* is the chiasma, the figure of inversion, and Eluard's purge poems are constructed according to this trope: the victors are vanquished, the executioners now face death, the language of the Nazis belongs to the Resistants. This chiastic structure is also the structure of the trial, as Eluard conceives of it in any case. In this respect Eluard's purge poems are structured like a trial. They present the evidence (the crimes committed by the Nazis and the collaborators), at times they allow for deliberation, and they issue the inevitable verdict (the execution of the "executioners"). Each poem repeats the same process, allowing only for small variations. The poems are more or

---

[16]In a 1942 article Brasillach called for the deportation of Jews in these terms: "we must completely separate ourselves from the Jews and must not keep the children ... *[il faut se séparer des Juifs en bloc et ne pas garder les petits ...]*" "Les Sept Internationales contre la patrie," *Je suis partout*, 25 Sept. 1942. See Michel Laval's discussion of this quotation in his book on the Brasillach trial (*Brasillach*, 118–19).

[17]"Resistance determination to see collaborators in the dock had more to do with a desire for *renversement* than with a desire for *renouvellement*." Novick, *The Resistance*, 140.

less precise in the designation of the criminals; they are more or less detailed in their presentation of the crimes; but they all follow this rigorous structure in which the crimes are denounced and the criminals punished. Furthermore, Eluard's use of traditional verse only adds to the rigor of this structure. The octosyllabic, decasyllabic, and alexandrine verse Eluard favors all draw upon principles of balance and harmony. Whereas a poem such as "Liberty" is based on a structure of repetition and substitution that could, theoretically, continue forever, each purge poem presents a variant or transformation of the same structure that has a clearly delineated beginning, middle, and end. The formal balance of the purge poems, both within individual verses and within the poems themselves, serves as a framework for an ethical balance that also goes under the names of justice, retribution, and revenge.

It is difficult to overestimate the extent to which *renversement*, or to be more blunt, revenge was a motor for the Communists during the purge. After Hitler's invasion of the Soviet Union in June 1941, the French Communists had regrouped and transformed themselves over the course of the war into what one historian has called "the single most unified and powerful force among all the metropolitan Resistance groups" (Tiersky, *French Communism,* 113). The Communists rapidly organized, created a political body, the National Front, and a group dedicated to carrying out military missions, the *Francs-Tireurs et Partisans*. After having called de Gaulle an "imperialist agent" of the "London bankers" in 1940, they nonetheless joined forces with him and decided out of opportunism or necessity to forgo their ambitions for a revolution. Still, they didn't forgo their hold on power in the postwar years, and the purge offered them an opportunity to solidify their base. Thousands of Communists were killed during the war, and though the figure of 75,000 executed often given by the party is an exaggeration, they nonetheless came out of the war bloodied and seeking revenge. The self-proclaimed *parti des fusillés,* the party of the executed, was much more violent in their calls for a purge than were the Gaullists. French Communists worked closely with the purge authorities, and many served as members of the juries during the trials. But the Communists were also extremely critical of what they saw as the laxity and indulgence of the purge courts and didn't hesitate to take the law into their own hands. Judging and condemning the collaborators became a communist imperative of sorts. The writer Claude Morgan went so far as to imply that judging collaborators was a sign of virility.[18] As Peter Novick writes, the Communists created an "image" of the hardest of hard-liners, the *"durs des durs."*[19]

In keeping with this image, the French Communist party created several paralegal groups whose task was to carry out their own brand of justice. In June 1944 they created the *Milices patriotiques*, made up of armed civilians entrusted with the power of purging fascists and collaborators. The Communists also set up a network of what they called *comités de vigilance*, a sort of neighborhood watch, whose role was to spy on, arrest, and, if necessary, punish suspected collaborators even before the purge tribunals had been established.[20] Ronald Tiersky has suggested that the Communists, along with a very real desire for vengeance, may also have been motivated by "an attempt to vacate sensitive positions of authority" that they could then fill with Communists (119). Whatever their motives, the Communists demanded a thorough purge and carried out that purge themselves when the situation demanded.

One can hardly open the pages of *L'Humanité* from this period without coming upon calls for retribution and a celebration of revenge. In September 1944, for example, the Central Committee of the French Communist party issued its three directives for the postwar period: the liberation of France, the empowerment of the people, and the swift punishment of the traitors.[21] Almost every day in the

[18]Morgan, "Refuser d'être juge ... c'est refuser d'être un homme." *Les Lettres françaises*, 11 Aug. 1945.
[19]Novick quotes headlines from *L'Humanité* protesting what the Communists believed to be the laxity of the purge courts. For the Communists "verdicts which were considered overly lenient were never 'ill-advised' . . . ; rather they were 'outrageous,' 'shocking,' or 'unbelievable.'" Novick, *The Resistance*, 179.
[20]"We must organize everywhere vigilance committees [*comités de vigilance*], in every neighborhood, in every street, in every building. These committees will check up on new renters and on suspect comings and goings." *L'Humanité*, 21 Aug. 1944.
[21]"Libérer la France, châtier les traîtres, donner la parole au peuple: tel est le

months following the Liberation *L'Humanité* published pictures of
notorious collaborators and called on its readers to apprehend or denounce these criminals on the lam. One such picture shows Laval
standing alone against a wall, as if he were awaiting the volley of the
firing squad. His hand rests in his vest, Napoleon style, and the picture bears the title "Bougnaparte," punning on *bougnat,* the sobriquet
given to coal salesmen from Laval's native region, the Auvergne. This
parody of the man *L'Humanité* called *"le misérable"* was created by a
self-styled "artist avenger" (*"artiste vengeur"*) as if a new category of
creator had replaced the Resistance poet or the worker intellectual
from another period.[22] Or again, at the end of September 1944,
L'Humanité ran an article condemning the "cozy" atmosphere at
Drancy, the infamous camp, which during the Occupation had been
the last stop of many Jews and Communists before deportation to
Auschwitz and which at the end of the war became a holding pen for
suspected collaborators. Calling the camp "Drancy-Palace" and accusing the collaborators of spending their time in prison "flirting,"
the author demands that they be punished in the name of the victims
of Nazi cruelty who "every day cry out for vengeance."[23] It is almost
as if the pages of *L'Humanité* were themselves laid out according to
the structure of vengeance that governs Eluard's poems. Directly under an editorial calling for the execution of Pétain, there is a picture of
a partially decomposed corpse, a victim the Nazis "didn't even bother
to bury" and whose miserable end, we are led to conclude, only
Pétain's death could avenge.[24] The Communists didn't have a mo-
nopoly on these calls for revenge, however. As I was researching this
subject, I came upon the Resistance card that had belonged to my

---

voeu du Parti Communiste exprimé hier par son Comité central." *L'Humanité,* 1
Sept. 1944. See also, for example, "Pour achever sa victoire, châtier les traîtres et
venger ses morts, le peuple en armes se bat sur le sol de la Patrie." *L'Humanité,*
4 Sept. 1944.

[22]*L'Humanité,* 3 Sept. 1944.

[23]"The 70,000 victims of Nazi barbarism cry out for justice. Those who are
still suffering and dying in German camps cry out for vengeance everyday."
Diquelon, "Drancy."

[24]Cogniot, "Pétain."

grandfather, an engineer at the Citroen plant, quai de Javel. The card is pink and slightly faded. It has spaces for the name, the address, a black-and-white photo, and the signature of the cardholder, Eugène Blaquart (he had, however, forgotten to sign it). In the center of the card there is the Croix de Lorraine, indicating that the group was Gaullist, and the card's heading bears the name of the Resistance group to which he belonged, Ceux de la Libération-Vengeance. It is as if in the final months of the war Liberation and revenge had become inseparable events. For the Communist party, they were. The sacrifice of many of its members during the Occupation and the subsequent calls for revenge became sacred acts on which the party based its legitimacy and its quest for power in the postwar years.

In this context it is difficult to see Eluard's poems as anything other than a direct reproduction of the calls for a popular justice issued by the Communist party. For all his love of humanity, from 1941, when in the poem "Patience" he first called for revenge, to 1946 Eluard was the proponent of a violent purge of fascists and collaborators. Aragon was right to call Eluard's poetry a "direct illustration" of the slogans of the Communists: the poet's voice is at the service of his party (Aragon, *L'Homme communiste*, 160). From the enumeration of the collaborators' crimes to his calls to "Kill," Eluard in every way toed the party line. Even his use of these poems as a site of justice can be read as a distrust of the purge courts. Creating a sort of literary *comité de vigilance*, Eluard's poems issue judgments independently of the purge tribunals. Still, Eluard was not writing slogans; indeed he rarely even published prose. His struggle was every bit as poetic as it was political. For the Resistance, poetry had a privileged status. It quickly became tied, both in the pages of *Les Lettres françaises* and in the popular imagination, to the prestige, to the "honor" of the nation. To publish a poem, for Eluard as well as for many others, was an act of personal courage and national pride. It was this prestige that made poems privileged vehicles of propaganda. But Eluard's poems are also a rich source for us in that along with their calls for revenge they initiate a reflection on form and on aesthetics, and while they are circumstantial, they also ask us to think about how poetry of circumstance may be intimately tied to the history of aesthetics.

Is there, then, a poetics of Eluard's purge poems? Does the poet reflect upon or ask the reader to reflect upon his project? What is the relation between Eluard's call to purge, indeed to kill, the collaborators and the lines of verse that vehiculate this call? Eluard's statements about the status of poetry are limited during the war years—the events call for action rather than theory, after all. Still, on several occasions Eluard sketches what he considers to be the poet's role and announces one of the major debates about aesthetics during the years of the purge. I want to begin this itinerary with several texts published by Eluard in the postwar years and then return to brief comments on the status of poetry that Eluard made during the Occupation. My starting point, then, is the preface to a 1947 collection titled *Deux Poètes d'aujourd'hui* [Two poets of today]. The two poets in question are Eluard and Aragon, who together decided to publish several of their poems after having refused to be included in an anthology of poetry compiled and edited by Jean Paulhan and Dominique Aury. The two poets are quite clear on their reasons: they refuse to publish with Paulhan, whose "views are foreign to them [*dont les vues leur sont diversement étrangères*]" (Eluard, *Œuvres complètes*, vol. 2, 141 [my translation]). The reference about the divergent—or rather "foreign"—views goes back, of course, to Paulhan's 1947 denunciation of the CNE blacklists and his defense of writers whom Eluard, Aragon, and other members of the National Writers' Committee considered to be traitors. In several articles and an interview collected in *De la paille et du grain* Paulhan had argued that, if the CNE were to apply the same criteria for judging writers of previous generations, they would be forced to conclude that both Romain Rolland and Arthur Rimbaud had betrayed France. This was more than the CNE could take, and they responded in *Les Lettres françaises*. The force of the debate was such that it continued five years later when Elsa Triolet published an editorial in which she mused about Paulhan's fascist tendencies. His defense of fascist writers seemed more than a little suspect to her.[25]

[25]Triolet, "Les Faits"; "Il ne saurait y avoir d'affaire Romain Rolland"; "Paulhan."

Triolet's husband, Aragon, and Eluard didn't go so far, but they did counter Paulhan's argument about what constitutes a traitor. Explaining their decision not to publish in Paulhan's anthology, they wrote: "we prefer sparing ourselves the commentaries of a man who not only calls Romain Rolland and Arthur Rimbaud traitors, in order to turn traitors into good fellows [*braves gens*] who made a mistake, but who also makes it his business to insult us." Once again Paulhan, this shadowy and somewhat mysterious player, returns in the debates about the status of literature. Once again he carries with him the complexity of the arguments around the purge. For Eluard, in any case, publishing a collection of poems in 1947 meant situating himself in direct opposition to his former ally. Though Eluard's poems in *Deux Poètes d'aujourd'hui* don't directly refer to the purge, publishing this alternative anthology meant continuing the verdicts, judgments, and sanctions of the purge.

In this collection Eluard published a poem that describes the goal of his political poetry. In "Poetry Must Have Practical Truth As Its Goal" Eluard aims "to explain the world and change it." Poetry, according to Eluard, is both a hermeneutic process and a practical action. But what does this mean for Eluard's purge poetry? A first indication can be found in a programmatic text published in his 1946 volume *Uninterrupted Poetry*. In this poem titled "The Poet's Work" (*"Le Travail du poète"*) Eluard outlines what he considers to be the poet's role. It is up to the poet to guarantee that "our hands and our eyes/ Come back from the horror open pure [*Je veux que nos mains et nos yeux/Reviennent de l'horreur ouvertes pures*]." Man has been trampled underfoot, he tells us, and it is up to the poet to avenge him: "I want to render justice to them / A justice without pity [*Je veux qu'on lui rende justice/Une justice sans pitié*]." Eluard's poet has a sacred function: he is the one who will purify society after the horror of the war. In this poem, as in others, Eluard, following the ideology of his party, associates the "executioners," that is, the Nazis, to the "masters," that is, the capitalists in postwar society. The poet must thus ensure the transition from Resistance to Revolution, but it is a transition that can only occur through a purge, through a purification ritual that takes place as much in the courts as it does between the covers of

Eluard's book. Eluard's poet is an "artist-avenger" whose work is to transform his text into the site of purification.

In *Uninterrupted Poetry* Eluard also outlines what he considers to be the role of the reader. From line 462 on, this narrative poem heads toward the final goal of personal and political fulfillment. Each new movement forward is introduced by the line "If we go up one degree [*Si nous montions d'un degré*]." The fifth segment in this series represents the violence of war and culminates in a reflection on judgment:

> Let understanding judge
> Error according to error
> If seeing were the lightning
> In the land of carrion
> The judge would be god
> There is no god
>
> *Et que comprendre juge*
> *L'erreur selon l'erreur*
> *Si voir était la foudre*
> *Au pays des charognes*
> *Le juge serait dieu*
> *Il n'y a pas de dieu*

These are but a few verses in a 687-line poem, but they constitute one of the essential links in its dialectic progression. In his gloss of *Uninterrupted Poetry* Aragon, who recommends that we read the entire poem as we would a newspaper article, considers that these lines are a direct reference to the purge. According to him, we must judge "Pétain according to Pétain's law, Brasillach and Goering according to Brasillach and Goering's law" (Aragon, *Chroniques,* 58). Aragon's (socialist) realist interpretation coincides with a theme prevalent among the writers at *Les Lettres françaises,* who claimed that judging the collaborators was an essential component in the identity of postwar (communist) man. Judgment, however, is also the work of the reader. With the phrase "Let understanding judge" Eluard reinforces the connection between two words that are at the center of his poetic lexicon. To understand is to judge, to judge understand. Poetic activity, for Eluard, amalgamates the hermeneutic and the critical processes, and in *Uninterrupted Poetry* this amalgamation takes place at precisely the moment when the poem calls upon the reader to judge those responsible for the Occupation of France. "To understand," which elsewhere in Eluard's work means to sympathize, here retains its links to an interpretative and ultimately juridical process. This, according to Eluard, is the work of the reader: to understand the poem and to turn this understanding into a political judgment. Eluard has tied the hermeneutic process, the decipherment of a poem, to the performance of justice.

We saw how Eluard's purge poems are structured according to an aesthetic of balance. His use of metered lines, the balance of the poems, and the *renversement* the poems effect in the final verses are all elements of a rigorous symmetry. This leads to a final consideration of the relation of poetry, purification, and aesthetics. In his 1943 introduction to *L'Honneur des poètes* Eluard justified politically committed poetry by tracing a literary genealogy:

> Whitman driven by his people, Hugo calling to arms, Rimbaud drawn into the Commune, Maïakovski exalted and exalting, it's toward action that poets with a broad vision are drawn, one day or another[...]Once more, poetry regroups when it is defied and rediscovers a precise meaning [*un sens précis*] in its latent violence, once more it cries, accuses, hopes.

Eluard's ideal of a politically committed poetry rests on two tenets. First, poetry gives voice to populist movements. Poetry is both action and expression, and in the introduction to *L'Honneur des poètes* Eluard's definition of poetic action almost imperceptibly slides from verbal acts—"Hugo calling to arms"—to physical acts—"Rimbaud drawn into the Commune." Second, for Eluard, poetry is a craft of precision. The poet's aesthetic ideal, according to Eluard, is to rediscover "a precise meaning." Rediscovering precision is a process of verbal control and mastery, but it is also a process of linguistic excision. Precision, as a rhetorical ideal, allows the poet to eliminate ambiguity, paradox, and deviance, for precision means not only accuracy, it also means an elimination and is linked through etymology to the act of cutting off, to excision. What exactly Eluard was cutting off from his poetry is made clear in a preface written by Aragon for another volume of Resistance poetry. Here Aragon had defined the poet's mission in similar terms: the role of the poet is to reappropriate a language that has been "distorted, perverted by the usurpers." And Aragon quotes as a model the celebrated line from Mallarmé's "Tombeau d'Edgar Poe": "Give a purer sense to the words of the tribe [*Donner un sens plus pur aux mots de la tribu*]" (quoted in Seghers, *La Résistance*, 326–27). Aragon's condemnation of the "perverted" language of the collaborators calls to mind the attacks during the purge on the perverted sexuality of the men and women accused of treason. For the Resistance poets purity and precision have become sexual, political, and rhetorical ideals. And when, in the preface to a volume of Resistance poetry, Eluard states that the poet rediscovers a precise meaning, he is implicitly arguing that poets must both excise the collaborators and purify their verse. Eluard's rhetoric of symmetry, transparency, and control has begun to sound like an *art poétique* of the purge.

Eluard returned to the question of poetic style in the notes accompanying the 1945 edition of *Au rendez-vous allemand*. Explaining his itinerary during the war, how he went from publishing with Gallimard to joining the Resistance and working for the clandestine press, Eluard writes:

> But poetry had to go underground. Poetry can never play on words for too long without taking risks. It was able to lose everything and stop playing and blend into its eternal reflection: a very naked and very poor and very fiery and always beautiful truth. And if I say "always beautiful," it is because it takes its place of beauty in the hearts of men. It is because it becomes the only virtue, the only good. And this good is immeasurable.[26]

Eluard did not wait until 1945 to renounce ambiguity and poetic "play," but perhaps nowhere does he more clearly, more precisely, distance himself from the surrealist aesthetic. Poetry is no longer an amusement for Eluard; it can no longer afford "to play" ("*jouer*"). When poetry goes "underground" (*prendre le maquis*), it takes risks, and writing in clandestine reviews becomes the equivalent to derail-

[26]My translation.

ing a train or cutting telephone wires. It is, of course, convenient for Eluard to describe his poetry as a reflection of a sublime truth, but one can hardly argue with him that at a time when freedom of expression has been squelched, writing the word *Liberté* could be considered a political act. While proclaiming their practical value, however, the terms Eluard uses also resituate his work within a clearly marked literary tradition. An aesthetic that responds to virtue, that conceives of language as an instrument, and that sees itself as a reflection of truth and beauty has a name: we call it classicism. This is precisely Henri Meschonnic's conclusion when he locates Eluard's classicism in his moralist's vision of the world and his poetic "control," a control that extends from the purity and precision of his language to his recovery of traditional forms of versification, such as the decasyllable and alexandrine verse, from his search for the truth to the metric balance of his texts (Meschonnic, *Pour la poétique III,* 119–43). Meschonnic's analysis extends beyond Eluard's war poetry, but *classicism* is, it seems to me, the word that best describes the aesthetic and the politics of Eluard's purge poems. These poems that are constructed around a "precise meaning" use a balanced structure, traditional verse, and formal control in order to call for a purge of writers who were politically and, Eluard tells us, sexually impure. In choosing a traditional and even retrograde model for his wartime poetry, Eluard is able to link his poetry to revenge and break away from his modernist past.

In the paragraph from *Au rendez-vous allemand* cited above, Eluard describes two movements: one defines an action, going underground, the other describes an aesthetic characterized by its quest for purity. The truth his poetry reflects is modified by four terms—*naked, poor, fiery,* and *beautiful*—which are all semantically linked to the notion of purity: naked by lack of artifice; poor because it connotes absence of corruption: the pure poet is the one who hasn't been paid, who hasn't rented his pen to the enemy; fiery through the purifying power of fire; and beautiful, the opposite of misshapen. If the act of going underground belongs to the Resistance, the quest for purity belongs to the purge. Eluard describes his poetics in the immediate postwar years as a purge (*épuration*) that takes place within the text itself. The acts of retribution against the collaborators—from summary executions to imprisonment—that Eluard's poetry advocated during the purge find their formal equivalent in the aesthetic of classicism.

For Aragon, Eluard's classicism was part of the working class's political reappropriation of a cultural heritage (Aragon, *L'Homme communiste*, 160). As we look at the purge archive, we realize that Eluard's fascination with precise meaning and pure form also places him at the center of a postwar debate about politics and aesthetics. For, while at the end of the war authors and intellectuals were vying for political position, while they were supporting or denouncing one another, they also engaged their work in a quarrel about classical aesthetics. A debate about form was never far behind their political action. One of postwar France's most ardent neoclassicists was Francis Ponge, whose itinerary was not so different from Eluard's. Ponge had been close to the surrealists but ultimately rejected their poetry and forged a style based on elegance and concision. During the Occupation Ponge had close ties to the Resistance, participated in numerous missions, and was even arrested during a raid (Martinoir, *La Littérature*, 213). Though he had been a member of the Communist party since 1937, Ponge's writing had little to do with the committed poetry of Eluard and Aragon. His first major work, *Le Parti pris des choses*, published by Gallimard in 1942, could even be considered, with its prose meditations on rain, on bread, on a cigarette, on an oyster, as the very opposite of militant poetry. Around this same time, however, Ponge began to write the long poem *Soap*, dedicated to this commodity that had become so scarce during the Occupation. But *Soap*, finally published in 1967, is also an ode to the virtues of French classicism. The effects of Ponge's soap lead to a rhetorical purity, an "ease of elocution," an "aesthetic perfection" (Ponge, *Soap*, 19). And it isn't a coincidence that the artists Ponge cites as predecessors—Chardin, La Fontaine, and Rameau—belong to the French classical tradition.[27] In *Soap* Ponge lays the foundations for an aesthetic that he will further develop in *Pour un Malherbe* and which will guide his writing until his

[27]For Ponge's relation to Rameau see Meadows, "Rameau," 626–37.

death.[28] It might be excessive to claim that *Soap* is another allegory of the purge, though it may very well have been written in reaction to the inflated rhetoric of wartime propaganda. Still, like Eluard's poems, *Soap* is a work that has as its ideal rhetorical purity and aesthetic perfection.

Two more brief examples show that the fascination for a rhetoric of purity was more widespread during the years of the purge than we might have imagined. In a 1946 essay Michel Leiris, speaking about the "dangers" of writing an autobiography, pointed to the necessity of preserving the truth from rhetorical "artifice," "quavers," and "flourish" that only serve to veil it. Ultimately, Leiris concludes, his stylistic model in writing *L'Age d'homme* is the "severity of classicism" (Leiris, *L'Age d'homme*, 19–21). It may be surprising to the reader of a later work such as *Fourbis* that Leiris considers his style classical—and when he does use the term in 1946 he places it in quotation marks, as if he did not entirely trust it. Still, Leiris's use of the term reveals that he too, like Eluard and like Ponge, is drawn to this ideal of a rhetoric of purity precisely at the moment when France is putting its "impure" writers—the ones France called *"les vendus"*—on trial. One more example comes from Sartre, whose conception of prose as transparent and of words as a "disclosure" (*"dévoilement"*) of the world, approaches the classical understanding of language as a tool (Sartre, *What Is Literature?* 37). When in "What Is Literature?" Sartre dismisses poetry from his considerations, he does so on precisely the grounds that it brings a materiality of language, an opacity that must be excluded from political discourse. All these writers, then, turn to a form of classical rhetoric at the end of the war. All espouse, to a greater or lesser extent, the transparency, the purity, the functionality, the order, the rigor, the control, and the balance associated with the aesthetic of classicism. Whether they were directly involved in the purge trials or more loosely associated with left-wing politics, they all instituted a rhetorical purge on their writing: Eluard eliminated the "game" of surrealist writing; Leiris excised the "effusions" of the confession; Sartre discarded the opacity of poetic language. At the

---

[28]For Ponge's relation to Malherbe see Chesters, "Malherbe."

moment when France is undergoing a purge, an *épuration* of collaborators, French writers are submitting their texts to a rigorous and measured aesthetic purge. In rediscovering classicism, they are turning to an aesthetic that Malherbe, the father of French classicism, described as *"l'épuration de la langue française."*

Is it possible that the power of the attraction of the purge was so strong that it pulled all these writers into its orbit? We saw earlier how writers and intellectuals during the purge set themselves the task of defining literature's role in society, and this definition often depended upon which side of the dock the writer stood. But Eluard's reflections on poetry intimate that the purge may have changed not only literature's function but also its form. To test this hypothesis we might look at writers who were themselves purged. Was *their* writing and their conception of literary form changed by the magnetic pull of the purge? Two purged writers did, in fact, address questions of literary form. Throughout his postwar work Louis-Ferdinand Céline constantly returned to questions of style, proposing a "pure" style, that is nonetheless the contrary of Eluard's classicism. If Céline played on the meaning of a pure style, it was precisely in order to counter the rhetorical and political control of the writers, and the lawyers, who attempted to purge him at the end of the war. Another writer also stepped into the fray at this time. Robert Brasillach, on trial for treason in January 1945, had been interested in classicism for a long time, publishing studies of Virgil and Corneille at the beginning of his career and ending with an extended comment on the neoclassical poet André Chénier.[29] Brasillach may have learned about classicism from Maurras, who saw in the Greeks a perfection of form based on measure, reason, and taste; in its organic conception of aesthetics and politics *L'Action française* was an authentic neoclassical movement.[30] By the end of the war, however, Brasillach turned away from this model. His *Anthology of Greek Poetry*, probably composed from April to July 1944, is a voluminous work in which the author sings the praises of

---

[29]Brasillach, *Œuvres complètes*, vol. 7. Brasillach, *Corneille*. I want to thank my colleague Benjamin Hicks for guiding me in Brasillach's reading of Corneille.

[30]For more on Maurras's attraction to ancient Greece see Carroll, *French Literary Fascism*, 71–86.

Greek sensuality and vitality (Brasillach, *Œuvres complètes*, vol. 9, 323). The collection is not without its explicit political references; Brasillach establishes what he calls "points of contact" (Brasillach, *Anthologie,* 323) between Greek and German poetry, and he praises Aristophanes as the "immortal enemy of democratic bellicosity" (475). More than anything else, however, Brasillach uses the anthology to distance himself from the classical poets. In his eyes Callimachus, the inventor of the alexandrine, the verse of classicism, has left nothing so much as a work of "considerable and majestic boredom" (497). Callimachus, he concludes, is the author of an "icy" official poetry. This might all seem like the somewhat arcane musings of a fascist aesthete, but Brasillach had already presented this theme in a January 1944 article titled "For an Impure Poetry," in which, singling out Aragon but also taking aim at Resistance poetry in general, he attacks the "icy" (*glacée*) contemporary poetry that relies on "regular verse" (Brasillach, *Œuvres complètes*, vol. 12, 600). In its place he calls for the "impure poetry" associated with the "oral style." This opposition between pure and impure poetry continues in one of Brasillach's last texts, *Chénier*, written while he was imprisoned in Fresnes, awaiting his execution. In this study of André Chénier, Brasillach establishes a kinship between himself and the poet guillotined during the Terror. Both were victims of a politically repressive regime and conceived ancient Greece as the land of tolerance and *"joie de vivre"* (Brasillach, *Chénier,* 24). But Brasillach also uses Chénier, the political martyr, to counter the likes of Aragon and Eluard. Chénier, the victim of the purge of 1793, is also, in Brasillach's words, the author of an "impure poetry" (43). His *Iambes* are the only works that can truly move a reader during a "revolutionary period" (44). As we read Brasillach, we cannot help but think that his *Anthology of Greek Poetry* and his essay on André Chénier served, along with an exculpatory function, as the author's foray into the debate about classicism during the postwar years. To praise an impure poetry during the purge, was also to make a political argument. Just as Eluard had linked the purge of fascists and collaborators to a poetry of precision, balance, and control, Brasillach argued on his own behalf through a reflection on impure poetry. Eluard's programmatic statements must be read not just as a rejection of his surrealist past but also as part of a larger dialogue about classicism and about the status of writing at the time of the purge. As proof that the political lines didn't always run parallel to aesthetic choices, I could cite the example of Raymond Queneau, vice president of the CNE and a contributing editor to *Les Lettres françaises*, but also a dedicated opponent of the heritage of French classicism.[31] More or less consciously, however, all these writers intertwined the political arguments of the purge with a series of literary arguments. Responses to the purge also took the form of a conflict about writing systems.

I do not mean to suggest that Eluard was more committed to purifying his verse than to purging French society. Rather, Eluard's reflections on poetry can lead us to two conclusions. First, the position taking, to retrieve Bourdieu's term, that took place in the political field at the end of the war found its equivalent in the aesthetic field. To the debates about guilt and innocence writers attached a debate about literature's very form. Second, the debate about form was directly tied to the process of purging France of the Vichyites. To claim that poetry should be pure (as Eluard did) or impure (Brasillach) was also to argue through indirection and, I might add, through allegory, for or against the purge. Eluard's classicism is not only about the purge as the French Communists envisioned it; the poet initiated this economy of style even before the war. Still, in the purge poems from *Au rendez-vous allemand* Eluard's search for a structural symmetry, his use of alexandrine verse, his rediscovery of a precise meaning in language are all inscriptions on a formal level of the political and moral imperatives of the purge. Eluard may well have rejected the "art for art's sake" credo, but his commitment to political action was also and primarily a commitment to poetic form.

Eluard's classical turn leaves us with one final paradox. His most celebrated wartime poem "Liberty" signaled a rediscovery, in his own words, of "freedom of expression." It is an ode against the control of Nazi and Vichy censors and reproduces in its very form the freedom it seeks. The seemingly endless repetition of its strophes, the uneven-

[31]See, for example, Queneau, *Bâtons*.

ness of the heptasyllabic verse give to the poem a verbal and structural freedom. By 1943–44, however, the purge poems have replaced this freedom of expression with verbal and structural control. Eluard has excised from his work all forms of linguistic and semantic play and replaced them with strict rules and constraints. It is as if Eluard's poetry reflected one of the fears that haunted France during the postwar years. The purge in its excesses, and especially when directed by the Communists, ran the risk of turning the freedom of the Liberation of 1944 into a reign of repression, censorship, and control. Eluard's poetry as it moves from ambiguity to precision, from freedom to rhetorical control is also, perhaps in spite of itself, a testimony that the purge, in punishing treason, also ran the risk of repressing poetic freedom.

CHAPTER 5

Céline:
Style Wars

To the attorney preparing his case before the purge tribunals Céline wrote that his "patriotic duty was to enrich French literature with new works" and that, whatever the verdict of his trial, "history will do [him] justice" (Céline, *Lettres à Tixier*, 36–37, 118). In these two sentences Céline is presenting in embryonic form the two main tendencies of his postwar writing: the creation of some of modernism's most innovative literary works and a plea of not guilty to the charges brought against him by the purge courts in France. From his earliest novels Céline was a self-conscious stylist. In the postwar works, however, the writing is overtaken by Céline's constant commentary on his fate as a writer, his place in the literary community, the sale of his books, his rivalry with writers who passed through the purge unscathed, and the exigencies of his style. More than in any of his previous texts, in Céline's postwar writings we see the author in the process of creating his works.[1] Not only his novels but also his letters, interviews, and legal papers are, in this respect, a

---

[1]Godard, *Poétique,* 303–40. Godard's study is the strongest formal analysis to date of Céline's style. My present concern is not to analyze the forms of the author's writing but rather to understand the function of his postwar theory of literature.

privileged site for examining the relation between the aesthetic space and the purge tribunals, between literary and legal arguments. Of all the postwar writers Céline is the one who most violently and repeatedly maligned the purge trials and vituperated against his fate. He is also the author whose style, themes, and metaphoric register remain most clearly tied to the arguments of the *épuration*. In this chapter and the next I look at the way Céline's writing balances between two poles: the author's reflections on style turn out to be inseparable from his revision of the purge trials, most notably his own; and historical revisionism in its most nefarious form takes place only through Céline's passionate and sustained commentary on the role of literature.

Céline remains one of the most intriguing cases of the postwar years. A hugely successful novelist in 1932 with *Journey to the End of the Night*, by the end of World War II he was a fugitive from justice, a man sought by the French purge courts, and a writer whose name appeared on every blacklist published by the CNE. Between 1937 and the end of the war Céline had written three of the most vitriolic anti-Semitic pamphlets ever published in France: *Bagatelles pour un massacre* (1937), *L'Ecole des cadavres* (1938), and *Les Beaux Draps* (1941). Though he was never one of the collaboration's official propagandists, his work had been used by French fascists as an alternative to the "polite" anti-Semitism of *L'Action française* (Kaplan, *Reproductions,* 117). When he sensed the coming defeat of Nazi Germany in June 1944, he fled France. His last days in Paris, his travels through war-torn Germany, his stay in Sigmaringen with Pétain and a coterie of French collaborators, his years of prison and exile in Denmark, and his return to France in 1951 — all these experiences later served the author as the material for his final novels. More than anything else, however, Céline was devoted until the end of his life not only to chronicling his experiences but to rewriting the terms and the verdict of his purge trial.

Like other writers accused of collaboration, Céline in exile in Copenhagen was first charged under Article 75 of the French Penal Code, the article that defines the crime of treason. Céline's legal status was tricky, for both *Bagatelles pour un massacre* and *L'Ecole des cadavres* had been published legally under the Third Republic — the Marchandeau decree outlawing racist literature had only gone into effect in April 1939—and his 1941 pamphlet, *Les Beaux Draps,* had been banned by the Vichy government. Still, Céline's two most notorious pamphlets had been reprinted during the Occupation, one with a new preface by the author, and the charges against him were considerable: he was accused of having written propaganda in favor of the collaboration, of being a member of the collaborationist Cercle Européen, of publishing anti-Semitic material during the Occupation, of supporting French fascist Jacques Doriot, of having fled to Germany, and of having been treated as a friend by the Nazis at the end of the war. If proven, these crimes constituted treason and were punishable by death. The French government's first move was to request Céline's extradition from Denmark, a process that lasted several years and ultimately failed, though Céline was imprisoned in Denmark for approximately a year. At this point, in November 1946, Céline wrote a twelve-page reply to accusations brought against him by the French courts (Céline, "Reply to Charges"). This legal brief contains the principal arguments of Céline's defense: that he never belonged to collaborationist circles, that he had never been a propagandist, that he had never supported Doriot, and that his German hosts had treated him worse than they treated their enemies. When replying to charges of anti-Semitism, he writes, "I do not remember having written a single anti-Semitic line since 1937" (Céline, "Reply to Charges," 532). Céline is forgetting, for reasons of his defense, the violently anti-Semitic pamphlet *L'Ecole des cadavres* as well as *Les Beaux Draps* and the numerous letters he wrote to the collaborationist press during the Occupation. But when he claims that *"the Jews should erect a statue to me for the harm which I have not done to them and which I could have done"* (532), one wonders if it's the desperation of his defense that leads him to write such statements or if his pen isn't once again guided by the malice that led him to write the pamphlets in the first place. For Céline the stakes were high. He was writing both in response to accusations of treason and to avoid extradition by the Danish authorities. A return to France in 1946, Céline knew, would have meant a trial and perhaps death. But even in his 1946 "Reply to Charges of Treason," when he risks losing everything, including his life, Céline's attempt to disavow his anti-Semitism turns out to reveal the stranglehold racial hatred had on his mind.

In 1949 Céline's case was reviewed by the purge courts, and he was charged a second time, but now under the terms of Article 83 of the Penal Code, a significant revision for the author since he was no longer accused of treason and could no longer be executed if found guilty. Though on the eve of his trial *L'Humanité* still claimed that Céline had been "an agent of the Gestapo,"[2] the French courts tried him solely on charges of having committed acts "harmful to the national defense." The author was found guilty, in absentia, sentenced to one year in prison, a 50,000-franc fine, and the confiscation of his property, and was declared in a state of "national indignity." A year later his attorney took advantage of a remission extended to veterans of World War I who had been convicted of crimes of collaboration and obtained amnesty for his client under his given name, Dr. Louis Destouches. The attorney never mentioned that his client was the infamous Céline. In 1951 Céline returned to France, signed a publishing contract with Gallimard, and began publishing what have turned out to be some of the strongest works of French postwar fiction: two volumes of the still untranslated novel *Féerie pour une autre fois* (1952) and (1954) and the three works known as the German trilogy: *Castle to Castle, North, Rigadoon.*

Though Céline's purge dossier was officially closed, his trial in the forum of public opinion has never really ended. Until the end of his life Céline railed against Article 75, exaggerated the charges against him (he frequently claimed that the purge authorities had accused him of selling the French fleet to the Germans), and compulsively repeated the arguments of his defense: he never collaborated, he never wrote propaganda, he was one of France's true patriots, the war left him destitute. All the arguments first laid out in the 1946 reply are repeated and reworked throughout the novels (Roussin, "Genèse," 159–67). What interests me here, however, is the manner in which the purge trials are inscribed in Céline's conception of literary style. Not

[2]"Louis-Ferdinand Céline était agent de la Gestapo," *L'Humanité*, 21 Jan. 1950.

only do the self-reflexive moments in Céline's postwar writings link his work to a certain modernist aesthetic, but they reveal that for all his outward attempts to detach himself from his anti-Semitic writings, Céline was never capable of transcending the political implications of his works that were at the heart of his trial.

A starting point for entering into Céline's text is the author's body. Céline's writing has always revolved around diseased bodies. From his earliest works he has described individuals as either ethereally sublime or as crowbait, flesh waiting for its chance to putrefy. Alice Kaplan has pointed to the connections between what she calls Céline's "tripe talk"—his fascination with bodily functions—the author's fragmentation of French syntax, and the death drive of fascism (Kaplan, *Reproductions,* 107–21). In his postwar writing Céline inscribes this sort of body language into his response to the purge. He carries on his flesh the marks of his trial, his exile, and his imprisonment: not only was his Paris apartment pillaged at the Liberation, he tells us, but his trials have left him debilitated, weak, wobbly, and practically toothless. He lives in a purged body, a shell. Pictures from the period show the author wrapped in tattered cloths, as if the cold of Denmark were forever cutting through him. And it is during the year in prison in Denmark that his body is quite literally purged. Not only does he claim to have lost 52 kilos while in jail, but since he is unable to defecate, his body is subjected to a series of enemas (*"lavements"*) (Céline, *Romans IV,* 174), which the narrator requests but which nonetheless make of his body the site of a purification by medical and political authorities.[3] Céline's prison term, his physical decay, and the enemas are all indices of the author's having undergone a purge that is as much physical as it is legal. If Eluard and Sartre, for instance, see the purge played out in terms of perverted or straight sexuality, Céline stages the purge in his intestines.

This is even more evident in his rivalry with Sartre, who in 1945 had accused Céline of having been paid for writing his anti-Semitic pamphlets. (I will return to the specifics of this argument a little

[3]Céline, *Romans IV*. Translations from both volumes of *Féerie pour une autre fois* are mine.

later.) Suffice it to say that Céline responds to this accusation by once again situating the purge in his body. Two of the insults he constantly uses to designate Sartre are "Artron" and "taenia." *Artron* is a neologism composed of *Sartre* and *étron*, the French word for turd. The neologism is scatological and juvenile, but it also transforms the purger, Sartre, into the very object Céline purges from his body. The effect is to sully the would-be purifier. Naming Sartre taenia, the tapeworm, serves several purposes. It indicates the parasitic nature of a writer who admittedly owes much to Céline's stylistic innovation. Sartre's *Nausea*, after all, carried an epigraph from Céline's play *L'Eglise,* and Sartre reportedly knew by heart entire pages from *Journey to the End of the Night.* But again, the taenia is most emphatically part of the world of the intestines. Sartre is the parasitic worm who is purging Céline from the inside. Sartre, the taenia, is the cause of the narrator's emaciated body. The historical event of the purge thus inscribes itself symbolically on the writer's body, in the form of enemas and tapeworms.

This purged body is also part of Céline's self-portrait as a victim: it serves to show and denounce what the author sees as the excesses of the purge, but we can also say that the body of the text has undergone a purge process. The elliptical, three-dot style of Céline's last works is a purged style; it is made up of a series of elisions and omissions that the reader must complete. Of course, Céline's elliptical style dates from before the war: *Death on the Installment Plan,* the 1936 novel, introduced this type of writing, and the 1941 pamphlet, *Les Beaux Draps,* begins with the author's assertions that, in order to avoid another trial, he is now writing "hermetically" with a "secret code accessible to the initiated reader."[4] Céline will nonetheless intensify his use of this secret code in the postwar works, and the rhetoric of allusion and omission is an integral part of the Holocaust negationism Céline espouses in these novels.

[4]Céline, *Les Beaux Draps,* 9 (my translation). In June 1939 Céline had been found guilty of libel for having accused a non-Jewish doctor of being Jewish in his pamphlet *L'Ecole des cadavres.* This is the ruling that precipitated the "hermetic" writing of the subsequent works.

If Céline's style can be called a purged style, it is also because the primary metaphor he uses to describe his postwar writing, the celebrated phrase *"rendu émotif,"* which Stanford Luce translates as "emotive yield," can just as efficiently be translated as "emotive vomit" (*rendre* in French means to regurgitate). In *Conversations with Professor Y*, his 1955 *art poétique*, Céline declares that he is a writer of emotion, and he opposes himself to writers such as Delly, a brother-and-sister team of popular novelists, who were never able to translate "emotion through written language" (Céline, *Conversations*, 17). Céline's *rendu émotif* evokes a poetics of retching, of uncontrollable spasms, and emotional excess.[5] But the *rendu émotif* also puts the author's work under the sign of a bodily purge. To write is to purge oneself of emotion, and indeed Céline's three-dot style is vituperative and spasmodic. If, for Kafka, "to write is to fast" (Deleuze and Guattari, *Kafka*, 20), for Céline to write is to vomit. Céline's writing transforms itself into a poetics of egesta; the fevers that regularly beset the narrator give way to emissions that are both physical and stylistic. Throughout his postwar writings Céline remains resolutely opposed to the purge of 1944–47: his texts attack the verdicts of the tribunals; he vituperates against members of the CNE; he limns himself as the purge's only true victim. This historical and political rejection of the purge finds its counterpoint in a reintegration in his text of a poetics of the purge, a writing that bears the marks of a stylistic and corporeal purification.

A purged body produces a purged text: Céline's trial for collaboration seems, at least at first, to have led the author to valorize style over all else. In a postwar survey Céline predicted that he would be one of the few authors read in France after the year 2000; in 1955 he claimed to be the inventor of a new style; a few years later he compared himself to Cézanne, who had found a new way of painting an apple; in 1957 he called himself a stylist who must write 80,000 pages

---

[5]Jean-Pierre Richard links Céline's early writings and his racism to poetics of vomit: "[Céline] delivers himself of his terrors by projecting them out of himself and investing them in others ... In order to get rid of nausea, all you have to do is *vomit*." Richard, *Nausée*, 52–53.

of manuscript to produce a 400-page novel.[6] This type of commentary on his style was not new for Céline. Beginning with the publication of *Journey to the End of the Night*, he had used interviews, correspondence, newspaper articles, advertising, and later, prefaces to comment on his works and attempt to control their reception. After the war, however, the author's commentaries on style become an integral part of his poetic practice; they pervade his work and take on a new tenor. When Céline presents his writing as nothing more than a stylistic monument, he often simultaneously claims that his writing is not about ideas, politics, or messages: "I have no ideas, myself! not a one! there's nothing more vulgar, more common, more disgusting than ideas!" he declares in *Conversations with Professor Y* (13). When he labels himself a stylist to the exclusion of everything else, he is quite consciously engaging in a campaign to disengage his work from his anti-Semitic rants and his earlier commitment to the political genre *par excellence*, the pamphlet. To demonstrate that his declarations about style are a form of self-defense, we need go no further than his 1946 reply to accusations, which sets the tone for his postwar literary theory: "I am probably the one well-known French writer who has remained strictly, jealously, fiercely, a *writer* and nothing but a *writer* without compromise" (Céline, "Reply to Charges," 532).

Writer must be read here as the opposite of intellectual and propagandist. Céline's declarations on style at this point are in line with the arguments about the autonomy of literature made by just about every writer accused of treason. Brasillach, Chardonne, Maurras, Rebatet all claimed during the purge that their investment in literary form attenuated their political responsibility. This line of defense was also repeated by Céline's defenders during his trial. In a letter to the court Marcel Aymé called Céline the "greatest living French writer" and compared him with the exiled Victor Hugo gearing up to write his *Châtiments*.[7] In the United States a group of American intellectuals including Milton Hindus, Henry Miller, and

---

[6]Céline, *Cahiers Céline 7*, 390; *Conversations*, 15; *Cahiers Céline 7*, 458; *Romans II*, 938.

[7]Quoted in Gibault, *Céline*, 231.

James Laughlin, Céline's editor at New Directions, circulated a petition calling for Céline's immediate release from his Danish prison. The authors of the petition, appealing to the principle of free speech and the writer's freedom to express "unpopular ideas," had, in an early draft, compared Céline with other writers, such as Villon, Molière, and Flaubert, who had been unjustifiably "condemned . . . by the righteous."[8] Even the phrase *"petite musique,"* which Céline often used to describe his style in the postwar years, leads us back to the purge trials,[9] for *petite musique* was the term Claude Jamet also used to describe Brasillach's writing style and defend the editor of *Je suis partout*: "There was in him [Brasillach] a little music [*petite musique*], sensitive, sad, gracious, insistent, that one finds everywhere, in his poems, in his essays, even in his quickly written articles" (Jamet, *Fifi Roi*, 207). The metaphor of writing and music is common enough in Céline: already in *Death on the Installment Plan* he describes his writing as the "opera of the deluge." What the passage from Jamet shows, however, is that after the trials the metaphor of writing as music served a specific juridical purpose. Céline's defense rests, not on claims of freedom of speech and of opinion, claims that, after all, carried little weight in the French judicial system, but rather on understanding the term *writer* in the intransitive sense. When writing is music, literature no longer has an object; it is no longer for anyone or about anything. The writer is absorbed in the labor of language. His work knows no end. Céline's writing, of course, never reaches this zero degree of content to which he aspires; even the desire to transcend ideology can be inscribed within the ideological debates of the purge trials. But as we read the author in the context of the trials, we realize that the pure stylist of the postwar years is indistinguishable from the purged writer of 1946.

In Céline's twisted logic he has become the victim of a universal persecution. One of the recurring themes in Céline's postwar work is

---

[8]"Statement in Regard to Louis-Ferdinand Céline," in Kaplan and Roussin, eds. "Céline, USA," 524.

[9]When asked in 1957 to characterize his writing, Céline responded, "A certain music, I've introduced a certain little music in style and that's it." *Cahiers Céline 2*, 20.

that he has become a scapegoat for all of France, the greatest, if not the only, victim of the war. From victimizer of the Jews, Céline turns himself into a victim, hated and hunted, not for his politics—and here is the twist—but for his style. When Céline attempts to understand the accusations against him, he can only find one answer: his accusers are jealous of his "pre-war success." Again the legal brief Céline wrote in 1946 gives a first indication of a theme that will run throughout his later work: "They wish, they seek desperately, to make me pay for, to expiate, my pre-war books, my pre-war literary and polemic success" (539). The agents of this persecution are here the CNE and the purge courts, but Céline also accused the Germans of participating in what he later calls his "expiation." Both his novels and his pamphlets were either "passed over in silence" or received "extremely malevolent criticism" (533) from the Nazi cultural officers. As for Otto Abetz, the German ambassador to Paris, Céline claims that "[he] always detested me, my books, my person, but *especially* my books" (533). "Then you were persecuted by those hating your style?" (Céline, *Conversations*, 23). By the time Professor Y asks this of Céline, there is no longer any question of a trial based on his "polemic success." Céline's defense rests on the assertion that he, or rather his work, is repulsive to both sides. How could he have been committed to fascism, he seems to ask, if the fascists despised him? That many officials in the Nazi ranks as well as in the Vichy government distrusted Céline is probably true enough. Céline's defense rhetoric, however, gives the reader a recycled, parodic, even hysterical version of the *poète maudit* cliché in order to deflect all charges of collaboration.

When he casts himself as a persecuted "writer," Céline is also consciously blurring the generic distinctions between his novels and his pamphlets. Again this move begins in the 1946 "Reply," when he uses the phrase "literary and polemic success" to designate all his works and amalgamates these successes in the general category "books." In *Féerie pour une autre fois I*, the first novel Céline publishes upon his return to France after the war, the author fantasizes about his literary itinerary: from the dream of writing operettas when he was a young man to the publication of a libretto, from the failure of this libretto to the reality of prose and a novel, *Journey to the End of the Night*, and then "handcuffs! dungeons! hatred!" (Céline, *Romans IV*, 21). While it would be fair to assume that the hatred is Céline's own, we are also led to believe that it is a hatred directed toward him. Céline's advice: "Never write [*n'écrivez jamais*]" (21). In the 1957 novel *Castle to Castle* Céline returns to this theme. Surrounded by hard-core collaborators, he nonetheless feels that he alone will have to pay for the crimes of the Occupation. In one passage he briefly mentions his pamphlet *Bagatelles pour un massacre* as a source of the enmity against him, but he quickly shifts the focus to his other works: "look at the books he's written ... " (Céline, *Castle to Castle,* 250), the collaborators whisper behind his back. Again Céline's advice to his reader is "never write" (250), as if writing itself had become the crime. Céline pushes this line of argumentation to its extreme when he claims that his first novel, *Journey to the End of the Night,* is responsible for his fate: "Nobody has forgiven me for the *Journey*" (61). And this nobody here includes not only the CNE and the purge tribunals but also the collaborators at Sigmaringen and Pétain himself. In his reaction to the accusations Céline translates his prosecution into persecution, and his anti-Semitic pamphlets into poetry: "poetry was my downfall! and still is! Worse and more of it! Ah, sacrificial victim? your ugly mug! ... your blood! your furniture! ... your lyre! ... your books! off to the dungeon! bastard!" (42–43).

Reading these claims, we are tempted to dismiss them as Céline's bad-faith attempt to deny any responsibility in the persecution of the Jews during the war. His use of the Romantic mythology of the misunderstood, hounded, and exiled poet hardly seems credible when one considers that his pamphlets were huge popular successes in France. Still, when Céline claims that his style led to the attacks against him, he is pointing, almost unconsciously, to the inextricable link he himself forged between poetry and politics. Already in *Bagatelles pour un massacre* Céline had placed the direct emotion of poetic language at the core of his racist diatribes.[10] The raging anti-Semitism

---

[10]"[Céline] made race the determining element of his poetics, but at the same time he proposed the realization of a poetic ideal as the ultimate purpose of his racism." Carroll, *French Literary Fascism,* 182. Before Carroll, Muray had already written that Céline's pamphlets were scandalous precisely because they

in this 1937 pamphlet becomes the site of the investment of all of Céline's stylistic procedures—from his trademark verve to his frag-
mented sentences, from his scatological humor to the sentimental
ballets. Céline's pamphlets are morally obscene works, and they are
stylistically overblown, repetitious, and sloppy. When in the postwar
years he maintains that he is persecuted for his "poetry," Céline is reaffirming, in a coded language, the poetic project of the pamphlets.
What seems at first to be a standard postwar defense, in which the accused writer claims irresponsibility and argues for the autonomy of
literature, turns into a defense of the project initiated in *Bagatelles
pour un massacre*. The writer, as Céline understands him, remains the
opposite of the intellectual, not because he has nothing to say, but
because he has fused style and ideology.

Throughout his career Céline was acutely aware of his position in
the literary field, and after the war he saw himself in conflict with almost every other writer still alive in France. Céline's voice is contradictory, oppositional, and revisionist, and his novels are ridden with
accusatory lists in which he denounces writers of all factions, especially in relation to the conflicts and crises of the postwar purge. In
Céline's understanding of the purge not only was he attacked for being a writer, but he claims to have been the only writer who didn't
taint himself in the collaboration. Céline reads the postwar literary
field as riddled with writers who slipped through the cracks of the
purge while he alone was made to pay. In "Reply to Charges of Treason" Céline claims to be one of the few French writers banned in
Germany and the only writer prosecuted by the French courts at the
end of the war:

> Thus were translated and printed, honored and feted under the Nazi
> regime: MAURIAC, MAUROIS, MARTIN DU GARD, JULES RO-
> MAIN[S]. During the Occupation other well-known authors, such as La
> Varende, H. Bordeaux, Guitry, Montherlant, Simenon, Giono, Marcel
> Aymé, Ed. Jaloux, Mac Orlan, Pierre Hamp, incessantly furnished
> comic or serious material to the newspapers of the Collaboration and

---

"put a 'revolutionary' writing at the service of racial hatred." Muray, *Céline*,
100–101.

even to Franco-German periodicals. They are no worse for it today. (Céline, "Reply," 533)

The list of authors in this passage recalls the CNE blacklists and even borrows their technique of putting names in capital letters. There is one significant difference, however. Céline's 1946 list has two components: a first set of writers, in capital letters, associated with the Resistance, and a second set of writers associated with the collaboration. Right-wing or left, Resistants or collaborators, all these writers have been either exonerated or "feted," while he alone is imprisoned.

In *Castle to Castle* Céline reproduces this type of accusatory list. Evoking the horrible conditions of his Danish prison he writes, "I'd like to see Montherlant, or Morand, or Carbuccia try it ... and see if they'd still be sipping cocktails with the best" (Céline, *Castle to Castle*, 115). Later he states that a stint in jail would cure writers of their desire to engage in politics: "I can see Achille [Gallimard], Mauriac, Loukoum [Paulhan], Montherlant, Morand, Aragon, Madeleine [Jacob], Duhamel and other political hotheads ... they don't know either! it would do them a hell of a lot of good! ... they wouldn't be giving any more cocktail parties!" (214–15). In a final example Céline tells of two musicians who had played for the Germans and who at the Liberation were charged under Article 75 "that Morand never got ... or Montherlant! or Maurois!" (253). It is surprising that Céline cites so many writers whose names begin with the letter M: Mauriac, Maurois, Martin du Gard, Montherlant, Morand, Madeleine Jacob. Perhaps he had in mind the celebrated "quatre M"—Mauriac, Maurois, Montherlant, Morand—four authors published by Grasset in the 1920s and 1930s and grouped together for marketing reasons. The repetition of names that begin with the letter M creates a phonic link between Céline's postwar writings, in this case the 1957 novel *Castle to Castle*, and the 1946 "Reply to Charges of Treason." This is one more example of the echoes between Céline's postwar novels and the legal brief he wrote in a Danish prison. We are led to conclude that when he wrote his last novels, Céline not only had his trial in mind, he may also have had his defense brief in hand.

Each cited passage from the novel *Castle to Castle* is closely connected with Céline's trial; they all evoke either the prison sentence or Article 75. Though he knows that Sacha Guitry had been imprisoned and that the CNE had blacklisted and opened files on both Morand and Montherlant, Céline is convinced that he is the only writer prosecuted at the end of the war. In all the accusatory lists Céline brings together writers from differing ideological perspectives, implying that there is a connivance among his enemies. In the cited passages writers who had little in common are placed side by side: Morand, who was the Vichy ambassador to Rumania; Montherlant, a supporter of the collaboration; Maurois, a Jewish writer who left France for New York during the Occupation; and Mauriac, the Resistance writer. Montherlant and Morand are mentioned in the same phrase as Aragon, a Communist committed to purging collaborators, and Madeleine Jacob, a journalist who covered Pétain's trial for the Communist newspaper *Franc-tireur*. When he is describing and denouncing his rivals in the literary field, Céline operates what we might call an ideological scrambling. By blurring the ideological differences between the "political hotheads," he can better assert his singularity and invalidate the legal accusations brought against him by the purge authorities. Céline's defense in this sense is the opposite of the "everyone was doing it" defense. Everyone else is guilty; he alone is punished. It is difficult not to fall into the language of psychoanalysis and see these accusatory lists as a massive projection of Céline's own guilt onto the other members of his profession. Projection is, after all, the psyche's final line of self-defense, and Céline writing after 1944 invariably returns to issues of guilt and innocence raised by the purge.

What also interests me here is that the author's self-defense mechanism becomes an aesthetic principle. Céline's projection of guilt onto writers from the Resistance and from the collaboration also serves to reaffirm his literary singularity. He denounces party politics and rejects "newspapers and periodicals" as a forum for his work. Céline is reaffirming an aesthetic ideal in which the "book" is a literary paragon, in a higher sphere than the habitual outlet for French intellectuals, the commissioned article. To be sure, there were exceptions to this aesthetic rule. During the Occupation Céline wrote some thirty letters to the editors of the collaborationist press, in which he reiterated the racist violence of his pamphlets. And though he never wrote a commissioned article, it is fair to say that no writer was more interested in money than Céline himself. Still, when he accuses other writers of having "furnished comic or serious material to the newspapers of the Collaboration" (Céline, "Reply," 533), he is reaffirming his position as a stylist, an author who remains autonomous from political pressures, even if he is persecuted for this autonomy.

Not everyone, of course, accepted unquestioningly Céline's declarations, in particular his claims to financial autonomy. We know that during the purge the charge of having been paid by the Nazis, of having profited from the Occupation, often served to prove a writer's treason. The treasonous writers, the courts repeatedly asserted, were *"vendus,"* intellectuals who had sold themselves to the Nazis. Though the courts never directly accused Céline of being on the Nazi payroll, as they did Jean Luchaire and Abel Hermant, for example, Sartre made just such an allusion in his 1945 article "Portrait of the Anti-Semite":

> anti-Semitism is a form of Manicheism; it explains the state of the world as the struggle of Good versus Evil. Between these two there is no possible accord: one of the two must triumph and the other must be annihilated. Take Céline: his vision of the universe is catastrophic; the Jew is everywhere, the earth is lost, the Aryan must never compromise, he must never cut a deal. But let him beware: if he breathes, he has already lost his purity, for the very air that penetrates his lungs is soiled. Doesn't that resemble the predications of a Cathare? *If Céline upheld the socialist doctrines of the Nazis, he must have been paid.* In his heart, he didn't believe it: for him there is no solution other than collective suicide, non-procreation, death.[11]

Sartre's accusation certainly served to distance the author of *La Nausée* from an author to whom he admittedly owed a great deal. The article in *Les Temps modernes* is the settling of old debts. Sartre is repaying Céline by accusing him of having been paid. Read today, Sar-

[11]Sartre, "Portrait de l'antisémite," 462 (my translation and emphasis).

tre's accusation also seems somewhat exculpatory, for though it follows the standard purge charge that the fascist writer sold himself to the Nazis, it also diminishes Céline's responsibility by claiming that he never believed what he wrote. Still, by the very fact that it mimics one of the accusations leveled at collaborators by the purge courts, Sartre's statement could have had costly implications for Céline. In the context of the purge, it is the equivalent of calling Céline a *vendu*.

Céline in any case certainly read Sartre's article as a denunciation, and from his earliest self-defense pleas he denies ever having received any remuneration from the Germans. On the contrary, the war brought him nothing but ruin, beginning with his flight to Sigmaringen, which cost him a small fortune:

> During all this time, I paid out of my own pocket for medicines which I administered to the sick, wrested from the local pharmacy with much difficulty. . . . Working day and night I spent about 600 000 francs of my own money in Germany, changed into marks and thrown to the winds in the form of gifts, loans, medicines, etc. (538)

Céline repeats this claim in exactly the same terms in *Castle to Castle*. To a German officer in Sigmaringen he declares that he must buy his own medicine: "I pay a fortune for it! ... My own money! [*le mien d'or!*] Not Adolf Hitler's! nor the Reich's!" (Céline, *Castle to Castle,* 237). Throughout his postwar writings Céline tells us that he committed no crime for which he has not already sufficiently paid. His impoverishment resulting from the war and his postwar indigence become a self-acquittal of sorts. There is a curious reversal at work in Céline's statements. In 1937 Céline had published his pamphlet *Bagatelles pour un massacre,* in which he accused the Jews of owning and controlling all the world's gold.[12] As horrible as it appears to us today, these claims made Céline rich. *Bagatelles pour un massacre* was a best-seller in its day, and Céline deposited the gold from his royalties in a safe-deposit box in a Danish bank. In a reversal typical of the purged writer, Céline asserts that he was ruined by the purge. His

---

[12]"[The Jews] pull all the strings. Propaganda, gold, advertisement, radio, press, 'little envelopes,' movies . . . the Jews own all the gold in the world." Céline, *Bagatelles,* 53–54 (my translation).

flight to Germany, his imprisonment in Denmark cost him "a fortune." From his "Reply to Charges of Treason" through his last novels Céline is staging the expiation through the payment in gold (*"le mien d'or"*) of crimes he elsewhere claims never to have committed.

Money, disbursements, acquittal, and gold are also at the heart of Céline's stylistic enterprise. To understand this point, I want to begin by returning to the author's conception of work. Throughout his postwar career Céline repeatedly tells us that he is physically consumed by the travails of his style. He writes in pain: "I don't write easily!" he tells one interviewer, "I work laboriously" (Céline, *Romans II*, 934, 937). Throughout the final novels Céline develops a cult of work, which, as he tells us, he learned from his parents when he was young and whose manifestation is now the stylistic labor on the literary text. While his rivals devote themselves to frivolity, he endlessly revises his texts, and the multiple versions of his novels, now reproduced in the prestigious Pléiade editions, attest to the compulsive corrections his works underwent. Céline's labor remains unrewarded, however. To hear him tell it, his books don't sell, his editor exploits him, and he lives in near poverty, reduced to a diet of cooked carrots and noodles. *Conversations with Professor Y* begins with the evocation of a crisis in the publishing industry:

> bookstores are suffering from a serious crisis in falling sales ... Matter of fact, nothing is selling ... bad times! ... Movies, TV, appliances, mopeds, big cars, little cars, middle-sized cars really hurt book sales ... credit merchandise! imagine! And weekends ... so, you know, buying a book! ... a camper? well! ... but a book? ... (Céline, *Conversations*, 3)

Throughout *Féerie pour une autre fois* Céline appeals to the reader to buy his book and even suggests a retail price: 2 pounds 50. In the opening fragment of *North* he claims that no one buys his books (Céline, *North,* 1). And in one of the last lines of his last book Céline complains that, even after having been published in the Pléiade edition, the remuneration remains minimal: "it's not the Pléiade and its four percent royalty that's going to put me on easy street! four percent is kidding the Muses" (Céline, *Rigadoon*, 259).

Poverty, for Céline, becomes proof of political and artistic integrity. Poor he remains pure, and because he is pure he remains poor. He didn't sell out during the Occupation, he tells us, and his books aren't selling in the postwar era. Céline quite literally writes for nothing. But this economic gratuity, what he calls "the writer working for free" (Céline, *Conversations,* 3) coincides with stylistic gratuity. Not only does he not get paid, but his investment in style is also a divestment from the traditional novel and its forms of representation: "the novel no longer has the mission it once had; it is no longer a vehicle of information;" "I make the story [*l'histoire*] conform to the style, just as painters no longer deal with the apple ... The object [of my writing] more or less disappears" (Céline, *Romans II,* 932, 937). All he would need to sell books is to tell a story, to write romances in the manner of the popular novelist Delly, for example. But by his own understanding Céline has evolved from best-selling novelist and pamphleteer to obscure modernist, ignored by the public because of his "quest for the aesthetic" (*Cahiers Céline 7,* 421). If Céline's postwar works sound at times like a modernist manifesto, it is in this apparent refusal of mimesis: his works reject representation, they claim to have no "object" and refuse to enter into a system of symbolic exchange, an exchange of words for "objects." The author's entire postwar literary enterprise seems to be directed against the theory of literature established by the purge courts and their supporters. By distancing his work from an economy of exchange, Céline is both refuting Sartre's accusations that he was paid and at the same time rejecting the Resistance credo that "to speak is to act." To hear him tell it, Céline's works participate in neither an economic exchange (he was never paid; his writing remains gratuitous) nor a symbolic exchange (his writing has no "object"; words cannot be exchanged for an apple). In this sense the postwar Céline resembles the postwar Blanchot. Both writers divest their literature from mimesis, transitivity, and an economy of representation.

This divestiture tells only half the story, however, for, if stylistic innovation is the source of Céline's poverty, poverty in turn becomes a source of his authority. In a passage from *Féerie pour une autre fois I* the writer bemoans his fate in prison. The purge authorities have made him pay—"'You'll pay for everyone!' they said!" (Céline, *Ro-*

mans IV, 159)—but now through his writing Céline will exact revenge. Targeting the members of the purge courts, Céline writes: "I want them to engrave their names in gold! in the granite of the Sainte Chapelle." He continues in this vein in reference to Paul Claudel: "I want another stone again there, engraved, for those who sold Odes to both sides" (159); or again, in reference to Sartre: "Artron he never screamed! ... He makes others scream in his plays! He makes his dough by denouncing!" (161). And then we return to the theme of the names engraved in stone:

> Oh, but I'll write, I'll avenge everyone, with my ass stuck to this stool, their historical names engraved in gold ... in the Sainte Chapelle! ... the power of the feeble writer! feeble poet, more feeble than anything! Watch out big Hercules dressed in togas! I'll have your names written in gold! They overturned my Amnesty. (162)

The movement of the text is typical of Céline's reactionary writing. Wronged by the judges, betrayed by his professional class, he vows to use his prose to rewrite the verdicts of the purge, denounce its judges, and humiliate his literary rivals. A golden thread ties these pages together, however. While Céline has had to pay, both Claudel and Sartre, he tells us, benefited monetarily from the Occupation: Claudel by selling his "odes" to both sides (and indeed Claudel wrote a poem to Pétain in 1942 and another to de Gaulle two years later); Sartre by denouncing others (Céline here sees himself as the principal victim of this denunciation). Céline accuses his rivals of precisely the crimes for which the purge courts accused the collaborators: venality and denunciation. His literary project includes a redistribution of what Céline considers a misbegotten wealth. He will carve his enemies' names in gold in the stones of the Sainte Chapelle, the Gothic church that adjoins the Palais de Justice, site of many purge trials. If we follow Céline from text to text, we see that the gold that, according to his "Reply," he spent in Germany buying medicine now miraculously reappears under his pen in the form of these gold inscriptions. Céline's texts are all about the circulation of gold: from *Death on the Installment Plan* to the pamphlets; from *Guignol's band*, where Boro strangles Van Claben in an attempt to have him regurgitate his

gold, to *North* (*Nord*), whose very title holds the gold (*or*) that moti-
vates Céline's northward quest. His postwar correspondence with his
editor, Gallimard, reveals an author obsessed with the terms of his
publishing contracts and the sale of his books.[13] But it is in *Féerie pour
une autre fois I* that we are confronted with a literary alchemy; the
losses Céline suffered during the purge and the gratuity of his writing
are turned into pure profit by the "feeble poet." What he has lost in
wealth and temporal power, he has regained in a symbolic authority,
an authority he will use to rewrite history and to avenge himself of his
fate during the purge. When Céline evokes the gold lettering of the
commemorative plaque at the Sainte Chapelle, he is predicting the future reception of his works in which his power as a poet will mark the
annals of history. Gold is a good investment. Céline knew this, and
today all of his novels, including this passage from *Féerie pour une
autre fois*, rest in the Pléiade edition, the collection that unites in de-
luxe and expensive form the great writers of France and the world.
Each volume is sold in its individual "coffer," and its covers, according to the advertisement, are embossed with gold.

Céline's investment in his literary future is intimately tied to his
rivalries with his peers. His complicated "art for art's sake" stance is
meant to distance him from his contemporaries' commitment to using literature as a political tool. And while Céline takes a scattershot
approach to denouncing his rivals, Sartre nonetheless seems to hold a
place of honor. Céline is as dedicated as Blanchot to refuting Sartre's
claims about literature, even though the two writers approached
these rebuttals through radically different methods. Céline's method,
more often than not, was the insult. Throughout the postwar novels
Céline engages in a running critique of Sartre, denouncing him as an
imitator and a sham: Sartre, now referred to as "Tartre," is nothing
but a vulgar plagiarist. "Tartre! the cream of the sewer! the way he
slandered me, moved heaven and earth to have me drawn and quar-
tered" (Céline, *Castle to Castle*, 56). Later, to denounce another literary rival, this time the right-wing Jean Hérold-Paquis, Céline claims
that he is "as shameless a liar as Tartre" (157).

[13]Céline, *Lettres à la N.R.F.*

In 1948 Céline wrote a short essay "A l'agité du bocal," in which he not only counters Sartre's accusation but also attacks his style (Céline, *Cahiers Céline 7*, 382–87). Céline accuses Sartre of being a *"Lamanièredeux,"* that is, of writing in "the style of" others such as La Bruyère and Céline himself in particular, a charge that reminds us that the author of *Nausea* had cited Céline as one of his influences. Sartre, the argument goes, is a writer devoid of originality, an imitator, a stylistic parasite; in a word a taenia, agitated in his formaldehyde bowl.[14] After having liberated Paris by bicycle (Céline, *Cahiers Céline 7*, 384), Sartre, according to Céline, is now running after the purge trials. Only, Céline warns Sartre, in order to become a true poet of the purge he must add music to his method:

> You must realize that horror is nothing without dream and without Music . . . Macbeth is only the Grand Guignol on a bad day without music, without dream ... You are evil, dirty, ungrateful, hateful, imbecilic, but that's not all J.B.S. [Sartre]! That's not enough ... You must dance as well! (385)

Céline ends his short essay with a parody of the purge, a play Sartre could write titled *Les Mouchards*, a grand parade of 200,000 murdered victims of the purge accompanied by the "Nuremberg hangman's choir." Céline thus responds to Sartre's charge in "Portrait of the Anti-Semite" by giving a highly stylized, parodic account of the postwar purge. His refutation of Sartre's accusation has turned into a lesson in literary style. In this moment of literary one-upmanship Céline is initiating his imitator in the art of rhetoric and the power of his *petite musique*.

The authority style obtains can also be seen in one of the most compelling passages from *Castle to Castle*, a passage that once again stages the rivalry between Sartre and Céline. One hundred pages into the novel Céline is about to begin what he calls his "chronicle" of Sigmaringen and its collaborationist refugees. Bedridden with a fever and under the sway of a *furor poeticus*, he once again mentions that his previous books haven't sold and that this latest one probably won't

---

[14]On this point see the parallel Pagès draws between Céline and Jules Vallès. Pagès, *Les Fictions*, 57–58.

fare any better: "I'm boycotted? ... what of it?" (Céline, *Castle to Castle,* 141). This boycott is, of course, the result of his wartime politics and of the CNE blacklists on which his name appeared, but Céline also understands it as a question of changing fashion. The postwar public and his literary rivals consider him "Out of date, decrepit!" (141). He is a writer in purgatory even before his death. Céline then turns this accusation on its head and compares his rivals to "rejects from the wax works!" (141) who each has one "idea" and who all need "rewriting." It is they and not Céline who are out of date. As for his own style, he compares it to the "painstaking" craft of a dressmaker he remembers from his past who made finely sewn garments of "flounces and embroidery" (142). In French Céline had used the terms *"flous et petits points,"* which can also be translated as "allusions and dots" and thus recall the author's allusive, three-dot style. Céline is recasting his style in nostalgic terms as the lost craft of dressmaking, and the comparison is particularly apt since "stylist" designates both the dressmaker and, in Céline's postwar novels, the writer himself.

This passage is one of the self-reflexive moments that constitutes a large part of the interest and the pleasure we take from Céline's last novels. The writing here seems to have no "object" other than writing itself. We see the novelist at work; we participate in the creation of his phrases and in the construction of meaning. Céline is putting his style on stage and letting us see, as if through the rent in a curtain, the work of the stylist. This moment of intimacy, however, also serves to reaffirm the authority of his writing. In Céline's argument contemporary writers, that is, his rivals, have lost the craftsmanship of the dressmaker. Céline's artisanal and finely woven style, the textuality of his writing, will permit him to outlast his peers: "I, who have seen Empires ground to hash, if I live long enough (coal and carrots), I'll witness the hash of our 'up-to-date' writers" (142). Céline uses the term *"actuels"* in the original to identify his up-to-date contemporaries, a term that makes us think of the writers at Sartre's *Les Temps modernes.* After the purge Céline gambles that a poetics based, at least in part, on nostalgia will assure his place in history. His style, made up of "allusions and dots," is the guarantee that, as he wrote to his attorney, "history will do [him] justice." Even in this self-reflexive moment he reaffirms his rivalry with those other modernists, the existentialists. Style for Céline is invariably caught in the literary rivalries of postwar France, to the point where even his most modernist, self-reflexive moments become part of a power struggle.

We thus arrive at a point in Céline's work where for the author style is power. More specifically, style is a power strategy.[15] Céline's books were always weapons in the struggle against what he perceived as forms of domination: military discipline, the family, educational institutions, the medical profession. Even his anti-Semitic pamphlets present themselves in the guise of a reaction against domination. If we can talk about Céline's text as the locus of a power relationship, it is because the postwar novels have as their objective to act upon their readers. As I have suggested, these novels can be read as an elaborate revision of the author's purge trial, and their ultimate goal is to convince the reader to deliver a favorable verdict. In this sense the investment in style presents itself as a divestment from politics; the author offers us a purged text along with his purged body. Critics in the 1970s and 1980s, perhaps in reaction to Sartre's method of reading and judging literature, often understood Céline's work as primarily a stylistic monument, purged of any racist or fascist ideology.[16] At the same time, however, it is precisely because of this investment that style for Céline becomes a strategy of power. Style is the means employed to attain a specific end: the revision of his trial by future generations of readers. Style, as his rivalry with Sartre makes clear, is the procedure used to gain an advantage over other writers. Style, as he tells his attorney, guarantees that he will be read in the year 2000. Far from simply being a way to deny his responsibility in the massacres of the Holocaust, Céline conceives of style as a weapon in his postwar works. As we read him, we realize that it is precisely at the moment when he seems to withdraw into literary autonomy that we find Cé-

---

[15] I borrow the term from Michel Foucault. Of Foucault's numerous writings on power see, for instance, "The Subject and Power," trans. Leslie Sawyer, in which the author sums up the different characteristics that constitute a "strategy of power." Dreyfus and Rabinow, *Foucault,* 208–26.

[16] For a response to this reading of Céline see Watts, "Postmodern Céline," 203–15.

line engaged in refuting accusations against him, overturning verdicts of the purge, and revising the history of the war. Seen in this light, Céline's postwar novels paradoxically illustrate the existentialist theory of literature as action. A commitment to style has become for Céline the most potent form of political commitment.

CHAPTER 6

Céline:
Denying History

O f all the arguments to come out of the postwar purge the most hateful and nefarious is undoubtedly what has come to be known as Holocaust revisionism, the attempts to deny the reality of the Nazi death camps. Pronounced by those Pierre Vidal-Naquet has called the "assassins of memory," revisionist arguments have taken various forms: voluminous pseudoscientific treatises, articles in the pages of a self-proclaimed nonconformist press, whole-page ads in college newspapers, insinuations by extreme right-wing politicians. Holocaust revisionism has become a rallying cry of anti-Semites of all stripes. While, as Vidal-Naquet has shown, current revisionism in France has its roots in both fascism and extreme left-wing movements (Vidal-Naquet, *Assassins,* 79–98), the trials of the postwar purge both in Germany and in France became a fertile ground for this new form of racial hatred. For someone like Maurice Bardèche, Robert Brasillach's brother-in-law and a radical critic of the purge, revisionism originates in his rejection of the verdicts of the Nuremberg trials and his desire to redo (*refaire*) the history of the war (Bardèche, *Nuremberg,* 11).

When critics have analyzed the politics of Céline's texts, they have up to now limited themselves to the pamphlets or the links between the first novels and the political discourse of the 1930s.[1] If Céline's anti-Semitism up to the end of the war is well documented, we must nonetheless ask ourselves about the postwar years. After 1944 Céline's anti-Semitism no longer relies upon the rhetorical violence of the pamphlets; one of Céline's main claims is that his style is no longer about politics at all. Rather, the legacy of anti-Semitism must be located in what we might call a rhetoric of silence and attenuation. From the end of the war, Céline and presently his widow maintained a ban on the pamphlets, which, among other things, serves to protect the memory of the author by erasing an entire part of his opus.[2] This ban is supported by all his published works, in which he refers to his pamphlets, if at all, simply as "books," no more, no less. Céline silences their function as anti-Semitic propaganda. At the same time Céline's vision of history has as one of its sources the revisionist attempt to falsify history and to silence the memory of the victims of the Holocaust. It is this second type of silence that concerns me here. When, in his novel *Castle to Castle,* echoing Bardèche, Céline writes that "the Nuremberg trials need doing over!" (Céline, *Castle to Castle,* 131), he reveals his project to do over (*"refaire"*), or rather to undo, through his fiction the verdicts delivered against the Nazi war criminals at Nuremberg. Céline sees writing as much in terms of competing narratives as in terms of competing styles. In *Castle to Castle* he declares that "History is written by the victors" (226) and then proceeds to write the history of those he considers the losers of the war. As Céline endlessly rewrote his texts—tuning his *"petite musique"* and working his sentences to find the right note—he was also revising the history of the war in terms that went beyond claims of innocence into the revisionist discourse that, though attenuated, must be read as a

---

[1]Kaplan has shown the extent to which Céline's racist discourse relies on the anti-Semitic press of his times. See Kaplan, *Relevé des sources.* See also Bellosta, *Céline*; Pagès, *Les Fictions.*

[2]Céline's widow and heir, Lucette Destouches, has also been instrumental in blocking compromising letters the author wrote to collaborationist newspapers during the Occupation. See, for example, her request in November 1994 that a recently published collection of letters from that period, titled *Lettres des années noires,* be seized. Her request was eventually denied, but it once again put into play the economic and moral forces at work in the author's heritage.

direct continuation of the anti-Semitism the author advocated until 1944.

Since the early 1980s a significant, precise, and committed critical work has dismantled the rhetorical strategies of Holocaust revisionism.[3] Still, for our understanding of Céline's postwar novels we must reopen the dossier on this discourse. My starting point is the claim made by revisionists and Nazi apologists that the real crimes of World War II were not the Nazi death camps at all, but the bombing of German cities by Allied planes, the atomic devastation at Hiroshima and Nagasaki, and the atrocities committed by the Soviets in their gulags. There is some evidence that this attitude was already prevalent before the end of the war. In a parody of collaborationist attitudes, published in 1945, Aragon gives us the interior monologues of a small-time traitor: "These horrible accounts of what goes on in concentration camps, in prison . . . Pétain's police, if we were to believe them would be like the inquisition. Of course, they never mention the bombed out cities, the bombs systematically dropped by the English to please the Jews in Washington on our hospitals, our schools, our kindergartens! Of that, not a word!"[4] Aragon's short *récit* was prescient, for this is precisely the attitude presented in one of the first texts to introduce the revisionist argument in France, Bardèche's 1948 pamphlet *Nuremberg ou la Terre promise*.[5] Before the war Bardèche, a scholar and critic, had cowritten a *History of the Cinema* with Brasillach. Since the war he has published studies of Balzac and Céline among others and has maintained a parallel activity as a self-declared "fascist writer" and editor of the neofascist publication *Défense de l'Occident*, which has consistently published the articles of Holocaust deniers.[6]

---

[3]Along with Vidal-Naquet's work see the following: Fresco, "Les Redresseurs," 2150–211; Finkielkraut, *L'Avenir*; Lipstadt, *Denying the Holocaust*; Rancière, "Un Négationnisme," 18–20; Taguieff, "La Logique," 28–30.

[4]Aragon, *Servitude*, 110–11 (my translation).

[5]Bardèche, *Nuremberg ou la Terre promise*. Two years later Bardèche published a companion volume *Nuremberg II ou les faux-monnayeurs*. My translation.

[6]Bardèche, *Qu'est-ce que le fascisme?* 9. See Kaplan's chilling interview with Bardèche in *Reproductions*, 161–92.

Immediately after Brasillach's death, Bardèche became one of France's most vocal critics of the purge. Vehemently opposed to the Nuremberg trials, as well as to the trials in France, Bardèche argues in *Nuremberg ou la Terre promise* that the accusations brought against the Nazis were entirely fabricated by the Allies in order to dissimulate what Bardèche calls the real crimes of the war, the destruction of German cities by Allied bombing raids: "if, by chance, [the Germans] hadn't been monsters, wouldn't the cities destroyed by thousands of phosphorous bombs have been a heavy burden indeed?" (Bardèche, *Nuremberg*, 17). As it turns out, the Allies had "the good fortune" (30) to discover the concentration camps in January 1945, a discovery that permitted them to divert world attention from the bombings to Nazi barbarism. Bardèche's rhetoric of comparison quickly gives way to his main argument: an attempt to raise doubts about the horror and indeed the very existence of the concentration camps. In the guise of scientific objectivity Bardèche demands "an impartial verification of the accusations [of extermination], a verification that has not yet taken place" (113). And his conclusion: "The true history of the camps has not been written [*l'histoire vraie des camps n'est pas faite*]" (150). Feigning to maintain a neutral tone, Bardèche is constructing the foundation of revisionist rhetoric: the comparison of the bombing raids to the concentration camps serves less to denounce the destruction of German or Japanese cities than to question the reality of Hitler's final solution. The attitude Aragon had parodied becomes the tragic ideology of Bardèche's pamphlet.

The structure of comparison is also at work in Paul Rassinier's *Le Mensonge d'Ulysse*, one of the first revisionist works that attempts to call into question the existence of gas chambers as weapons of extermination.[7] Rassinier, a Socialist and member of the Resistance who was deported to Buchenwald and Dora, set out, upon his return to France, to contradict what he felt were mendacious accounts about the Nazi concentration camps. Targeting David Rousset, whom he accuses of *"bolcheviko-philie"* (Rassinier, *Le Mensonge,* 247), Rassinier

[7]Rassinier, *Le Mensonge d'Ulysse.* I am quoting from the 1955 edition (my translation).

fingers the Communists, rather than the Nazis, as the real culprits.[8] Not only did Communist prisoners impose a "reign of Terror" within the camps, but after the war the Soviets fixed world opinion on Auschwitz in order to conceal the horror of the gulag (315). The Nuremberg trials and the purge, Rassinier maintains, were their way of avoiding the dock. Behind this *tu quoque* reasoning is Rassinier's main argument: a "definitive judgment" on the gas chambers cannot yet be made (249). But in the meantime Rassinier is willing to give us his opinion: "My opinion on the gas chambers? There were some: but not as many as they think. There were also exterminations by this method: but not as many as they say" (254). The seeds of Robert Faurisson's bitter fruit are planted in these lines. A denunciation of the crimes of the "victors" of the war only makes sense if the revisionist can simultaneously show that the mass murders in the Nazi camps were a fabrication. And if we should have missed the point, in the 1955 introduction to *Le Mensonge d'Ulysse*, Rassinier criticizes those who condemn German atrocities without mentioning the "hundreds of thousands of people—women, children and elderly too!—exterminated [*exterminés*] at Leipzig, Hamburg etc. (Germany), Nagasaki and Hiroshima (Japan) in conditions that we know were just as atrocious" (29). Rassinier's use of the term *exterminated* is not innocent. He has little interest in speaking on behalf of the victims of Allied bombings. Rather, his use of the word *exterminated* is meant to complete a process of substitution in which the victims of Allied bombings replace the millions who died in the Nazi death camps.

One last example, this one taken from the satirical review *Le Crapouillot*, indicates that revisionist discourse in France is not limited to the pamphlets of a handful of Nazi apologists. In his 1945 *Journal* Jean Galtier-Boissière had described the "horror" he felt upon discovering the existence of the death camps. Strangely, however, this horror is mitigated by two factors. First, he writes in April 1945, that one particularly gruesome detail is that prisoners of the camps would,

[8]David Rousset had been deported to Buchenwald and returned with an account of this tragic, "ubuesque" world.

for a supplemental ration, light the crematory ovens themselves. Second, he denounces the hypocrisy of the French man in the streets who is "horrified" (*"soulevée d'horreur"*) upon learning of the camps but who becomes joyous (*"s'épanouit"*) upon reading that a small city has been destroyed by phosphorous bombs (Galtier-Boissière, *Mon Journal*, 218, 224). The author's complacency in morbid details also reveals an attraction to the terms of compared atrocities: the camps cannot be evoked without another element being introduced to deflect the reality of and the responsibility for the Final Solution.

Galtier-Boissière had founded the periodical *Le Crapouillot* in 1914 as a reaction to the bellicosity of the *union sacrée*, France's quasi-unanimous enthusiasm for sending troops to fight the Germans. The monthly review quickly became the voice of the right-wing anarchist milieu. The self-proclaimed nonconformist journal is still publishing today and runs cover stories on such topics as turncoat politicians, society's greed, the gangsters of Montmartre, or the history of sex. An issue from 1950 promises to present the great crimes and massacres of history but invariably returns to the recent past, as evidenced by an article written by Galtier-Boissière titled "Compared Atrocities: From the English Pontoons to the Nazi Reprisal Camps—From Oradour-sur-Glane to Hiroshima."[9] The title itself is revealing: by using the phrase "Nazi Reprisal Camps" Galtier-Boissière suggests that they were a site of justified revenge. Furthermore, the very comparison of the camps to nineteenth-century English prison ships confirms that we are in a rhetoric that seeks to diminish the horror of the death camps. The article makes full use of the structure of compared atrocities announced in the title; indeed the first atrocity mentioned is the bombing of civilian populations: London but also, and especially, Hamburg and Berlin. And in a later development the Nazi camps are downgraded to "prisons," and the article tells us that these "prisons" "were modeled on Soviet reeducation camps . . . and pros-

---

[9]*Le Crapouillot*, no. 11 (1950): 12–23. In 1985 *Le Crapouillot* published a special issue devoted to exposing and denouncing the purge. This issue gives considerable space to the crimes of the unauthorized purge, such as the shearing of women, and publishes an article by Lucien Rebatet on his imprisonment at the end of the war, "On ne fusille pas le dimanche," *Le Crapouillot*, no. 81 (1985).

pered in France." The reversal is only complete, however, when the article speaks of the French "concentration camps" of 1939–49. Nothing new under the sun. By a semantic displacement typical of revisionist thinking, the Nazi death camps have become prisons, and these prisons are shown to have always existed, even in modern-day France, where coincidentally they are once again called "concentration camps." This issue of *Le Crapouillot* is less concerned with an apology of the Nazis than with a denunciation of the purge. To be sure, Galtier-Boissière quotes Bardèche and Rassinier as his historical sources, but the issue also ran an article by Marcel Aymé which denounced the atrocities that followed the Liberation. What is most troubling, however, is that *Le Crapouillot* disguises its revisionism as a nonconformist version of history. The issue casts itself as a resistance to what it calls the public's "brainwashing" about "Hitler's atrocities." The revisionist now sees himself in a struggle against Communist and Gaullist conformity; he wants to be an iconoclast, a destroyer of myths, and the purveyor of a new historical truth.

The rhetoric of the revisionists progresses incrementally from almost meaningless generalities, such as a denunciation of *all* atrocities, to the specificity of their main argument. They work through a structure of comparison, and their trope is the analogy. But if one term of the comparison is true—the Allied bombings and the Soviet camps were indeed responsible for the deaths of countless civilians—the analogy itself remains fraudulent. For the revisionist the bombing of Dresden seems to cancel the horror of Auschwitz; denouncing the Soviet camps somehow exculpates the Nazi leaders. Furthermore, the revisionist discourse in the late 1940s and 1950s depends upon what we could call a rhetoric of insinuation and allusion.[10] Bardèche does not openly deny the existence of the death camps; he claims their "true history" has not yet been written. Rassinier does not directly deny the existence of gas chambers; he denies the role and the importance others gave to them. The editors of *Le Crapouillot* do not deny the reality of the Nazi camps; they show that these types of camps

---

[10]For an analysis of the rhetoric of insinuation see Rancière, "Un Négationnisme," 18–20.

have always existed. This rhetoric of insinuation in the early revisionist texts may have been the result of an attempt to avoid the censors of the Fourth Republic. Upon its release, copies of Bardèche's *Nuremberg* were seized and pulped, and the author was condemned and jailed for what the French call "apology of the crime of murder" (*"apologie du crime de meurtre"*). It is perhaps due to this fear of censorship that revisionists often resort to interrogatory phrases or to sentences that seem to stop short of their goal. More than this, however, the rhetoric of insinuation demands the participation of the reader, who is called upon to finish the author's thought, to make the final leap from facts to a denial of facts. The reader of the revisionist tract is called to enter into complicity through this rhetoric of innuendo.

We know that Céline read the works of Bardèche and Rassinier while he was writing his novel *Féerie pour une autre fois* in Denmark. Critics have been reluctant to acknowledge, however, that these revisionist tracts constitute one of the important ideological intertexts of Céline's postwar novels. To understand the role revisionism plays in Céline's work, we must begin by looking at some of the numerous letters he wrote during the last years of his life. In his correspondence with Albert Paraz, a French novelist and right-wing anarchist, though he repeatedly mocks Bardèche, he nonetheless praises *Nuremberg* and writes: "the end is idiotic [*conne*] but the arguments [*le développement*] are solid."[11] In a letter dated 9 October 1950, Céline asks his correspondent to send him four copies of Rassinier's *Le Mensonge d'Ulysse*, for which Paraz had written the preface, and he concludes his letter with this comment: "[*Le Mensonge d'Ulysse*] seems to me a splendid work and worthy of the best salons" (Céline, *Cahiers Céline* 6, 269). The following month, after having read the work, Céline reiterates his claims: "Rassinier is certainly an *honnête homme* ... His admirable book is going to make a big noise—AFTER ALL it raises doubts about the magic *gas chamber*! ... that permitted EVERYTHING!" (276). How can we avoid thinking that when Céline writes these lines, his perspective on the war is oriented by Rassinier's revisionism? At times Céline seems close to acknowledging the horror of the

[11]Letter dated 13 Jan. 1949, in Céline, *Cahiers Céline 6*, 123.

concentration camps, if only to defend himself against accusations of anti-Semitism. In 1948 he wrote to Jean Paulhan that he "didn't want [*je n'ai pas voulu*] Auschwitz, Buchenwald." But even in this letter, in which the author declares his pacifism, he cannot avoid the type of comparison the revisionists were fond of. During the next war, Céline tells Paulhan, the massacres will be even more devastating: "we'll see one hundred times better, or worse! [*on verra cent fois mieux, ou pire!*]." And in a 1957 letter to Roger Nimier, Céline holds the Jews directly responsible for the Holocaust: "The Jews and their whining bore me . . . If they hadn't made France declare war, they would never have known Buchenwald and everything else . . . All they had to do was follow the advice I gave in *Bagatelles* [*pour un massacre*]."[12] Céline will show signs of this type of thinking until his death, for as late as 1960 he asks his German correspondent Hermann Bickler[13] for information concerning "an official institute of Historical Research in Bonn whose headquarters are in Munich . . . which, after much research would have discovered that there never were gas ovens [*fours à gaz*] at Buchenwald, Dachau etc. *nor anywhere else in* Germany ... There were some in construction but they were never completed ... according to this *Institute*. If you obtain some documents these would greatly interest me ..."[14] A number of different rhetorical moves come out of Céline's correspondence, all of which belong to revisionist discourse and appear in the novels. To Paulhan in 1948 he claims irresponsibility. To Nimier nine years later he adopts the strategy of blaming the victim. And in his letters to Paraz and Bickler we see what Pierre-André Taguieff has called the dubitative moment of revisionism (Taguieff, "La Logique," 28–30). Without ever openly

---

[12]Céline, *Lettres à la N.R.F.*, 53–54, 373 (my translation).

[13]Hermann Bickler, an officer in the German secret police during the war, helped Céline flee to Denmark at the end of the war. He was tried and sentenced to death *in absentia* in 1947.

[14]Quoted in Gibault, *Céline III*, 328. In all likelihood Céline was referring to the Institute for Contemporary History in Munich, whose director, Martin Broszat, wrote a letter to a German daily, *Die Zeit* (19 Aug. 1960), to correct an error of a journalist who had claimed that there were gas chambers at Dachau. On how Broszat's historical points have been picked up and distorted by the revisionists, including Bardèche, see Kaplan, *Reproductions*, 191–92.

denying the Holocaust, Céline is attempting, through "research," to put into doubt the reality of the Shoah.

While these fragments are revealing, they were never destined for publication. In reading Céline, we must still determine if his public, literary works, the texts that are based on the writer's *"petite musique"* and the only texts that, as far as Céline is concerned, should interest us, are the vehicles of a revisionist ideology. What makes this reading particularly difficult is that the same rhetorical devises used by the revisionists—allusions and insinuations, in particular—seem at first glance to prevent a precise historical reading of the novels.

In 1946, when he begins to write *Féerie pour une autre fois I*, Céline is conscious of his role as both political pariah and literary innovator, and this paradoxical situation determines the construction of his text. Written in part while Céline is still in prison, the novel juxtaposes events from Montmartre in 1944 to the imprisonment of the author in Denmark two years later. *Féerie pour une autre fois* is also the thinly veiled defense plea of an author who fears the firing squad if ever he were to be extradited to France: Céline first calls his novel a *"petit mémoire,"* a term most frequently used to refer to a legal brief (see Céline, *Romans IV*, 1113). It is important to remember that Céline begins to write this novel at the same time that he is composing his 1946 "Reply to Charges of Treason," in which he answers the accusations of anti-Semitism and treason. While transforming history into a *féerie*, that is, a magical spectacle, the novel nonetheless attempts to exonerate the author and denounce the purge, and it is in this interplay between history and féerie that the commentaries on the Nazi death camps begin to appear.

The narration in *Féerie pour une autre fois* is often interrupted by a series of exchanges between the narrator and an anonymous and hostile reader, who confronts Céline with his responsibility as regards the death camps. Céline neither ignores nor suppresses the horror of the camps, but every mention of the camps serves ultimately to alleviate the author's guilt. Every reference can be seen as part of Céline's attempt to revise his own trial. Thus, he can only conceive of the suffering endured by the victims of the camps in relation to his own suffering and the hardship he has endured in the Danish prison cell. One of the first references to the camps comes in an attack by the "aveng-ing reader" (Céline, *Romans IV,* 31) against the author, who has just detailed the symptoms of the scabies he contracted in "Blaringhem," the name Céline gives to the German town Sigmaringen, where he and the Vichy government ended up in June 1944. Here, then, is the reader challenging Céline:

> Well then, what about Augsbourg! it wasn't papulous skin patches! it was a total shredding! All the skins for A.A. lanterns! Lampshades and burnt bindings, kazoos, Walkyries, Odine sabbaths and gas ovens! (31)

Only in the final revision of his manuscript did Céline change Auschwitz to Augsbourg and S.S. to A.A., but even with these changes, and despite the speed at which these lines pass in the narra-tion, we are able to decrypt the allusion. The camp, like everything else in the novel, is part of the author's spectacularized vision of the war. The absolute horror of the images such as lampshades made of human skin is accompanied by the sound of a kazoo (*mirliton*) and Wagnerian Walkyries. But this description of the horror also allows the author to decline all responsibility: "I declare that it's not my fault! [*j'y suis pour rien*] neither my ass, nor Augsbourg! I didn't de-clare this war, I didn't declare anything, but 'Long Live France and Courbevoie! Down with the Slaughterhouse!'" (31) Without naming them, Céline maintains that his pamphlets were pacifist and patriotic writings and not anti-Semitic tracts, and he thus reformulates the central claim of his plea: "it's not my fault." At the same time the dia-logic form of the text reproduces the structure of compared atrocities on a personal level. Augsbourg and the author's scabby ass are equated in his imagination. Céline is once again averring what he had already written in his "Reply to Charges of Treason" about his stay at Sigmaringen: "it is impossible to be more unfortunate [than we were], even at Buchenwald" (Céline, "Reply to Charges," 537). At first, then, evoking the atrocities of the camps is more beneficial to Céline than denying them; the denial will come later. By having a hostile reader accuse him, Céline can respond that he is the true and perhaps the sole victim not only of the purge but of the war itself. While it escapes rationality, Céline's hyperbole is nonetheless a logical development of the postwar revisionists' rhetoric of compared atrocities.

While Céline denounces the violence against him with his own voice, the horror of the camps arrives at the text through the voice of another, the "avenging reader." But this dialogic construction also reveals a progressive attempt by the author to erase the testimony of the camps. When his interlocutor evokes Cassel—Dora in the earlier versions—Céline answers: "you weren't there either! Don't talk to me about tortures!" (Céline, *Romans IV*, 32). Later in *Féerie pour une autre fois* the imaginary reader again forces the author to consider the reality of the camps: "What about Claunau [Dachau]?" to which Céline responds, "Good point! I complain, but I'm pampered! but were you at Claunau? ... Bullshit! but yelling a thousand times as if you were!" (66). If, in a first movement, Céline seems to admit that his fate is not the worst—he was "pampered" compared with the victims at Dachau—he almost instantly attacks the hypocrisy of a reader who accuses him without having suffered. *Féerie pour une autre fois*, then, stages a confrontation between two voices: the reader's and the author's. But little by little the avenging reader's voice is shown to be hypocritical and, therefore, unreliable. Céline denounces the cant of his enemies, and it is not unfair to claim that during the purge certain individuals used sanctimonious condemnation of collaborators for personal gain. But Céline also uses these passages to put into doubt the testimonies of the camps. The writing of history, as Céline's novels present it, can only be based on the direct testimony of personal experience, and the only experience Céline acknowledges is his own.

Comparison, refutation—in the end the dialogue between the reader and the narrator also permits the revision of history. After having evoked the horrors of "Lünebourg" (the camouflaged name of Buchenwald), Céline responds in a characteristic way: "Were you at Lünebourg? They're dead at Lünebourg! did you replace them? ... avengers, replacements, it's all the same! ... Conjurers of History! . . . Lünebourg, well I'll tell you! there were whorehouses [*poufs*] at Lünebourg, not just mass graves!" (66). Again Céline refuses all testimony except that of an eyewitness, but this witness is nonexistent because he is dead. Furthermore, the phrase "conjurers of History"

Céline uses to characterize his accusers resembles Bardèche's claim that in their revelation to the world of the death camps, the Allies perpetrated a "falsification" or an "alteration of History."[15] If Céline does not explicitly deny the atrocities of the camps, he nonetheless attempts to deny all testimony about them. With one stroke of the pen Céline strikes out the history of the camps. Once this testimony is silenced, he proposes his own version of events. Just as Bardèche had called for a verification of the Holocaust, Céline attempts to rewrite history: "I'll tell you! there were whorehouses at Lünebourg." The association of death and prostitution, of war and eroticism has been one of the author's main themes since *Journey to the End of the Night*. Nonetheless, this type of association is precisely one of the strategies of revisionist rhetoric: as Pierre Vidal-Naquet has shown, to claim that the camps were also sites of pleasure participates in an attempt to deny that they were sites of extermination.[16] The rhetorical work that begins in a desire to silence all testimony but the author's own ends up in a revision of history that, though it depends on allusion, attempts to attenuate the atrocities of the camps. The references to the Shoah constitute only a few lines of a 300-page novel that brims with references of all sorts. But these references are quintessential. Not only do they allow the author to reiterate his innocence, but they tie Céline's novels to the discourse of Holocaust revisionism. Céline's postwar novels are also the chronicle of the author's rediscovery of an ideology of hate.

With the publication of the second volume of *Féerie pour une autre fois* in 1954, the structure of compared atrocities is once again put into play. The work of attenuation initiated in the first volume is followed by 400 pages dedicated to representing the destruction of Montmartre by Allied bombs. At first glance *Féerie pour une autre fois II* does not seem to be a political text. The events appear to give way to a fantastic tale, in particular when Céline describes his comrade, the paint-

[15]Bardèche, *Nuremberg*, 9; *Nuremberg II*, 11.
[16]"Because Jewish weddings were celebrated at Maidanek, near Lublin, it will be pretended that the camps were, if need be, places of rejoicing. But who does not perceive that such phases were the temporal and social conditions necessary for the proper functioning of the killing?" Vidal-Naquet, *Assassins,* 86.

er Jules, orchestrating the bombing from his windmill. Céline saturates his text with a colorist terminology, transforming fire and explosions into a palette of colors: "one of those blazes on Renault! the height of the clouds! blue! ... orange! ... green flames! ... and giant zigzag candles ... " (185). The investment in style here reaches its apogee and reminds us of the analogy with painting that Céline uses in 1956 to describe his own writing. Like the impressionists, who changed their painting with the advent of photography, the author wants his writing to forget its "object" and to have the same emotional impact as *plein-air* painting (Céline, *Conversations*, 22–23). More than any other of Céline's texts, *Féerie II* becomes the site of stylistic innovation. Added to this aestheticization are numerous references to the operetta, to antiquity, and to biblical mythology—*La Bohème* but also Vesuvius, the Apocalypse, the Deluge—which seem to remove the text from its historical reality (Bellosta, "*Féerie pour une autre fois I et II*, 31–62).

It is precisely at the moment of greatest stylistic investment, however, that we rediscover the historical dimension of Céline's text. It turns out that the cataclysmic vocabulary that Céline borrows to transpose the bombings echoes the vocabulary used in political writings of 1944 to denounce the Allied bombing raids. The transformation of the end of the Third Reich into the end of the world was a common trope of French collaborators and fascists. Bardèche, for example, uses the expression "apocalyptic destruction" when describing the ruins of Dresden (Bardèche, *Nuremberg*, 22). Targeting the Allied D-Day invasion, the collaborationist journalist Claude Jamet writes, "We may be at the limit that precedes the Apocalypses, the great Devastations, the Catastrophes of the world."[17] And in July 1944 Brasillach publishes an article in which he claims that since D-Day and the Allied bombing raids "the Apocalypse had entrenched itself in France." A Revelationist tone runs throughout Brasillach's piece: to describe the destruction of French cities he writes that "fire from

[17]Jamet, "L'Heure H moins 5." Jamet published an interview with Céline in the first issue of *Germinal*, 28 April 1944, and in an article titled "Bombing Parties" he condemned the allied bombing raids on Paris.

heaven scatters the venerable wall [of the city] [*le feu du ciel jette au vent les murailles vénérables*]."[18] Even several years after the war the Allied bombing of France remained a sore spot for apologists of Vichy France. In 1952, the year *Féerie I* was published, the review *Rivarol*, whose slant even today remains Pétainist and nostalgic, printed an article on the 1944 destruction of Saint-Lô, "as related by a witness" (*Rivarol*, 25 July 1952). To "bear witness" to Allied bombing raids is already to participate in a discourse that condemns these acts of war and begins to exculpate the partisans of collaboration. Céline's postwar text can be located at the border between literary and historical descriptive systems and seems to refute any reading that threatens to fix its meaning. But this is precisely the gamble of the vocabulary in *Féerie II*. If Céline assimilates his writing to medieval chronicles, it is in part because these chronicles find themselves between literature and historiography.[19] When Céline transforms the bombing of Montmartre and Billancourt into a painterly Apocalypse, he is simultaneously transcending historical events and repositioning his novel next to articles from the collaborationist press intent upon denouncing Allied actions.

We need not leave the text to find its historical dimension, however, for from the very beginning of the novel Céline asserts his role as an eyewitness: "I am the simple eyewitness" (190); "I won't lie about a thing" (204). Just as he had denied the testimony of the avenging reader, Céline is providing us with his experience of history. Furthermore, Céline presents his work as a historical document: "much later they'll buy my books, much later, when I'm dead, to study the first seismic activity of the end" (191). He is writing against the "100,000" (190) false witnesses intent upon contradicting his account of the war. Céline's testimony of the bombing of Montmartre claims to reveal a truth ignored by the public: "they don't know yet, but they will" (191). The reader is thus confronted with a work that, though it may be hallucinatory, though it may be at the limit of an intransitive writing, also claims the status of historical document. If the fantastic

[18]Brasillach, "Devant l'Apocalypse," in *Œuvres complètes*, vol. 12, 714–16.
[19]Anderson, "Joliment actuelles."

seems to dominate the novel when we see Jules on his windmill, *Féerie II* nonetheless delivers a series of precise references that permit us to read the novel in the context of the Second World War. The planes dropping the bombs come from London (188), drop their "murderous melinite" (190), and execute a precise strategy: "they hit the 'target' only at the end! ... everything around it must burn first" (189). Then they flee: "they drop their load and then fly away! cowards! poltroons! pigs!" (190).[20] What is more, Céline insists upon the fact that his professional training as a doctor forces him to examine and identify the charred remains of the numerous victims of the "burning magnesium" (226): "they're gray all over and shriveled up" (226). The autopsy of the burn victims leaves little to the imagination: "I'll perform the autopsy myself ... I'll open them ... I'll cut the thorax in two! ribs turned down ... their lungs will be all gray" (226). In his *Nuremberg* Bardèche had already written that "the phosphorous bombs are well worth the concentration camps" (Bardèche, *Nuremberg*, 230), a phrase exemplary of the structure of compared atrocities that we find at the heart of revisionist arguments. How can we not think of this comparison when Céline describes the charred bodies and repeats that the bombing raids have turned Paris into an "oven" ("*four*") (Céline, *Romans IV*, 196 *et passim*)? If the oven in Céline's text at first seems to be the kiln of the sculptor Jules, there is no doubt that this word evokes the exterminations performed by the Nazis. Not satisfied with denouncing the bombings, Céline's text insinuates that the crematoria could be found in Paris as well as in Auschwitz, an insinuation that is unthinkable to anyone who has not learned the "lessons" of the revisionists.

Céline had originally planned to write a third and perhaps a fourth volume in the *Féerie pour une autre fois* series, but the commercial failure of the first two forced him to change his plans or in any case his title. Yet, that he stopped with *Féerie pour une autre fois II* shows the hold the structure of compared atrocities had on him.

[20]Céline uses the same term, *lâches* (cowards), that Vichy propagandists used to denounce Allied bombers at the end of the war. This term was frequently seen in the Paris region on posters that showed Allied planes flying home after a raid that left Parisian neighborhoods in ruins.

While the first volume tries to attenuate and indeed to silence the horror of the death camps, the second volume seeks to replace the memory of Auschwitz with a hyperbolic rendition of the Allied bombing of Paris. In this logic there was no need for a continuation.

Three years later, in 1957, when Céline published *Castle to Castle,* in which he recounts his exile in Sigmaringen, he was responding to the expectations of the French reading public. Vichy is once again generating interest. Louis Noguères published *La Dernière Etape: Sigmaringen* in 1956, a diplomatic history with a series of letters between Pétain, Laval, and Otto Abetz. At the same time an article in *Annales* mentioned the simultaneous publication of three studies on Vichy (Michel, "Lumières," 510–25). That year de Gaulle released *L'Appel,* the first volume of his wartime autobiography. As the history of Vichy and the collaboration is being written, Céline is more and more convinced that his writing must serve to refute a history written by those he calls the "victors" of the war (Céline, *Castle to Castle,* 266). Even though Céline is no longer being pursued by the purge tribunals, even though the novels that constitute the German trilogy— *Castle to Castle* (1957), *North* (1960), and *Rigadoon* (1969)—present a farcical vision of the war and a parodic portrait of its political actors, the author continues to plead his case before the public and reiterates the revisionist project initiated during the purge trials.

In one of the first sequences of *Castle to Castle* Céline asks himself where a doctor who gives "a risky prescription" to his patients might wind up: "In the criminal courts ... the Tenth Chamber? ... Buchenwald? Siberia? ... " (8). Later a digression on the success of the song *Lili Marlene* brings about the association of the concentration camp and tourist sites: "Buchenwald, Key-West and Saint-Malo" (194). A description of the wood-collecting chore at Sigmaringen incites Céline to write: "the Volga ... Buchenwald ... the Great Wall of China ... Nasser and the Pyramids ... the same racket! swift kicks in the ass are nothing new!" (241). In *North* Céline associates Buchenwald with the "Russian labor camps" and the "atomic ashes" and concludes "life goes on" (5). Later the concentration camp is compared to Montrouge (353), the fortress where Pétain was imprisoned and Brasillach executed at the end of the war. And when Céline reflects upon the fate of a German doctor hanged during the Nuremberg trials, he concludes: "Gebhardt, war criminal, hanged! ... for all sorts of genocides, little intimate Hiroshimas ... oh, not that Hiroshima makes me flip!" (126). What is more, Gebhardt is hanged, Céline tells us, while Truman, the president responsible for the bombing of Hiroshima, is free to play the piano. The moral of this story? "just wait a while ... kill a lot of people and wait ... that does it" (126).

Has the author's attitude changed since *Féerie pour une autre fois*? The style is certainly less violent, and, more than anything else, these references reveal Céline's cynicism toward the fate that History has in store for men. Still, Céline has revived the rhetoric of compared atrocities: the demon of analogy is active once again. For Céline the victims of Buchenwald can be assimilated not only to the victims of Hiroshima but also to the prisoners of the gulag, to common criminals, to the collaborationist refugees at Sigmaringen, and to the leaders of the collaboration. Céline's use of analogy serves two purposes: it turns the collaborators executed at Montrouge into martyrs of the purge and transforms the victims of the camps into everything but what they really were: the victims of the racist and anti-Semitic politics of European fascism, to which the author himself contributed. If, according to Céline, persecutor and persecuted are equal, if every nation and every time period has known some form of genocide, then the responsibility of the anti-Semitic author is erased, transformed into pure historical contingency. I certainly have no desire to defend Truman's policy: that the Allies were responsible for their share of atrocities is not the question. Céline's historical relativism is not simply the work of a skeptical and anarchistic mind, though. The repetition of those historical analogies ties Céline's work to the writings of Bardèche and Rassinier and presents in a literary and allusive form their revisionist claims.

Revisionist discourse, whatever form it takes, is characterized by a regression from analogy to denial. At some point the rhetoric of analogy inevitably unveils itself, revealing a desire to deny not only the specificity but the very fact of the Holocaust. This is as true with

Céline as with any other author. Thus in *North*, the second volume
of the trilogy, Céline and his companions meet a group of Gypsies
in the German town of "Zornhof." Céline asks himself how these
Gypsies were able to survive the war and, in a meditative moment,
he adds:

> weren't the Gypsies supposed to be eliminated according to the Nurem-
> berg Laws? ... highly contaminating! ... crypto-Asiatics! ... a Gypsy free
> and shooting the shit! might as well say the war was a waste of time! ...
> Hitler's New Order, let's not forget, was just as racist as that of the
> blacks of Mali or the yellows of Hankow ... we'd see what we'd see! ...
> luckily, we've seen nothing [*on a rien vu, heureusement*]! (Céline, *North*,
> 199)

Céline's English biographer, Patrick McCarthy, sees in this passage a parody of Nazi racist laws and an admission of the defeat of
this ideology (McCarthy, *Céline*, 301–2). But is this passage really a
parody of Nazi doctrine? The phrase denouncing "Hitler's New Order" shows the type of insinuation Céline's text puts into practice, for
if the sentence opens by reminding us that Hitler was a racist, a fact
that no one has forgotten, it ends by telling us that this racism exists
everywhere on earth. The construction of the sentence forces us to
understand the phrase "just as racist as" in the sense of "not more
racist than." The reminder of Hitler's racism thus seems to transform
itself into an apology. Furthermore, the final phrase in this passage—
"luckily we've seen nothing!"—reproduces the erasure already at
work in *Féerie pour une autre fois*. This phrase can be read two ways.
Literally it denies the possibility of any testimony on the event;
"we've seen nothing" is a challenge to the witnesses and the victims of
the Holocaust. And if Céline speaks of Gypsies, he never mentions
the Jews, thus literally erasing the largest population of the victims of
the "Nuremberg Laws." Read in the figurative sense, "we've seen
nothing" is a synonym of "nothing happened," and the phrase thus
transforms itself into a denial of the atrocities of the death camps. Either way this sentence can be read as a response to the phrase that in
Bagatelles pour un massacre opens the way for Céline's anti-Semitic
ravings: "Ah, you're going to see some anti-Semitism! ... Ah, you're

going to see some revolt!" (Céline, *Bagatelles,* 41). Through a reversal of this phrase and a play of the verb *to see* the text not only erases the testimony of the victims, but it attempts to suppress the historical reality of the genocide; all the while this passage expresses the relief of an author who had called in the most violent terms possible for the persecution of the Jews.

As we saw in *Féerie pour une autre fois*, in the structure of revisionist discourse the testimony about the camps is not only annihilated, it must be replaced by an account of the destruction wrought by the Allies. In Céline's final novels the author again bears witness to the bombings while telling us that he is revealing a version of history about which "they never say a word" (Céline, *Castle to Castle,* 246). In *Castle to Castle*, after a paralipsis in which the author feigns that he doesn't want to talk about the bombing raids—"who gives a damn" (33)—he goes so far as to give us the names and the address of the victims in Paris—"the Poirier family on the rue Duhem" (33). Göttingen, Cassel, Osnabrück, he tells us were transformed into *"pots-au-feu"* (33), and Dresden, the "Mecca of the arts," became the site of 200,000 dead (243) "roasted alive in Germany beneath the spreading wings of democracy" (246). Just as Céline had devoted the entirety of *Féerie pour une autre fois II* to the representation of the bombing of Montmartre, he spends numerous pages of *Rigadoon*, his final novel, describing the destruction of Hamburg and Hanover by the Allied flying fortresses. In this last novel Céline finds himself once again amid the ruins, the witness to an Apocalyptic event. The vocabulary, the same as in *Féerie pour une autre fois II*, is replete with an aesthetic terminology that seems to transform the destruction into a poetic spectacle: "every rubble heap, these green and pink flames were dancing around ... and around ... and shooting up at the sky! ... those streets of green ... pink ... and red rubble ... you can't deny it ... looked a lot more cheerful ... a carnival of flames" (Céline, *Rigadoon,* 130). To be sure, the passage reveals a self-reflexive moment: when, in order to describe the bombings, Céline uses a musical and lyric vocabulary, it is difficult not to think of the *"petite musique"* he used to characterize his style. We must nonetheless not confuse this poeticization of the bombing with a rejection of the historical project, as some readers of Céline have suggested.[21] Céline speaks of "fortresses" (130), the American B-17s, of "incendiary gook" (130), the phosphorous bombs, and of the "complete destruction" (130) they leave behind. Later, the text confirms that "Hamburg had been destroyed with liquid phosphorous" (191). Far from withdrawing the text from an ideological interpretation, these passages from *Rigadoon*, like the pages from *Féerie pour une autre fois II*, present a constant oscillation between highly stylized writing and precise historical referents. In his final novels Céline is again taking us on a journey, but this time the textual work that seeks to deny the historical reality of the Final Solution ends in a testimony about the "complete destruction" of German cities. The journey is now complete. We have reached the end of the night. Faced with the accumulation of evidence, we are forced to conclude that Céline's final novel, and indeed his entire postwar literary production, for all its linguistic brilliance also reveals, at its core, a stylized version of the revisionist program to rewrite the history of the war and erase the memory of the Shoah.

If Céline's style presents a poeticization of his revisionist sources, we cannot ignore that his work has been the object of a revisionist reception. As early as 1950 Rassinier borrows a phrase from Céline, "legends are being toppled," in order to advertise the first edition of *Le Mensonge d'Ulysse*.[22] Most likely through the intervention of Albert Paraz, Céline's name served as a guarantee for one of the founding texts of revisionism. Robert Faurisson, a professor of literature at the University of Lyon and a man intent upon proving the gas chambers never existed, also gives great credence to Céline's declarations about the genocide.[23] Starting in the 1970s, Faurisson presents himself as

[21]Kristeva reads the representation of the bombings in *Rigadoon* as examples of "scription as the laying bare of meaning," which would deny all "ideological interpretation" of his texts. Kristeva, *Powers*, 154.

[22]See Dauphin and Fouché, eds., *Bibliographie*, 50B4. Dauphin and Fouché cannot locate the source of this phrase and claim that it is probably apocryphal.

[23]See Faurisson, "A quand la libération," 4–5; "Céline," 3: 4–8; 4: 5–6. Faurisson first published his revisionist tracts in Bardèche's *Défense de l'Occident* in 1978, that is, *after* claiming that Céline's genius lay in his pamphlets.

Céline's attorney of sorts against charges dating from the purge and demands that Céline's pamphlets be republished since it was there that the author "discovered and perfected his style." But Faurisson also uses Céline to support his own revisionist claims, and considering the chronology of his publications, we are led to wonder if Faurisson doesn't arrive at his revisionist claims as a result of having frequented Céline. In a first article in the *Bulletin célinien*, a review published in Belgium for Céline enthusiasts, Faurisson recommends that we read the "admirable pamphlets," which prove that "if the gas chambers never existed, then the greatest crime of the last war becomes Hiroshima or Nagasaki or Dresden." In the following issue of the review Faurisson quotes Céline's phrase on the "magic gas chamber," which, he says, "suits him perfectly." Céline's phrase must be a favorite in revisionist circles since Vidal-Naquet gives the example of a Ph.D. candidate in Nantes who also quoted the phrase during his doctoral defense in 1985 (Vidal-Naquet, *Assassins,* 115).

Céline, in fact, consistently reappears as an authority for contemporary revisionists both in France and in the United States. In October 1992 several Céline scholars applying for a grant from the National Endowment for the Humanities, received an evaluation of their project from a scholar who used this occasion to deny the fact of the Holocaust. Comfortably hidden behind the veil of anonymity, the revisionist evaluator proclaims his suspicion of "the usual hidden agenda," something he seems to identify with "politically correct speech." From the grant application the evaluator quickly turns to the Holocaust, and the sham arguments that characterize revisionists begin to flow—phony statistics, falsified quotes—all in an attempt to clear Céline's name. The evaluator approvingly quotes Céline's phrase about the "magic gas chambers" as proof that the Holocaust was a hoax and concludes that Céline scholars should all become acquainted with the work of Faurisson. This letter to the NEH is insane, but it offers proof that Céline has become an authority of sorts for Holocaust revisionists.[24] Though they do not bring out the links between

[24]One of the more recent flare-ups in France came to be known as the "Affaire Abbé Pierre." Abbé Pierre, a long-standing supporter of the poor, the

Holocaust revisionism and Céline's last novels, all these revisionists cite Céline in their desultory and mendacious arguments. At the same time, in its cult of Céline, the revisionist clique reveals the links between the explicit prewar anti-Semitism and the closeted and almost disavowed anti-Semitism of postwar revisionist thinking. The two are, it turns out, inextricably tied to one another. Faurisson's rehabilitation of Céline's pamphlets defies reason: in his view the anti-Semitic pamphlets are proof that Allied bombings are "the greatest crime of the last war." As Nadine Fresco has shown, this is precisely the type of rhetorical incoherence the revisionist discourse depends upon. More than this, however, Faurisson's articles clearly show an ideological itinerary from prewar persecution of the Jews to denial of the Shoah, an itinerary of which Céline's final novels are, unfortunately, exemplary. If we return to Céline after all this, it is with a renewed vigilance that, never denying the pleasure of the text, refuses the defeat of memory to which the text incites us.

---

homeless, and the downtrodden of all sorts recently came out in support of the revisionist claims of Roger Garaudy, a former Stalinist. In 1995 Garaudy published a revisionist history titled *Les Mythes fondateurs de la politique israélienne* at La Vieille Taupe, a publishing house that is also the haunt of extreme leftists turned revisionists. At a press conference in support of Garaudy, Jacques Vergès, Klaus Barbie's lawyer, read a letter by Abbé Pierre, the "so-called pope of the outcasts," praising Garaudy. Before publishing his book, Garaudy had also written for the neofascist and revisionist journal *Nationalisme et République*, which places itself under the symbolic patronage of Jacques Doriot and Céline. See Videlier, "Zones," 3.

Conclusion:
The Spirit of the Trial

In *Testaments Betrayed*, his 1992 essay on the art of fiction, Milan Kundera concludes that the literature of our century is haunted by what he calls the "spirit of the trial" (Kundera, *Testaments*, 234). Since World War I writers have increasingly been confined, accused, repressed, and made to feel guilty by an array of forces, from the Soviet revolutionary tribunals and Nazi censorship to the postwar purge of fascist sympathizers and the *fatwa* against Salman Rushdie. In the late twentieth century the complexity of reading has, according to Kundera, given way to cursory judgments, to agitprop, and to the annihilation of "this century's culture" (234). Perhaps, Kundera suggests, for reasons even the author himself could not have suspected at the time, Kafka's novel *The Trial*, in which a character's every move is read as a manifestation of his guilt, has become the emblematic text for our time. Kundera's essay is an impassioned plea for intellectual freedom from an author who was himself the victim of a politically and culturally repressive regime and who lives in a society, contemporary France, still coming to terms with the intimate relation between literature and politics which prevailed throughout this century. But while he envisions a time when moral and political judgments will no longer impede understanding of the novel, there is perhaps no better proof that we are still haunted by this spirit of the trial than Kundera's eloquent essay. His appeal on behalf of the novel, this "realm where moral judgment is suspended" (6), his panegyric on humor, can also be seen as an elaborate plea for an art form he considers beleaguered. Rather than dissolve the spirit of the trial, Kundera has joined the trial as an attorney for the defense.[1]

Kundera's essay characterizes an attempt among certain writers in Europe today to move away from the trials, accusations, judgments, and position taking that have dominated the literary field in the twentieth century. While refusing the "art for art's sake" model of previous generations, these novelists, poets, playwrights, and critics are also distancing themselves from the roles and models designed for literature during the Cold War. Kundera himself has seen and written about the disastrous effects for both art and politics when literature collaborates with the state. But just as his essay participates, however reluctantly, in the spirit of the trial, so too have several contemporary writers and thinkers remembered the arguments of the purge at precisely the moment they were attempting to forget the past. What was true in the late 1940s is still true today: the purge remains a moment of unresolved conflicts that makes the task of concluding complex, if not impossible.

That the divisions of the purge still structure certain approaches to literature is evidenced by the texts of two authors who lived through the war but who came into their own as writers and thinkers sometime after the purge trials had died down. Forty years after the end of the war Marguerite Duras and Jacques Derrida published texts in which they addressed questions about guilt, responsibility, and the status of literature which were at the heart of the trials of fascist and collaborationist intellectuals. Though they came to these questions in different ways and for different reasons, their approaches and the solutions they propose seem at times eerily close to one another. Duras's texts *The Lover* and *The War: A Memoir* as well as Derrida's 1988

---

[1]With its emphasis on laughter and on musicality Kundera's strategy for defending certain writers is not so different from the one elaborated in the 1940s by Céline, whom Kundera mentions on several occasions as a victim of "the conformism of popular opinion." Ibid., 234.

response to the revelations about Paul de Man's journalism for a collaborationist newspaper participate in what can be characterized as an entire generation's violent rediscovery of the trauma of the Occupation, a rediscovery that Henry Rousso has called the "obsessive phase" of the Vichy syndrome. Duras and Derrida come to the question in particular ways, however, for while their texts give voice to their nation's obsession with and equivocation toward Vichy, they also participate in a revision of the purge trials and force us to reflect on what it means to return to and rewrite the trials nearly half a century after the war.

In the 1980s Marguerite Duras published a series of texts that addressed questions of guilt and innocence, of judgment and culpability which had first surfaced in France during the purge. These works, the best-selling novel *The Lover* and several of the stories in *The War: A Memoir*, evoke or center on the horrors of the war and the legacy of the Holocaust. One of the few critics to have noted the importance of Duras's return to the purge is Lynn Higgins, who in her recent book, *New Novel, New Wave, New Politics*, reads Duras's representations of the trauma of the war as both a "historiographic project" (Higgins, *New Novel*, 172) and a return to "a still earlier trauma" (176). Turning to "Albert of the Capitals," a story from *The War* that stages the torture of a Nazi informant by a woman of the Resistance, Higgins points to both the moral and stylistic ambiguities of the text and concludes that the representation of this torture "takes place under the ominous sign of reversal" (183). Names are reversed in this short tale, victims become executioners, and executioners turn into cowering victims as the torture of the informant becomes increasingly violent and useless. "Albert of the Capitals" presents both the trial by torture of an informer and the denunciation of this torture. I take Higgins's suggestive comments as my starting point: Duras's writing about the purge is equivocal. What remains to be seen is the relation between this equivocation, the purge archive, and Duras's literary aesthetics.

Another story from *The War*, "Monsieur X, Here Called Pierre Rabier," gives us certain clues for understanding this relation. This story tells of the relationship between the narrator, presumably the author herself, and a member of the Gestapo, who may or may not have information about the narrator's recently arrested husband and who may or may not be trying to seduce her. As the story progresses, the narrator finds herself in a more and more untenable position: her friends in the Resistance are asking her to deliver Rabier, but at the same time she needs Rabier alive in order to gather information about her missing husband. Parallel to what might be called the political intrigue of the text, there is the story of the seduction and attraction of the two characters, a story that ends in a cul-de-sac and which at times strikingly resembles Duras's 1958 text, *Moderato cantabile*. By the end of the *récit*, however, we learn that Rabier was executed during the winter of 1944–45, that is, at the height of the purge, and that the narrator's testimony against him, more than any other, was responsible for his execution. The story thus ends with the narrator testifying before the French purge courts, and we realize that the 40 or so pages we have just read can, in fact, be understood as a deposition by the narrator presented against "Pierre Rabier." "Monsieur X. Here Called Pierre Rabier" is, more than anything else, a testimony brought against a member of the Gestapo by what the French call a *témoin à charge*, a witness for the prosecution.

It is precisely when we begin to read the text as a testimony, however, that we encounter the problem of its ambiguity. The narrative itself gives us both sides of the trial, it is both prosecution and defense, it accumulates proof against Rabier and simultaneously presents a series of extenuating circumstances. Through a sort of "on the one hand ... on the other hand" system of argumentation, it both condemns and pardons. On the one hand, Pierre Rabier is a member of the Gestapo who has sent individuals to the gas chambers of the concentration camps; on the other, he is incapable of arresting a Jewish family after he sees the drawings made by one of the children (Duras, *The War*, 103–4). On the one hand, Rabier can be ruthless, but on the other, his violence is more posturing than pure ideological commitment; ultimately he is a solitary being. On the one hand, Rabier may believe in the victory of Nazi Germany, but on the other it is only in order to be able to fulfill his dream: to open a fine-arts bookstore. Duras even writes early on in the story: "I found this out afterward. Rabier was fascinated by French intellectuals, artists, authors.

He'd gone into the Gestapo because he hadn't been able to buy an art bookshop" (79).

This declaration might seem scandalous, but, in fact, the extenuating circumstances Duras evokes reproduce quite precisely the defense strategies of accused fascists and collaborators during the purge trials. When Duras speaks of Rabier's inability to arrest a Jewish family, she is arguing that he was an attenuating force within the Gestapo (103–4). When she writes that Pierre Rabier was a solitary individual, she is again subtly elaborating a plea on his behalf. Whereas, in his portrait of the collaborator Sartre saw solitude as the mother of vice and of ill-fated politics, Duras uses individualism to distance her character from all forms of ideology. Furthermore, the type of solitude or individualism she evokes in depicting Rabier carried with it positive connotations, not only in Duras's literary universe, where solitude is constantly mythologized, but during the purge trials themselves. If Sartre condemned solitude in the name of solidarity, Simone de Beauvoir, in her February 1946 article on Brasillach, praised the courage of the lone collaborator.[2] Indeed de Beauvoir and Duras describe the accused in similar terms. Surrounded by journalists, lawyers, judges, and jury, Brasillach was alone as he approached the end: "And alone in his box, cut off from everybody else, was a man whom the circumstances were stimulating to show the very best that was in him. There he was face to face with his death, and consequently with his life too, whose whole burden he had to assume, now that he was about to die."[3] If we return to Duras's description of Pierre Rabier at his trial, we find a similar terminology: a defendant, alone in the dock, facing his accusers with courage and dignity: "[Rabier] is alone in the dock. He isn't anxious, he seems supernaturally brave, so indifferent does he appear to the death that awaits him" (98). In both cases the defendant was executed, but in both cases the writers—de Beauvoir and Duras—mitigate their judgment of the accused through a sort of mythologizing gesture.

As for the third extenuating circumstance concerning Rabier, that

[2] de Beauvoir, "Œil pour œil," 813–30.
[3] de Beauvoir, "Œil pour œil," quoted in Kaplan, "Literature," 970.

he was always more interested in literature than in politics, that he became a Nazi in order to pay for rare editions of Mallarmé and Gide, it echoes one of the recurring defense strategies of French fascist sympathizers. I will not rehearse the arguments from the time; we have seen them throughout this study. Suffice it to recall, for these concluding remarks, that not a single fascist or collaborationist intellectual went on trial during the purge without claiming, in one form or another, that his status as a writer somehow compensated for and attenuated his commitment to a totalitarian ideology.

"Monsieur X.," then, stages an equivocation, the undecidability of the narrator in the face of a trial. This equivocation is put into narrative form at the end of the story as the narrator tells us that she testified twice against Rabier, once for the prosecution and then again in his defense. Her undecidability triggers the rage of the judge, who screams at her: "'Make up your mind—first you accused him, now you defend him. We haven't time to waste here!'"(111). This then is the imperative of the purge tribunal: "Make up your mind [*Il faudrait savoir*]." Duras, however, is quite consciously using the purge as a matrix of unknowability. The back and forth movement of the story, the alternating vision of Rabier find their legal equivalent in the narrator's double testimony before the courts. The extent to which the purge is tied to equivocation in Duras's writing can be seen if we compare "Monsieur X." to the transcript of the trial at which Duras did, in fact, testify in December 1944 against the Gestapo agent Charles Delval. In his recent book on Mitterrand's eerie association with the Vichy regime, the journalist Pierre Péan gives us an indication that Duras modified at least one aspect of the story when she wrote it. For while Duras did indeed testify twice at Delval's trial, once for the prosecution and again in his defense, the reaction of the judge is not the same in the trial transcript as it is in Duras's *récit*. Instead of declaring "make up your mind," the representative of the court actually told Duras that her need to come before the court to give a second, more nuanced testimony honored her: "*ce scrupule vous honore*" (Péan, *Mitterrand*, 469). Whether Duras wrote "Monsieur X." in the immediate postwar years or shortly before its publication in 1985 is impossible to gauge for the time being. What a comparison of the text to manuscript does tell us, however, is that the writing process for Duras is intimately connected with undecidability. By placing in the judge's mouth the imperative to know, to choose, to decide, Duras has highlighted literature's uncertainty in the face of the purge. Duras uses the purge as the historical support for an *art poétique*: the irresolution of the historical event serves as a means of anchoring her writing in hesitation and doubt.[4]

When Duras couples her literary aesthetic to the debates of the purge, she also takes us back to the trials of collaborationist writers. In order to see how this return to the past operates, I want to examine a moment approximately midway through the 1984 autobiographical novel *The Lover,* when Duras turns her attention from her childhood in Vietnam to the years she spent in Paris during the Second World War. *The Lover* is a text built through the accumulation of fragments of memory that echo one another. About halfway through the book we encounter one series of fragments that begins with a recollection of the narrator's murderous older brother, whom she compares to the Nazis occupying France. Recycling the cliché of the Occupation as a sexual violation of France, Duras writes that both the brother and the Nazi occupiers thought nothing of stealing, imprisoning, penetrating, and "occupying the delightful territory" of the body of others (Duras, *The Lover,* 63). A few pages later the tone of the writing changes: from the horrors of the Occupation we progress to another fragment recounting a collaborationist *salon* held in the home of Betty Fernandez, the wife of Ramon Fernandez, the journalist and literary critic who, until his death from an embolism in 1944, had supported Jacques Doriot's fascist and populist party, the Parti Populaire français. Duras briefly evokes literary luminaries of the Occupation who frequented the salon:

> Once Drieu la Rochelle was there . . . Maybe Brasillach was there too, but I don't remember, unfortunately [*je le regrette beaucoup*]. Sartre never came. There were poets from Montparnasse, but I don't remember any

[4]In her 1993 text *Ecrire,* a work in which Duras examines the art of writing, she made this idea more explicit: "doubt is writing [*le doute c'est écrire*]," and a little later she claims that "writing is the unknown [*l'écriture c'est l'inconnu*]" (26).

names, not one. There were no Germans. We didn't talk politics. We talked about literature. (67)

Duras then praises Ramon Fernandez's literary talent and what she calls his "sublime courtesy" (68) and concludes with a passage that has become fairly notorious in Duras's work:

> Collaborators, the Fernandezes were. And I, two years after the war, I was a member of the French Communist party. The parallel is complete and absolute. The two things are the same, the same pity, the same call for help, the same lack of judgment, the same superstition if you like that consists in believing in a political solution to the personal problem. (68)

There are several things at work in these two passages, not the least of which is the nostalgia with which Duras evokes the literary salon, a world haunted by Drieu la Rochelle, Brasillach, and Ramon Fernandez, three collaborationist writers who died at the end of the war. *The Lover* is, at least in part, an educational novel, the story of a woman's transformation and in particular of the author's coming to writing. In this sense the collaborationist salon plays the role of a transitional moment from the violence and eroticism of her youth to the sophistication, delicacy, and "courtesy" of the Parisian literary world. We may ask ourselves why Duras chooses to write about this aspect of the Parisian literary world since, after all, she also frequented the Resistance and its writers. The answer lies in the fact that Duras's coming to writing, at least as she sees it in the 1980s, is intimately tied to the purge of collaborationist intellectuals. In a 1984 interview on the French literary talk show *Apostrophes* Duras came back to the question of the purge, denouncing what she considered to have been its excesses: the shearing of women suspected of collaboration and the execution of Robert Brasillach. Why should she have been spared, she asks the host, Bernard Pivot, and Brasillach executed: "Why whitewash me [*me blanchir*] and then soil Brasillach, for example? What did he do, Brasillach? How old was he? He was very young." Pivot is unable to answer Duras's question—what did Brasillach do?—and can only echo that Brasillach was indeed quite young. To be sure, when Duras draws an equivalence between collaboration and communism, she is distancing herself from the commitment to communism that marked the early part of her career. When in the *Apostrophes* interview Pivot asks her where she stands politically she replies: "I am nothing. I am for Mitterrand [*Je suis mitterrandienne*]," and then adds that she is attracted to him "because he has no ideology." Mapping this move away from ideology, Julia Kristeva has used the term "blankness of meaning" to describe Duras's style (Kristeva, *Black Sun*, 258). Duras's move away from political ideology in general only takes on its full significance, however, when we understand it in relation to the singularity of the purge. Duras is not only forging a new form of writing, she is repeating, replaying, and revising what was at stake for literature in the immediate postwar years.

Duras as a public intellectual remained vigilantly antifascist most of her life, and she was certainly not motivated by the same interests as some of the extreme right-wing factions in France who dedicated themselves to turning Brasillach into a martyr. Rather, her rehabilitation of Brasillach and of Ramon Fernandez, her nostalgic portrait of the collaborationist salon, are, more than anything else, part of an aesthetic move. The world of the Fernandezes, she tells us, is a hermetic, literary world, a world of "poets from Montparnasse." Duras refined this point in her interview with Pivot when she spoke of *"l'écriture pure"* as a literary ideal. Pure writing or pure literature as she sees it is a space in which social, political, and moral considerations were relegated to a secondary role, a site in which moral judgment was suspended.[5] Now Duras is certainly not alone in searching for a writing devoid of reference, a pure writing. What happened to her in the mid-1980s, however, shows the extent to which the purge forged the way postwar France came to understand the relation of literature and politics. Duras's attempt to attain this modernist ideal of a *pure writing* passes through a valorization of writers who were *purged* at the end of the Second World War. Her historical sensibility is such, or perhaps it is due to the force of the purge, that she equates *écrivains*

[5]Duras returned to this idea in *Ecrire*, in which she claims that writing is without reference: *"L'écriture a toujours été sans référence aucune"* (38).

épurés such as Brasillach and Ramon Fernandez with *écriture pure*. Anyone familiar with Brasillach's anti-Semitic diatribes from *Je suis partout* or with Fernandez's somewhat less strident but equally ideological articles in *Le Cri du peuple* might be hard pressed to understand how Duras accesses a pure writing through a rehabilitation of these two characters. Again the purge archive hands us a key to this peculiar logic. In order to counter the accusations of treason made against them, the collaborationist writers, almost without exception, began claiming that they, the *purged* writers, were the real proponents of a pure literature. Céline rechristened himself a "pure stylist" after the war; Lucien Rebatet, the author of the pamphlet *Les Décombres,* spent his days in jail looking for what he called *"le mot propre"* (not *"le mot juste"*); even Charles Maurras, imprisoned in Lyons, abandoned politics and spent his time translating Horace. At their trials Céline, Rebatet, Maurras, and others all pleaded not only that they were innocent—that is, politically pure—but also that they were the true defendants of pure literature. It is precisely this bad-faith argument, this legal chicane, that Duras has internalized and reproduced in the pages of *The Lover* when she describes, in nostalgic terms, the collaborationist salon.

If we needed further proof that Duras is revising the trials, and that the purge is revisiting Duras, we could turn to her comments about Sartre in the 1984 *Apostrophes* interview. Sartre, for Duras, represents the polar opposite of her pure writing ideal. Sartre, she tells Pivot, "never wrote. He didn't know what writing was. . . . He never confronted pure writing. Sartre is a moralist." Forty years after the purge and three years after his death, Sartre still represents a prosecutorial and political voice. Sartre was also, of course, the writer who refused to sign the petition in favor of Brasillach, who during the purge elaborated a theory for judging literature, and who expressed suspicion toward "pure writing." Duras's reaction to Sartre may seem peculiar, since her writing never really participated in Sartrean ideals of committed literature. Still, her need to return to this figure is one more link in a textual network that brings together the purge tribunals, the defense pleas of Vichyite intellectuals, Duras's best-selling novel, and the theory of literature she elaborated in the last years of her life.

Part of the richness of Duras's texts comes from her sensitivity to the traumas of history, to the intersection between the public and the private. But it is this same sensitivity that leaves her caught in a dangerous paradox. In a text such as *The Lover* Duras does not simply purge ideology from her writing. In order to free her work from political ideology, she returns to the ideological debates and the political positions of the postwar purge. In order to attain a pure writing, she repeats and revises the trials of the postwar purge. Finally, in order to arrive at what Kristeva calls a blankness of meaning, she must, as if she were a defense attorney at a purge trial, ask the reader to blank out the publishing history of the very writers she is remembering.

Three years after Duras published *The Lover* and two years after *The War*, the *New York Times* ran a story revealing to the American academic community that from 1940 to 1942 Paul de Man had published numerous articles in the collaborationist Belgian daily newspaper *Le Soir*.[6] Among the recent aftereffects of the Second World War few have had as drastic an impact, at least within American universities, as these revelations about a celebrated, and at times almost sanctified, literary critic. Reactions to this discovery were swift, violent, and varied. Whether in the American press or in academic publications the responses to Paul de Man's early journalism and in particular to anti-Semitic statements he made always insistently returned to questions of guilt and innocence and ranged from exculpation to a condemnation that held de Man responsible not only for condoning the persecution of Jews during the war but for continuing his wartime work in later years through an attempt to erase the memory of the Shoah.[7] When reading the various responses to de Man's journal-

[6] "Yale Scholar Wrote for Pro-Nazi Newspaper," *New York Times*, 1 Dec. 1987.

[7] Among the responses that call for extenuating circumstances in the judgment of de Man, see the texts by Bahti, Balfour, and Hamacher in Hamacher, Hertz, and Keenan, eds., *Responses*. To my mind the most serious accusations are those that implicate de Man and deconstruction in a form of Holocaust negationism. See the responses by Corngold and Mehlman in ibid.

ism, one has the feeling of being caught in a vertiginous spiral of accusations, rebuttals, counteraccusations, and parries. It isn't my intention to offer yet another response to the revelations about de Man's past. In the last ten years others have expressed, sometimes many times over, the range of emotions and the intellectual reevaluations many of us were supposed to have undergone at the time. What concerns me here is Jacques Derrida's 1988 response in particular, not only for what he has to tell us about de Man and the accusations brought against this man who was his friend but for what he reveals about the difficulty of breaking with attitudes and a rhetoric inherited from the postwar purge.

Derrida's response stands out for several reasons. He was, after all, a friend of de Man, and he tells us that his reactions to de Man's wartime journalism were conditioned by his friendship. He was also deeply implicated in the fallout of the affair since behind the attacks on de Man, critics were often targeting deconstruction and Derrida himself. Furthermore, his is the lone French voice in a scandal that affected mainly the American academic institution. This might seem irrelevant, especially considering that Derrida's academic reputation, one might even say his fame, was made in the United States. But on several occasions Derrida draws our attention to the fact that he is French, that his voice is French, and that he consciously engaged against the "hatred which certain *American* newspapers displayed" (Derrida, "Like the Sound," 128 [emphasis added]) in the weeks following the revelations about de Man's past. And there is more, for not only did Derrida read de Man's early articles in French, but he wrote his response in French, and what he calls the "equivocality" of certain French expressions points to the "murkiness" of translation (129). There is little doubt that "*American* newspapers," in Derrida's mind are ill-suited to understanding equivocality or deciphering murky translations. When Derrida identifies his voice as French, he is telling us something about both a reading methodology and an intellectual and cultural position. But as we will see, he is also bringing to the debate something of the specificity of the French historical context.

On several occasions Derrida claims that he is not "speaking . . . as a judge, witness, prosecutor, or defender in some *trial of Paul de Man*" (146). Because de Man is dead, it is impossible "to organize a trial in order to judge [him]" (128). He deliberately positions himself against anyone who would use the revelations about de Man's wartime journalism to become "an authorized prosecutor or clever inquisitor" (151). He claims that to read responsibly one must "avoid the totalizing process and trial: of the work and the man" (154). De Man's work, Derrida writes, will always be of more interest than those who "are in a hurry to judge"; his writings will always outmaneuver the apparatus of the trial: "judge, prosecutor, defense lawyer, witnesses, and, waiting in the wings, the instruments of execution" (156). For Derrida "purification," "purge," and "totalization" are synonymous (154), and he sees the "purge" trial of Paul de Man as a form of dogmatism, of simplification, of totalizing, indeed totalitarian thought, that threatens the equivocality not only of de Man's insights but of "reading" itself (153). Thus, while Derrida's 1988 response clearly participates in a scandal of interest to American academics primarily, it also directly alludes to the postwar purge trials in France and denounces them in terms that are similar to the terms employed by Milan Kundera and Marguerite Duras.

Just like these two other writers, Derrida's attempts to be done with the spirit of the trial resembles the defense plea of an attorney responding to accusations of the purge. If he refuses to participate in "some *trial of Paul de Man*," it is in order to avoid "a general judgment with no possibility of appeal" (147). What more could the defense attorney of a guilty client ask for, however, than the possibility of appeal? Derrida's defense of de Man is based on what he calls a rhetoric of "recurrent alternation" (134). On the one hand, he locates an incriminating ideological coherence in de Man's articles for *Le Soir*. This "first, painful reading" (134) reveals the collusion between de Man's journalism and components of totalitarian ideology, namely, the irrevocability of the victory of Nazi Germany, the question of nationalism, and the persecution, deportation, and murder of European Jews. But at the same time, and on the other hand, Derrida claims that this collaborationist and fascistic discourse "is constantly split, disjointed, engaged in incessant conflicts" (134–35). De Man's articles are constructed according to a principle of irony and don't say what they seem to say. Even when de Man seems closest to championing Nazi Germany's anti-Semitic policies and cultural program, Derrida identifies his work as "ambiguous and sometimes anticonformist" (147), a subversive force in a pro-Nazi context. The articles force us to suspend our judgment because they are all constructed according to what Derrida calls a *"double edge"* and a *"double bind"* (135). From collaborationist intellectual, de Man becomes, in Derrida's reading, a "nonconformist smuggler" akin to "so many others" who "in France and in Belgium," "inside or outside the Resistance" (143) patiently and silently worked against the occupiers.

There is another expression for what Derrida calls the double bind, and that is "double game," in French *"double jeu."* Derrida's response to Paul de Man's wartime journalism seems to be tiptoeing around this expression, without ever daring to pronounce it, perhaps precisely because it was the major defense strategy of notorious collaborators at the end of the war and also because, since it first appeared in the trials in 1944, it has been thoroughly discredited. Beginning in 1944, the infamous double-game strategy began to appear in the defense briefs of politicians, bureaucrats, and at times writers who were accused of collaboration and who found themselves in the dock. From Pétain to René Bousquet, the accused claimed that, no matter what appearances suggested, no matter what the evidence said, no matter how involved in the collaboration they seemed, they had been working for the Resistance all along. It was a defense based on ambiguity, on the claim of anticonformism. The most common variant of the double-game strategy was the shield theory employed by Marshal Pétain and most of his ministers. Without them as intermediaries between the Nazis and the French public, they liked to claim, things would have been much worse. According to this line of defense, the collaboration was the lesser of two evils, a "shield" that permitted France to survive during the war. This argument rarely worked, at least for top-level collaborators, and since Robert Paxton's study of Vichy France revealed that the Vichy regime implemented

many of its programs, including its anti-Semitic policies, well in advance of Nazi demands, the double-game theory is rarely, if ever,
given credence today.[8]

This dismal success rate notwithstanding, writers no less than
politicians attempted to transform their ideological commitment into
a political equivocation. Charles Maurras, for example, claimed that
his support of Pétain was concomitant to a "resistance" to the
"desires and demands" of Nazi Germany" (Pujo, *L'Action française*,
22–23). If Maurras and *L'Action française* seemed to conform to the
ideology of Nazi Germany, it was only a ruse, and the proof was that
Maurras never gave in to any of the occupiers demands without pronouncing the slur *"Boche"* (London, *Le Procès*, 53). An even more frantic, yet equally significant version of this double-game strategy appeared during the trial of Jean Luchaire, a hack journalist who became the editor of the collaborationist daily *Les Nouveaux Temps*
during the Occupation. According to the prosecution, one of the
proofs that Luchaire had betrayed France lay in an article he had written in which he called members of the French Resistance "bastards"
and accused them of being responsible for the death of "hundreds of
thousands" of French men and women. Here was irrefutable proof of
a journalist putting himself at the service of the enemy. Luchaire,
however, did refute this accusation. Even if his article appeared in a
pro-Nazi newspaper, even if it seemed to denounce the Resistance, it
was, in fact, Luchaire claimed, an equivocal, ambiguous, and nonconformist piece of writing. This article, he told the jury, was a text
with two meanings (*"à double sens"*). All his articles, he went on to
add, were coded messages to the Resistance. To these claims the government's commissioner could only reply in biting terms: "In other
words, you were writing to the Resistants, and to make sure they
opened the envelope you addressed the letter 'Dear Bastards'" (Garçon, ed., *Les Procès*, 398–99).

It is perhaps unfair to compare Derrida to Maurras and Luchaire.
Luchaire was trying to save his skin. Derrida was defending a friend's

[8]For the details of this line of defense and proof that it wasn't an accurate
representation of the politics of Vichy France, see Paxton, *Vichy France*, 358–59.

beleaguered reputation and elaborating an ethics of reading. Still, Derrida's theory of the message with a double edge and the Vichyites recourse to a double-game strategy have several things in common. They are defenses of last resort, trotted out at precisely the moment when the evidence against the accused seems overwhelming. They seek to blur the meaning of a text or an action through recourse to ambiguity and double meanings. They claim that the defendant was involved in secret activities of which there is, in fact, no evidence: Luchaire's coded messages to the Resistance, for example, and de Man's life as a secret "smuggler"—a word that is not only loaded but has connotations of heroism. Finally, the strategy of the double game and of equivocal meanings problematizes questions of guilt and attempts to deny or at least attenuate the accused subject's legal, moral, and intellectual responsibility.

This term *responsibility* brings us to a final consideration on the relation between Derrida's response to de Man's wartime journalism and the postwar purge in France. For behind his response to de Man and to American newspapers Derrida is also targeting Sartre and existentialist models of reading and judging literature. Derrida begins his considerations with precisely the problem most closely associated with Sartre's name in the postwar years, the question of responsibility. Indeed the first line of the article evokes not only responsibility but also another Sartrean concept, the situation (127). From the very first paragraph, however, we know that Derrida's responsibility is different, more problematic, less decisive than Sartre's. It is introduced as a question, a deferment rather than a judgment and a decision: "is it not an act to assume in theory the concept of responsibility?" (127). We are a long way from Sartre's 1945 statement that he held "Flaubert and the Goncourts responsible for the repression that followed the Commune because they didn't write a line to prevent it" (Sartre, *What Is Literature?* 252). That is, it seems to me, at least one of the points of Derrida's article: to defer responsibility by redefining it; to say "what *responding* and taking a *responsibility* can mean" (Derrida, "Like the Sound," 128); to pass responsibility from the writer to the reader, from the individual to a collectivity. Indeed, Derrida's responsibility seems to be the very opposite of the definition Sartre gave at the end of the war. The existentialist model of responsibility was based on the notion of literature as a transparent and unequivocal signifying system. For the author to be responsible, literature must be an act of "disclosure" (Sartre, *What Is Literature?* 37) that says what we think it says and can be directly assigned to an originating subject. For Derrida responsibility is caught in an aporia: if it is necessary, it is only because it is impossible; if reading requires it, it is only because we are not sure "if there is any" (Derrida, "Like the Sound," 151). Responsibility for Derrida involves not just the subject but also the voice of the other either through transference or through the trope of prosopopeia, the voice from beyond the grave. In either case for Derrida assigning responsibility to an existential subject, to a subject who can be identified, named, incarcerated, or executed is an impossibility since the voice, and the subject, are invariably absent. Derrida leaves no doubt that behind his defense of de Man he is aiming at Sartre. To read without hearing the ruptures, equivocations, and displacements that the deconstructionist hears in the text is, in Derrida's words, nothing more than "good old existential psychoanalysis of the immediate postwar period!" (152).

Forty years after the trials in France and 3,000 miles away the purge is playing itself out once again. Derrida's response to de Man's articles and to the de Man affair resembles Duras's reactions to the purge in several ways. Both writers are making the case for hesitation and undecidability. Both Duras and Derrida are designating Sartre as the foil and the representative of a totalizing thought. Both exclude Sartre from their literary considerations. Duras claims that Sartre is a moralizer rather than a writer. Derrida for his part, while he makes the case for the undecidability of de Man's early journalism, never considers that Sartre's texts may give rise to the same type of splits and ruptures. Finally Duras and Derrida both revise the trial of accused collaborationist intellectuals, but both misread the purge precisely in their foiled attempts to get beyond it. Their attempts to evacuate the spirit of the trial leads them to repeat some of the very legal and intellectual arguments that characterize it.

According to one historian, the purge never really ended: "It dragged on for years" (Judt, *Past Imperfect,* 72). Even today, though we have perhaps arrived at the end of an era, the values, debates, and positions passed on to us from the purge constitute an important part of our intellectual field. Certainly the reflections of both Derrida and Duras on the purge are symptomatic of France's equivocation toward the postwar trials. Their hesitations, their attempts to break out of ideological constraints, their reinscription of guilt and responsibility—all these moves confirm that the French nation has yet to resolve a fundamental historical crisis. The trials, verdicts, executions of the purge remain present today and yet because they are elusive, strangely absent. The spirit of the trial continues to haunt us as it haunted writers and readers fifty years ago.

The debates around the purge, from the immediate postwar years to the present, also ask us to reflect upon the status of literature. Perhaps because it was a moment of fast-paced position taking, of excess, of ideological dogmatism, and cursory judgments, the purge is seen today, at least by some, as the antithesis of a literary ideal. According to this view, the debates of the purge produced only stalwart doctrines and totalizing discourse; in a word, they produced only Sartre. But contrary to what Duras and Derrida claim, Sartre's work points us in the direction of the complications, equivocations, and contradictions of the literary responses to the purge. And that it does so at times unconsciously does not make these complications any less important. Sartre may have "judged too much," as Paulhan claimed, but he knew that it is not a simplification to say that literature engages our responsibility and solicits our judgment. The literary texts I have examined over the course of this book also confirm that we are perhaps inescapably caught in the spirit of the trial. In that case, rather than trying to purge this reality, we might be better off asking literature to tell us about the strategies, the dissemination, and the stakes of the spirit of the trial as long as we remember that literature is an unreliable witness and that it never allows us to have the last word.

Bibliography

Bibliography

Anderson, Kirk. "Joliment actuelles: Les Chroniques médiévales et la trilogie allemande." *Actes du colloque de Toulouse*. Tusson: Editions du Lérot, 1990.

Aragon, Louis. *Chroniques du bel canto*. Genève: Skira, 1947.

———. *Les Communistes*. 2 vols. Paris: La Bibliothèque française, 1949.

———. *L'Homme communiste*. Vol. 2. Paris: Gallimard, 1953.

———. *Servitude et grandeur des Français. Scènes des années terribles*. Paris: La Bibliothèque française, 1945.

Aron, Robert. *Histoire de l'épuration: Le Monde de la presse, des arts, des lettres . . . 1944–1953*. Paris: Fayard, 1975.

Assouline, Pierre. *L'Epuration des intellectuels*. Brussels: Complexe, 1985.

———. *Gaston Gallimard*. Trans. Harold J. Salemson. New York: Harcourt Brace Jovanovich, 1988.

Aymé, Marcel. *La Tête des autres*. Paris: Grasset, 1952.

———. *Uranus*. Paris: Gallimard, 1948.

———. "L'Epuration et le délit d'opinion." *Le Crapouillot* 11 (Apr. 1950).

Bardèche, Maurice. *Lettre à François Mauriac*. Paris: La Pensée libre, 1947.

———. *Nuremberg ou la Terre promise*. Paris: Les Sept Couleurs, 1948.

———. *Nuremberg II ou les faux-monnayeurs*. Paris: Les Sept Couleurs, 1950.

———. *Qu'est-ce que le fascisme?* Paris: Les Sept Couleurs, 1961.

Bataille, Georges. *L'Erotisme*. Paris: Minuit, 1957. Reprinted in *Oeuvres complètes*. Vol. 10. Paris, Gallimard, 1987.

———. "L'Inculpation d'Henry Miller." *Critique* 3–4 (1946): 380–84.

———. "Nietzsche est-il fasciste?" *Combat*, 20 Oct. 1944.

Bellosta, Marie-Christine. *Céline ou l'art de la contradiction: Lecture de Voyage au bout de la nuit*. Paris: PUF, 1990.

———. *"Féerie pour une autre fois I et II*: Un Spectacle et son prologue." *La Revue des lettres modernes*. Vol. 3. Paris: Minard, 1978.

Béraud, Henri. *Quinze Jours avec la mort ou la chasse au lampiste*. Paris: Plon, 1951.

Bersani, Leo. *Homos*. Cambridge, Mass.: Harvard University Press, 1995.

Blanchot, Maurice. *Faux pas*. Paris: Gallimard, 1943.

———. *L'Instant de ma mort*. Paris: Fata Morgana, 1994.

———. *La Part du feu*. Paris: Gallimard, 1949.

———. *Lautréamont et Sade*. Paris: Editions de Minuit, 1949.

Boschetti, Anna. *The Intellectual Enterprise*. Trans. Richard C. McCleary. Evanston: Northwestern University Press, 1988.

Bourdel, Philippe. *L'Epuration sauvage 1944–1945*. Paris: Perrin, 1988.

Bourdieu, Pierre. *The Rules of Art: Genesis and Structure of the Literary Field*. Trans. Susan Emanuel. Stanford, Calif.: Stanford University Press, 1995.

Brasillach, Robert. *Anthologie de la poésie grecque*. In *Œuvres complètes*. Vol. 9. Paris: Au club de l'honnête homme, 1964.

———. *Chénier*. Paris: Club du libraire, 1957.

———. *Corneille*. Paris: Arthème Fayard, 1961.

———. "Devant l'Apocalypse." *La Chronique de Paris*, July 1944. Reprinted in *Œuvres complètes*. Vol. 12. Paris: Au club de l'honnête homme, 1964.

———. "Lettre à quelques jeunes gens." *Révolution nationale*, 19 Feb. 1944. Reprinted in *Œuvres complètes*. Vol. 12. Paris: Au club de l'honnête homme, 1964.

———. "Naissance d'un sentiment." *Révolution nationale*, 4 Sept. 1943. Reprinted in *Œuvres complètes*. Vol. 12. Paris: Au club de l'honnête homme, 1964.

———. *Notre Avant-Guerre*. Paris: Plon, 1941. Reprint, Paris: Livre de Poche, 1973.

———. "Pour une poésie impure," *Révolution nationale*, 8 Jan. 1944. Reprinted in *Œuvres complètes*. Vol. 12. Paris: Au club de l'honnête homme, 1964.

———. *Présence de Virgile*. In *Œuvres complètes*. Vol. 7. Paris: Au club de l'honnête homme, 1964.

———. "Les Sept Internationales contre la patrie." *Je suis partout*, 25 Sept. 1942. Reprinted in *Œuvres complètes*. Vol. 12. Paris: Au club de l'honnête homme, 1964.

Brossat, Alain. *Les Tondues: Un Carnaval moche*. Paris: Manya, 1992. Reprint, Paris: Pluriel, 1994.

Caillois, Roger. "Des excès de la littérature." *Cahiers de la Pléiade*, Apr. 1946.

Camus, Albert. "Justice et charité." *Combat*, 11 Jan. 1945.

Carroll, David. *French Literary Fascism: Nationalism, Anti-Semitism, and the Ideology of Culture*. Princeton: Princeton University Press, 1995.

Céline, Louis-Ferdinand. *Bagatelles pour un massacre*. Paris: Denoël, 1937.

———. *Les Beaux Draps*. Paris: Nouvelles Editions françaises, 1941.

———. *Cahiers Céline 2*. Ed. Jean-Pierre Dauphin and Henri Godard. Paris. Gallimard, 1976.

———. *Cahiers Céline 6*. Ed. Jean-Paul Louis. Paris. Gallimard, 1980.

———. *Cahiers Céline 7*. Ed. Jean-Pierre Dauphin and Pascal Fouché. Paris: Gallimard, 1986.

———. *Castle to Castle.* Trans. Ralph Manheim. New York: Delacorte Press, 1968.

———. *Conversations with Professor Y.* Trans. Stanford Luce. Hanover, N.H.: University Press of New England, 1986.

———. *Lettres à la N.R.F. 1931–1961.* Paris: Gallimard, 1991.

———. *Lettres à Tixier.* Paris: La Flûte de Pan, 1985.

———. *North.* Trans. Ralph Manheim. New York: Delacorte Press, 1972.

———. "Reply to Charges of Treason Made by the French Department of Justice (Copenhagen, 6 November 1946)." Trans. Julien Cornell. *South Atlantic Quarterly* 93, no. 2 (1994): 531–39.

———. *Rigadoon.* Trans. Ralph Manheim. New York: Delacorte Press, 1974.

———. *Romans II.* Ed. Henri Godard. Paris: Gallimard, 1974.

———. *Romans IV.* Ed. Henri Godard. Paris: Gallimard, 1993.

Césaire, Aimé. *Discourse on Colonialism.* Trans. Joan Pinkham. New York: MR, 1972.

Chandet, Henriette. *Le Procès Maurras.* Lyon: Editions de Savoie, 1945.

Chardonne, Jacques. *Détachements.* Paris: Albin Michel, 1963.

Charle, Christophe. *Naissance des "intellectuels" 1880–1900.* Paris: Editions de Minuit, 1990.

Chesters, G. "Malherbe, Ponge and Revolutionary Classicism." In *The Classical Tradition in French Literature.* Ed. H. T. Barnwell et al. London: Grant & Cutler, 1977.

Cogniot, Georges. "Pétain au Poteau." *L'Humanité,* 1 May 1945.

Cohen-Solal, Annie. *Sartre: A Life.* Trans. Anna Cancogni. New York: Pantheon Books, 1987.

Compagnon, Antoine. *Chat en poche: Montaigne et l'allégorie.* Paris: Seuil, 1993.

Contat, Michel, and Michel Rybalka, eds. *The Writings of Jean-Paul Sartre.* Vol. 1, *A Bibliographical Life.* Trans. Richard C. McCleary. Evanston: Northwestern University Press, 1974.

Dauphin, Jean-Pierre, and Pascal Fouché, eds. *Bibliographie des écrits de Louis-Ferdinand Céline.* Paris: Bibliothèque de littérature française contemporaine, 1983.

de Beauvoir, Simone. *Faut-il brûler Sade?* Paris: Gallimard, 1952.

———. "Œil pour œil." *Les Temps modernes* 5 (Feb. 1946): 813–30.

———. *The Prime of Life.* Trans. Peter Green. New York: World Publishing, 1962.

Decour, Jacques. "Manifeste du Front National des Ecrivains." *Les Lettres françaises* 1 (Sept. 1942): 2.

de Gaulle, Charles. *The Complete War Memoirs.* Trans. Jonathan Griffin and Richard Howard. New York: Simon and Schuster, 1964.

Deleuze, Gilles, and Félix Guattari. *Kafka: Toward a Minor Literature*. Trans. Dana Polan. Minneapolis: University of Minnesota Press, 1986.

de Man, Paul. *Blindness and Insight: Essays in the Rhetoric of Contemporary Criticism*. Minneapolis: University of Minnesota Press, 1983.

——. "La Circularité de l'interprétation dans l'œuvre critique de Maurice Blanchot." *Critique* 229 (Jun. 1966): 547–60.

Derrida, Jacques. "Like the Sound of the Sea Deep Within a Shell: Paul de Man's War." Trans. Peggy Kamuf. In *Responses on Paul de Man's Wartime Journalism*, ed. Werner Hamacher et al., 127–64. Lincoln: University of Nebraska Press, 1989.

Les Deux Justices ou Notre J'accuse. Paris: Edition de la Seule France, 1948.

Diquelon, Roland. "Drancy deviendra-t-il villégiature pour la 5e colonne?" *L'Humanité*, 28 Sept. 1944.

Domenach, J.-M. "La Justice sans la révolution et sans l'Eglise." *Esprit* 136 (Aug. 1947): 184–93.

Dreyfus, Hubert, and Paul Rabinow. *Michel Foucault: Beyond Structuralism and Hermeneutics*. Second edition. Chicago: University of Chicago Press, 1983.

Drieu la Rochelle, Pierre. *Journal 1939–1945*. Paris: Gallimard, 1992.

——. *Secret Journal and Other Writings*. Trans. Alastair Hamilton. New York: Howard Fertig, 1973.

Duhamel, Georges. *Tribulations de l'espérance*. Paris: Mercure de France, 1947.

Duras, Marguerite. *Ecrire*. Paris: Gallimard, 1993.

——. *The Lover*. Trans. Barbara Bray. New York: Random House, 1985.

——. *The War: A Memoir*. Trans. Barbara Bray. New York: Pantheon Books, 1986.

Eluard, Paul. *Au rendez-vous allemand*. Paris: Editions de Minuit, 1945.

——. "Courage." *Les Lettres françaises*, Jan.–Feb. 1943.

——. "L'Esprit de suite dans le mal." *Les Lettres françaises*, Sept. 1943.

——. "L'Etendard sanglant est levé." *Les Lettres françaises*, Sept. 1943.

——. *Œuvres complètes*. Ed. Lucien Scheler and Marcelle Dumas. 2 vols. Paris: Gallimard, 1968.

——. *Uninterrupted Poetry: Selected Writings of Paul Eluard*. Trans. Lloyd Alexander. New York: New Directions, 1951.

——. "Les Vendeurs d'indulgence." *Les Lettres françaises*, 17 Mar. 1945.

——, ed. *L'Honneur des poètes*. Paris: Editions de Minuit. N.d.

Eluard, Paul, Claude Morgan, and Edith Thomas. "L'Agonie de la Nouvelle Revue Française." *Les Lettres françaises*, July 1943.

——. "L'Esprit de la maison." *Les Lettres françaises*, July 1943.

Fabre-Luce, Alfred. *Au nom des silencieux*. Paris: n.p., 1945.

Faurisson, Robert. "A quand la libération de Céline?" *Les Nouvelles littéraires*, no. 2388 (1973): 4–5.

————. "Céline devant le mensonge du siècle." *Le Bulletin célinien* no. 3 (1982): 4–8.

————. "Céline devant le mensonge du siècle." *Le Bulletin célinien* no. 4 (1982): 5–6.

Felman, Shoshana, and Dori Laub, M.D. *Testimony: Crises of Witnessing in Literature, Psychoanalysis, and History*. New York: Routledge, 1992.

Fineman, Joël. "The Structure of Allegorical Desire." In *Allegory and Representation*. Ed. Stephen Greenblatt, 26–60. Baltimore: Johns Hopkins University Press, 1981.

Finkielkraut, Alain. *L'Avenir d'une négation. Réflexion sur la question du génocide*. Paris: Seuil, 1982.

Fresco, Nadine. "Les Redresseurs de la mort." *Les Temps modernes*, no. 407 (1980): 2150–211.

Galtier-Boissière, Jean. *Mon Journal depuis la Libération*. Paris: La Jeune Parque, 1945.

Garçon, Maurice, ed. *Les Procès de la collaboration: Fernand de Brinon, Joseph Darnaud, Jean Luchaire*. Paris: Albin Michel, 1948.

Genet, Jean. *Funeral Rites*. Trans. Bernard Frechtman. New York: Grove Press, 1969.

Gibault, François. *Céline*. 3 vols. Paris: Mercure de France, 1985.

Godard, Henri. *Poétique de Céline*. Paris: Gallimard, 1985.

Goriely, Benjamin. "La Politique littéraire en URSS." *Critique* 5 (Oct. 1946): 475–80.

Guitry, Sacha. *60 Jours de prison*. Paris: Librairie Académique Perrin, 1964.

Halpern, Joseph. *Critical Fictions: The Literary Criticism of Jean-Paul Sartre*. New Haven: Yale University Press, 1976.

Hamacher, Werner, Neil Hertz, and Thomas Keenan, eds. *Responses on Paul de Man's Wartime Journalism*. Lincoln: University of Nebraska Press, 1989.

Higgins, Lynn. *New Novel, New Wave, New Politics: Fiction and the Representation of History in Postwar France*. Lincoln: University of Nebraska Press, 1996.

Holland, Michael, and Patrick Rousseau. "Blanchot: Bibliographie I." *Gramma* 3/4 nos. 3–4 (1976): 224–45.

————. "Blanchot: Bibliographie II." *Gramma* 5 (1976): 124–32.

Hollier, Denis. *Les Dépossédés*. Paris: Editions de Minuit, 1993.

————. *The Politics of Prose: Essay on Sartre*. Trans. Jeffrey Mehlman. Minneapolis: University of Minnesota Press, 1986.

————, ed. *The College of Sociology 1937–39*. Minneapolis: University of Minnesota Press, 1988.

Isorni, Jacques. *Le Procès de Robert Brasillach*. Paris: Flammarion, 1946.

Jameson, Fredric. *Postmodernism, or, the Cultural Logic of Late Capitalism*. Durham: Duke University Press, 1991.

Jamet, Claude. "Bombing Parties." *Germinal*, 5 May 1944.

——. *Fifi Roi*. Paris: Les Editions de l'Elan, 1947.

——. "L'Heure H moins 5." *Germinal*, 2 Jun. 1944.

——. "Un Entretien chez Denoël avec Louis-Ferdinand Céline. *Germinal*, 28 Apr. 1944.

Joseph, Gilbert. *Une si douce occupation ... Simone de Beauvoir et Jean-Paul Sartre 1940–1944*. Paris: Albin Michel, 1991.

Judt, Tony. *Past Imperfect: French Intellectuals, 1944–1956*. Berkeley: University of California Press, 1992.

Kaplan, Alice Y. "Literature and Collaboration." In *A New History of French Literature*. Ed. Denis Hollier, 966–71. Cambridge: Harvard University Press, 1989.

——. "Paul de Man, *Le Soir*, and the Francophone Collaboration (1940–1942)." In *Responses on Paul de Man's Wartime Journalism*, ed. Werner Hamacher et al., 266–84. Lincoln: University of Nebraska Press, 1989.

——. *Relevé des sources et des citations dans Bagatelles pour un massacre*. Tusson: Edition du Lérot, 1987.

——. *Reproductions of Banality*. Minneapolis: University of Minnesota Press, 1986.

Kaplan, Alice Y., and Philippe Roussin, eds. "Céline, USA." *The South Atlantic Quarterly* 93, no. 2 (spring 1994).

Kristeva, Julia. *Black Sun: Depression and Melancholia*. Trans. Leon S. Roudiez. New York: Columbia University Press, 1989.

——. *Powers of Horror: An Essay on Abjection*. Trans. Leon Roudiez. New York: Columbia University Press, 1982.

Kundera, Milan. *Testaments Betrayed*. Trans. Linda Asher. New York: HarperCollins, 1995.

Laborie, Pierre. *L'Opinion française sous Vichy*. Paris: Seuil, 1990.

Laval, Michel. *Brasillach ou la trahison du clerc*. Paris: Hachette, 1992.

Leiris, Michel. *L'Age d'homme*. Paris: Gallimard, 1946.

Lipstadt, Deborah. *Denying the Holocaust: The Growing Assault on Truth and Memory*. New York: Free Press, 1993.

London, Géo. *Le Procès de Charles Maurras*. Lyon: Bonnefon, 1945.

Loselle, Andrea. "The Historical Nullification of Paul Morand's Gendered Eugenics." In *Gender and Fascism in Modern France*. Ed. Melanie Hawthorne and Richard J. Golsan, 101–18. Hanover, N.H.: University Press of New England, 1997.

Lottman, Herbert. *The Purge*. New York: William Morrow, 1986.

Marrus, Michael R., and Robert O. Paxton. *Vichy France and the Jews*. New York: Basic Books, 1981

Martinoir, Francine de. *La Littérature occupée. Les années de guerre 1939–1945*. Paris: Hatier, 1995.

Mauriac, François. *Le Baillon dénoué après quatre ans de silence*. Paris: Grasset, 1945.

———. "Le Cas Genet." *Le Figaro littéraire*, 26 Mar. 1949, 7.

Maurras, Hélène. *Souvenirs de prison de Charles Maurras*. France: Editions du Fuseau, 1965.

McCarthy, Patrick. *Céline*. New York: Viking Press, 1975.

Meadows, Patrick. "Rameau and the Role of Music in Ponge's Poetry." *The French Review* 68, no. 5 (Mar. 1995): 626–35.

Mehlman, Jeffrey. *Legacies: Of Anti-Semitism in France*. Minneapolis: University of Minnesota Press, 1983.

———. "Prosopopeia Revisited." *Romanic Review* 81, no. 1 (Jan. 1990): 137–43.

———. "Writing and Deference: The Politics of Literary Adulation." *Representations* 15 (summer 1986): 1–14.

Meschonnic, Henri. *Pour la poétique III*. Paris: Gallimard, 1973.

Mesnard, Philippe. "Maurice Blanchot, le sujet de l'engagement." *L'Infini*, no. 48 (1994): 103–28.

Michel, Henri. "Lumières sur Vichy." *Annales ESC* (July–Sept. 1956): 510–25.

Montherlant, Henry de. *L'Equinoxe de septembre. Le Solstice de juin. Mémoire*. Paris: Gallimard, 1976.

Morand, Paul. *Le Dernier Jour de l'Inquisition*. Paris: La Table Ronde, 1947.

———. *Le Flagellant de Séville*. Paris: Fayard, 1951.

———. *Fouquet ou le soleil offusqué*. Paris: Gallimard, 1961.

———. *Vie de Guy de Maupassant*. Paris: Flammarion, 1942.

Morgan, Claude. "Les Indulgents." *Les Lettres françaises*, 11 Aug. 1945.

———. "Refuser d'être juge ... c'est refuser d'être homme." *Les Lettres françaises*, 13 Dec. 1946.

Muray, Philippe. *Céline*. Paris: Seuil, 1981.

Newmark, Kevin. *Beyond Symbolism: Textual History and the Future of Reading*. Ithaca: Cornell University Press, 1991.

Noguères, Louis. *La Dernière Etape: Sigmaringen*. Paris: Arthème Fayard, 1956.

Novick, Peter. *The Resistance versus Vichy: The Purge of Collaborators in Liberated France*. New York: Columbia University Press, 1968.

Ory, Pascal. *Les Collaborateurs 1940–1945*. Paris:Seuil, 1976.

Pagès, Yves. *Les Fictions du politique chez Louis-Ferdinand Céline*. Paris: Seuil, 1994.

Paulhan, Jean. *De la paille et du grain*. N.R.F. Paris: Gallimard, 1948.

———. *Lettre aux directeurs de la Résistance*. Paris: Les Editions de Minuit, 1952. Reprint, Paris: Ramsay, 1987.

———. "Lettre sur la paix." In *Œuvres complètes*. Vol. 5. Paris: Cercle du livre précieux, 1970.

———. "Note." *Cahiers de la Pléiade* 3 (winter 1948): 9.

Paxton, Robert O. *Vichy France: Old Guard and New Order, 1940–1944.* New York: Knopf, 1972.

Péan, Pierre. *Une Jeunesse française: François Mitterrand 1934–1947.* Paris: Fayard, 1994.

Ponge, Francis. *Soap.* Trans. Lane Dunlop. London: Jonathan Cape, 1969.

Poulet, Robert. *L'Enfer ciel. Journal d'un condamné à mort.* Paris: Plon, 1952.

Pujo, Maurice. *L'Action française contre l'Allemagne: Mémoire au juge d'instruction.* N.p.: Editions de la Seule France, 1946.

Queneau, Raymond. *Bâtons, chiffres et lettres.* Paris: Gallimard, 1965.

Rancière, Jacques. "Un Négationnisme ordinaire." *Passages,* no. 56 (1993): 18–20.

Rassinier, Paul. *Le Mensonge d'Ulysse.* Paris: Editions Bressanes, 1950. Reprint, Paris: La Librairie française, 1955.

Rebatet, Lucien. *Les Décombres.* Paris: Denoël, 1942. Reprint, Paris: Pauvert, 1976.

———. *Les Mémoires d'un fasciste II 1941/1947.* Paris: Pauvert, 1976.

Richard, Jean-Pierre. *Nausée de Céline.* Paris: Fata Morgana, 1973.

Rousset, David. *L'Univers concentrationnaire.* Paris: Editions du Pavois, 1946.

Roussin, Philippe. "Genèse, versions et procès." *Critique* 574 (Mar. 1995): 159–67.

Rousso, Henry. *The Vichy Syndrome: History and Memory in France since 1944.* Trans. Arthur Goldhammer. Cambridge, Mass.: Harvard University Press, 1991.

———. "L'Epuration en France. Une histoire inachevée." *Vingtième Siècle* 33 (Jan.–Mar. 1992): 78–105.

Roux, Georges. "Un Epuré considérable et peu connu." *Ecrits de Paris,* May 1956.

Sapiro, Gisèle. "Complicités et anathèmes en temps de crise: Modes de survie du champ littéraire et de ses institutions, 1940–1953 (Académie française, Académie Goncourt, Comité national des écrivains)." Ph.D. diss., Ecole des hautes etudes en sciences sociales, 1994.

Sartre, Jean-Paul. *Baudelaire.* Trans. Martin Turnell. New York: New Directions, 1950.

———. *Being and Nothingness.* Trans. Hazel E. Barnes. New York: Simon & Schuster, 1966.

———. "Drieu la Rochelle ou la haine de soi." *Les Lettres françaises,* Apr. 1943.

———. "L'Espoir fait l'homme." *Les Lettres françaises,* July 1944.

———. *L'Idiot de la famille.* Paris: Gallimard, 1971.

———. "La Littérature, cette liberté." *Les Lettres françaises,* Apr. 1944.

————. *Mallarmé. La Lucidité et sa face d'ombre*. Paris: Gallimard, 1986.

————. "Portrait de l'antisémite." *Les Temps modernes*, 3 Dec. 1945.

————. *Saint Genet. Comédien et martyr*. Paris: Gallimard, 1952.

————. *Situations I*. Paris: Gallimard, 1947.

————. *Situations III*. Paris: Gallimard, 1949.

————. *Situations IX*. Paris: Gallimard, 1972.

————. *What Is Literature? and Other Writings*. Ed. Steven Ungar. Cambridge, Mass.: Harvard University Press, 1988.

Scullion, Rosemarie, Philip H. Solomon, and Thomas Spear. *Céline and the Politics of Difference*. Hanover, N.H.: University Press of New England, 1995.

Seghers, Pierre. *La Résistance et ses poètes*. Paris: Seghers, 1974.

Simonin, Anne. *Les Editions de Minuit 1942–1955. Le Devoir d'insoumission*. Paris: IMEC, 1994.

Stoekl Allan. *Politics, Writing, Mutation*. Minneapolis: University of Minnesota Press, 1985.

Syrotinski, Michael. "Some Wheat and Some Chaff: Jean Paulhan and the Post-War Literary Purge in France." *Studies in Twentieth-Century Literature* 16, no. 2 (summer 1992): 247–63.

Taguieff, Pierre-André. "La Logique du soupçon." *Passages*, no. 56 (1993): 28–30.

Teitgen, Pierre-Henri. *Les Cours de Justice, Conférence du 5 avril 1946*. Paris: Le Mail, 1946.

Tiersky, Ronald. *French Communism 1920–1972*. New York: Columbia University Press, 1974.

Triolet, Elsa. "Les Faits." *Les Lettres françaises*, 14 Feb. 1947.

————. "Il ne saurait y avoir d'affaire Romain Rolland." *Les Lettres françaises*, 14 Feb. 1947.

————. "Jean Paulhan successeur de Drieu la Rochelle." *Les Lettres françaises*, 7 Feb. 1952.

Ungar, Steven. *Scandal and Aftereffect: Blanchot and France Since 1930*. Minneapolis: University of Minnesota Press, 1995.

Vercors. *Les Mots*. Paris: Editions de Minuit, 1947.

————. Response to a survey. *Carrefour*, no. 25, 10 Feb. 1945.

Verdès-Leroux, Jeannine. *Refus et violences: Politique et littérature à l'extrême droite des années trente aux retombées de la Libération*. Paris: Gallimard, 1996.

Vernier, Richard. *"Poésie ininterrompue" et la poétique de Paul Eluard*. Paris: Mouton, 1971.

Vidal-Naquet, Pierre. *Assassins of Memory: Essays on the Denial of the Holocaust*. Trans. Jeffrey Mehlman. New York: Columbia University Press, 1992.

Videlier, Philippe. "Zones d'ombre et coup monté." *Le Monde diplomatique*, June 1996, 3.

Watts, Philip. "Postmodern Céline." In *Céline and the Politics of Difference,*
eds. Rosemarie Scullion, Philip H. Solomon, and Thomas Spear, 203–15.
Hanover, N.H.: University Press of New England, 1995.

Weber, Eugen. *Action française: Royalism and Reaction in Twentieth-Century France.* Stanford, Calif.: Stanford University Press, 1962.

White, Edmund. *Genet.* London: Chatto & Windus, 1993.

Index

In this index an "ff" after a number indicates a separate reference on the next page, and an "ff" indicates separate references on the next two pages. A continuous discussion over two or more pages is indicated by a span of page numbers, e.g., "57–59." *Passim* is used for a cluster of references in close but not consecutive sequence.

Library of Congress Cataloging-in-Publication Data

Watts, Philip.
    Allegories of the purge : how literature responded to the
postwar trials of writers and intellectuals in France / Philip Watts.
        p. cm.
    Includes bibliographical references and index.
        ISBN 0-8047-3184-5 (cloth : alk. paper). —ISBN 0-8047-3185-3
(pbk. : alk. paper)
        1. French literature—20th century—History and criticism.
2. World War, 1939–1945—Collaborationists—France.   3. World
War, 1939–1945—Literature and the war.   4. France—History—
German occupation, 1940–1945.   5. Trials (Treason)—France—
History—20th century.   6. Trials (Treason) in literature.
7. Intellectuals—France—Political activity.   I. Title.

PQ307.W4W38   1999
840.9'.358—dc21
                                                        98-35347
                                                            CIP

This book is printed on acid-free, recycled paper.

Original printing 1999
Last figure below indicates year of this printing:
08   07   06   05   04   03   02   01   00   99